PLATE 1. *See pages 26, 27*

FOUR EARLY IRON LIGHTING DEVICES ON RARE SEVENTEENTH CENTURY TRESTLE TABLE
From Burton N. Gates' Collection, Worcester

Colonial and Early American Lighting

By

ARTHUR H. HAYWARD

Third Enlarged Edition
With a new Introduction and
Supplement, "Colonial Chandeliers"
By JAMES R. MARSH

illustrated

DOVER PUBLICATIONS, INC.
NEW YORK

Published in Canada by General Publishing Company, Ltd., 30 Lesmill Road, Don Mills, Toronto, Ontario.
Published in the United Kingdom by Constable and Company, Ltd., 10 Orange Street, London WC 2.

This Dover edition, first published in 1962, is an unabridged and unaltered republication of the second revised edition of *Colonial Lighting*, published by Little, Brown, and Company in 1927, to which has been added the following new material especially prepared for this Dover edition by James R. Marsh:

Standard Book Number: 486-20975-X
Library of Congress Catalog Card Number: 62-6720

Manufactured in the United States of America
Dover Publications, Inc.
180 Varick Street
New York, N.Y. 10014

DEDICATION

To the one whose enthusiastic interest, devotion, and self-sacrifice has been a constant inspiration and without whose loving and loyal companionship my collection and this record would have been impossible

TO MY WIFE

Melrose, Massachusetts

INTRODUCTION TO DOVER EDITION

AN interesting aspect of early American folklore is the fascinating story of lighting devices. To my knowledge the only complete book on this subject covering the colonial period is Arthur H. Hayward's Colonial Lighting, *a truly prodigious work.*

Mr. Hayward's research brought him into contact with important collectors of his day, which circumstance enabled him to present pictures of many varieties of lighting devices with valuable descriptive material. In his book, he supports the illustrations by a running comment of names, places, inventions and events of the times. His tales of wicks and candlemaking, the ceaseless struggle to control the flickering flame and prolong its life, the tinderbox days before the modern match, the variety of oils, waxes and grease, all indicate what our forefathers went through to get illumination. His story goes back to ancient times and describes the material used by artists and craftsmen who embellished many forms of oil containers and candleholders. He also points out that the ancient grease lamps used by the Egyptians, Greeks and Romans worked on the same principle as the seventeenth-century "Betty" lamps used by our New England pioneers.

Chandeliers were about the only type of illuminating device not extensively represented in the early editions of this book. Formerly few collectors were interested in acquiring them, for they were designed for suspension and could not be stood on tables or shelves. But today the architect, interior designer and museum curator regard them as important keynotes.

In colonial days, the crystal and Flemish style chandeliers were the most elegant, and adorned important buildings and homes. Outstanding examples of the crystal chandelier may be seen in the White House in Washington and the Governor's Palace in Colonial Williamsburg, Virginia as well as in many museums. The Flemish style was made of brass, bronze, silver or pewter and is also well represented throughout the country; Stanford White's New York Harvard Club has two enormous beauties in the dining hall. This style chandelier was made mostly by highly skilled craftsmen in Europe and was brought to the colonies.

Early chandeliers made of ordinary materials such as iron, copper, pewter and wood were part of the American folk art which also produced carved wood figures, weathervanes and other handcraft. In making wood spindles, metal leaves, cones, curving arms, fluted candle cups and pierced designs, the artisan added touches of his own with interesting results. With simple tools he displayed a taste that excites admiration today. Among his creations is the so-called tin chandelier, made actually not of tin but of sheet iron with only a thin coating of tin to prevent rusting. Tin is the principle alloy of pewter.

The chandelier maker of the colonial period left little evidence of how he conducted his business. No doubt he had a shop and traveled with his wares in the same manner as the itinerant sign and portrait painter. Old prints show the lamp fabricator costumed in an array of sconces, candleholders and lanterns announcing his samples. Also there is little record of the actual buildings from which the surviving originals came, although occasionally some information is revealed as described in the following story.

Several years ago I acquired a double-tier beauty with

a gayly colored wood center. Later I discovered a pair of the same with added leaves in the ballroom of the Frary House in Old Deerfield, Massachusetts. In my recent search for material for this edition I found a similar pair at the Wadsworth Atheneum, home of the fine Wallace Nutting collection, in Hartford, Connecticut. Mr. Henry P. Maynard, Conservator of Furniture, probed into the history and found it was a gift from the Goodwin Collection and that the chandeliers came from a church near Bridgeport, Connecticut. An illustration in a 1952 issue of Antiques Magazine *showed a chandelier with exactly the same design, and the caption "an unusual American piece . . . Used in a church in Virginia during the early 1800's and evidently represents some native craftsman's rendering, in simple materials he had at hand, of the elaborate scrolled designs of European brass and silver chandeliers of the seventeenth and eighteenth centuries."*

In my opinion there seems to be no doubt that such duplication of design was the work of one artisan. It is possible that he spent the winters in his shop fabricating these and other designs of chandeliers and sconces, then traveled about in the summer making sales, deliveries and contacting prospective clients. Of course, general tinsmiths and blacksmiths made lighting devices as well as hardware and other implements, but I believe there were those who had a flare for lighting fixtures and specialized in them. Whatever the case, their creations are worthy of being brought to the attention of the collector, interior designer and architect.

The pictures of early chandeliers in the supplement were selected from the fine collections of leading museums and restorations whose generosity in permitting them to be published makes it possible to visualize and appre-

ciate their character in a far better way than through the written word.

For their help in making their collections available, I wish to thank Mr. James Biddle, Acting Curator, American Wing, The Metropolitan Museum of Art, New York; Mr. John M. Graham, Director and Curator of Collections and Mrs. A. Willard Duncan, Associate Curator, Colonial Williamsburg, Virginia; Mr. Kenneth M. Wilson, Curator and Mr. Herbert C. Darbee, Assistant Curator, Old Sturbridge Village, Massachusetts; Hedy Backlin, Curator of Decorative Arts, Cooper Union Museum, New York; Samuel Chamberlain, Marblehead, Massachusetts; Mr. Charles F. Montgomery, Director and Mr. Milo M. Naeve, Secretary, the Henry Francis du Pont Winterthur Museum, Winterthur, Delaware; Mr. Henry P. Maynard, Conservator of Furniture, Wadsworth Atheneum, Hartford, Connecticut; Mr. James Candler, General Merchandizing Manager, Henry Ford Museum and Greenfield Village, Dearborn, Michigan; Alice Winchester and Mr. Lawrence Ross, Antiques Magazine.

JAMES R. MARSH

Fiddlers Forge
Pittstown, New Jersey
April, 1961

INTRODUCTION AND APOLOGY

THIS book is not the very last word on the subject. It is the observations, random notes and studies made at various times and in various places, bits of wisdom gathered from many a lover of the old things much more learned than the author, extending over quite a period of time, on a subject which has so far seemed to have almost entirely escaped the pen of the chronicler; and gathered and arranged so as to show a connected and cumulative record of the wonderful progress which artificial illumination has made in this land of ours from the time

> *"When a band of exiles moored their bark*
> *On the wild New England shore"*

up to the day when the advent of gas and kerosene relegated the old lamps and candlesticks to the closet shelf and the attic. More than that, I have here tried to show that there was an intimate parallel in the purely material development which kept pace with, and was closely linked with, the changing and expanding intellectual, social and moral growth of that sturdy, solid, and, in some aspects, somber and narrow Colony, which, from its small beginning on the forbidding shore of Massachusetts Bay, spread a network of influence and stamped its character upon a vast territory stretching across the mountains and prairies to the farthest West and South, peopled by men of many races and far different habits; and the influence of whose deeds, habits and thoughts, lives to-day in so many of our laws and institutions.

I am as keenly aware as my reader of the enormity of such a task, and my only apology for undertaking it at all is that as there has not been up to the present time, so far as I am aware, any attempt to write a book of this kind, some one must make a beginning. My purposes then in writing this chronicle are these: first, to try to crystallize the fragmentary and confusing bits of information which one picks up, here and there, into a connected and coherent picture, or, series of pictures, in orderly array setting forth the various steps by which the crude, early, dim, inadequate lamps of the early sixteen hundreds gradually evolved into the elegant and fairly satisfactory lighting of the early eighteen hundreds; and putting it in such fashion, with adequate illustrations, that the average collector may have a comprehensive and intelligent grasp of the subject — where before was more or less confusion. Secondly, to try to treat this subject in such a way as to awaken in the mind of the casual reader love for and desire to acquaint himself personally with the great art of collecting, and thus add a few more to that array of congenial souls, scattered all over the country, who find delightful relaxation, as well as a vast fund of interesting information, in getting together a collection of the relics of past generations; and lastly, and, I think, perhaps the most important of all, to make more real in the minds of my readers, particularly the younger people, by means of these bits of by-gone days — links connecting the present with a long-buried and half-forgotten past — the character, the thoughts, and the habits and, particularly, the ideals of those splendid fathers and mothers of our great Republic — for they were men and women of strong and splendid courage, of loyal devotion to their own conception of duty, of deep love for truth and civic and social righteousness, and of faith in a wonderful future for this new land which by their self-sacrifice they were helping to found. And if I can help to visualize to my readers those who daily used these lamps and candlesticks, their modes of life, their virtues, their strong points as well as their weaknesses, their daily habits of thought and action, I feel that I shall have done something at least to help us of the present day to solve wisely and rightly some of the many problems which seem just now to be threatening the very life itself of our democracy, and to get back to those principles of right living and right thinking, in our relations with our fellow men, which were so firmly and deeply rooted in them.

The author realizes, perhaps more keenly than the reader, the many shortcomings of this book. As the reader gets into it, he will doubtless note that there are some types of lamps with which he is more or less familiar or which perhaps are in his own collection which are not illustrated or perhaps not even mentioned. This is due to the fact that the field is so immense that it was simply an impossible task to describe or, even, to know all the variants of the different lighting devices which have appeared from time to time in the widely scattered settlements of this country. Another source of disappointment will be the fact that few authoritative dates are assigned to the varied types of lamps shown.

As many of the older lamps continued to be made and used long years after improved models came into use and many different kinds were in use during the same period in different sections, it is only very occasionally, when one can authenticate some particular specimen with absolute sureness, that a date may be ventured; however, this book should be considered in the light of a primer — the A B C of lamp collecting.

I have been greatly helped by many friends and collectors, in fact without their assistance, I should not have had the courage to put pen to paper. They have given me generously from their stores of knowledge, opened their collections for my inspection and camera, and helped me in every way possible.

My grateful thanks are due particularly to the family of the late Doctor C. A. Quincy Norton, whose untimely death forced the scattering of probably the largest and most comprehensive collection of lamps ever made in this country and the abandon-

ment of the publication of a book on this subject for which he had been collecting a great amount of material, which would have been a really splendid memorial for his years of devotion to the subject. I am indebted to the Anderson Galleries of New York City for courteously allowing me the use of some ten or more plates, illustrating the choicest of Doctor Norton's collection with accompanying notes. Mr. Burton N. Gates of Worcester, Massachusetts, has aided me with much valuable material and notes and has allowed me to photograph some of the best pieces of his collection. Mr. V. M. Hillyer of Baltimore, Maryland, whose collection of lighting devices is a most extensive one, has furnished some fine plates, as well as much information, on this subject in which he has so great an interest. Mrs. Geo. W. Mitton of Jamaica Plain, Boston, has rendered valuable assistance in allowing me to photograph from her large collection of rare Sandwich glass. Mr. Henry Ford of Dearborn, Michigan, has an extensive collection of early lighting devices containing many rare pieces from which he has sent me some excellent pictures which you will find herein. To Mr. C. Lawrence Cooney of Boston, whose home is the old Iron Master's house in Saugus, filled with treasures of all kinds, gathered from Colonial days, and which, together with an inexhaustible fund of antique lore, has been freely opened to me, I am deeply indebted. Also to Mr. Daniel F. Magner of Hingham by whose aid I have added many interesting lamps to my own collection. My sincere thanks are also due Miss Mary Harrod Northend of Salem, the author of books and articles on Colonial days, who opened her rich and extensive collection of photographs for my use; and to the Jordan Marsh Company of Boston for their valuable coöperation in my study of early glass.

To all of these and to the other many friends and collectors who have most generously aided me with photographs of their choice pieces and much valuable information, I wish to express here my grateful acknowledgment of their kindness and generosity. In all this I would not forget Mr. E. B. Luce of Worcester, and F. E. Colby and W. S. Snell of Boston, whose skilled work with lens and camera has placed before my readers, much more vividly than mere words could do, many a rare lamp.

So, gentle reader, if there is found any virtue in these pages it is due in large measure to many good friends; the mistakes are my own.

ARTHUR H. HAYWARD

FOREWORD TO THE SECOND PRINTING

Absence of adverse criticism and the many letters of appreciation from people otherwise unknown to the author, coupled with the fact that the first edition is exhausted and letters from collectors and others seeking to buy the book are being received, makes him feel that another edition at this time would be welcomed.

The further facts that no other book on this subject has as yet been written, and that a constantly increasing number of collectors are interesting themselves in this particular branch of antiques, would seem to justify its reprinting.

That no serious errors have been brought to his attention is very gratifying. A number of friendly suggestions have, however, been made, and he has carefully gone over the text, modifying such statements and making other slight changes as these suggestions would seem to warrant.

As the only text-book on the development of lighting appliances in the New England colonies, it has, within the limits of a small first printing, found a place in the homes of collectors, the shops of dealers, the shelves of public libraries and the studios of architects and decorators.

This, of course, is very pleasing to the author, but he feels in duty bound to respond to the letters recently received, and to share his enthusiasm and knowledge (so far as it goes) with the large numbers who have heretofore not known, or have been unable to secure copies of the first printing, hence this edition.

ARTHUR H. HAYWARD

January 1, 1927

CONTENTS

ILLUSTRATIONS

DRAWINGS BY THE AUTHOR

SUPPLEMENT ILLUSTRATIONS

PLATE NUMBER | PAGE

Colonial and Early American Lighting

CHAPTER I

LAMPS OF ANCIENT DAYS

To one who is at all interested in the subject of the development of lighting from the crude primitive lamps of early New England Pilgrim days, the study of artificial illumination from the earliest times is very essential, as furnishing not only a starting point but a fitting background from which the remarkable changes of the last three centuries stand out with great vividness.

If we pick up one of the "Betty" lamps, the little iron open wick lamps which the first New England pioneers brought over on the *Mayflower* and subsequent ships, and which, filled with rank-smelling fish oil, furnished what little light they had, aside from the blazing logs in the crude fireplaces of the log huts, during those gloomy winter days of 1620 and following years; we must hark back thousands of years, for this Plymouth lamp of 1620 A.D. is identical in design and principle with lamps found in excavating the buried cities of Greece, Rome and other once famous and populous countries of Asia, Europe and Africa — but now only a memory — some of them dating as far back as 6000 B.C. Compare the Plate 2 with Plate 4 showing a collection of lamps from Doctor Norton: the resemblance is startling, which brings us to the astounding fact that while civilization was advancing steadily and at times swiftly, and remarkable progress was being made in art, science, learning and handicraft of almost every kind, such an essential and important thing as artificial lighting remained practically at the same point for at least ten thousand years, and it is only within the last two hundred years that the tremendous advance was accomplished.

The origin of the first lamp is hidden in the dark and mysterious recesses of time at the beginning of history. For myself I can see a picture of some vigorous and powerful specimen of a cave man, returning from a successful hunt, his stone weapons in his hand and his quarry flung across his shoulders. He comes to the entrance of his cave house and flings down his burden while he seeks rest and warmth by the open fire which is carefully guarded and kept alive from the smouldering embers of the last great thunder storm when jagged bolts of lightning started a devastating forest fire. His female companion takes the slaughtered animal, crudely dresses it and props it up in front of the fire for roasting. Idly watching, the cave man sees that some of the fat from the roasting meat has dripped down on the rock and has formed a tiny pool, and into this as he looks, from one of the logs just placed on the fire, drops a tiny bit of dry moss, all ablaze. It floats about on the surface of the oily pool, sending up a spiral of smoke from its tiny flame. His attention is called away by some sounds in the forest yonder and he forgets it for the time. After a bit his eyes idly light on it again to observe that it still floats and burns with increased energy. The meat is now ready and he tears off a portion for himself and then the rest is distributed among the others of his family. When he has finished and he goes to renew the fire which has burned down to a bed of embers, he notices the floating moss still burning with a small, hot, steady flame and then and there is formed the idea of the first lamp. He goes out and picks up from the refuse heap the skull of some small animal, into which he puts some of the hot, melted fat and lighting a piece of dry moss drops it in, and the first lamp made by the hand of man has come into being.

When one considers how much of the world's business and

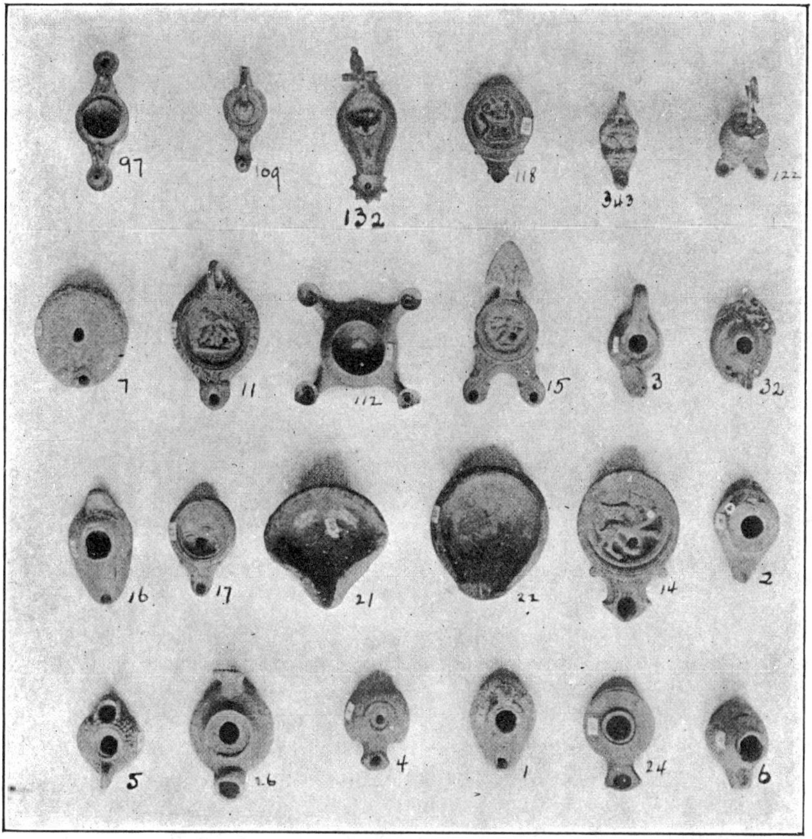

PLATE 2. *See pages 3, 9, 10*

Ancient Pottery and Bronze Lamps
From Dr. C. A. Q. Norton's Collection

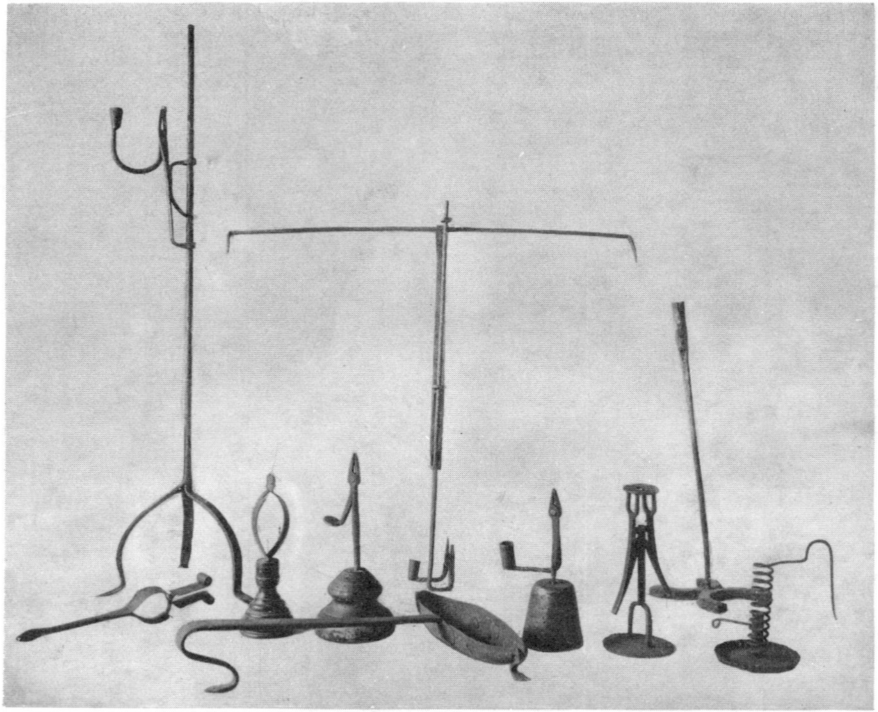

PLATE 3.

GROUP OF EARLY IRON RUSH-LIGHT HOLDERS
Collection of Mr. V. M. Hillyer, Baltimore

See pages 8, 92, 93

pleasure has been done after the sun has disappeared, it seems strange that the ingenuity of man, so abundantly exercised in other directions, should not have been turned to the subject of artificial lighting and that the absurdly inadequate and crude methods of those very ancient days should have been accepted, apparently without serious protest, almost up to the present. When, however, the change did come, it was most rapid and from the glittering, gorgeous "White Way" of a twentieth century metropolis back to the days of our Pilgrim forefathers seems like a journey of innumerable ages, while it is really only a span of some six or eight generations.

It may be fairly assumed that, next to implements of warfare, stone and clay lamps were among the first articles for domestic use made by the hand of man. Almost all the large museums of the world have collections of lamps which have been found in excavating the sites of cities which have grown to prominence and fame, been the seat of opulence, luxury and the higher civilization of the times and have finally disappeared and been covered by the dust and debris of centuries and then quite frequently furnished the sites of yet other cities which have passed through the same cycle.

This little drawing is of an old lamp of sun-dried clay from the collection of Doctor Norton of Hartford, Connecticut. It was found many feet beneath the surface on the site of the city of Nippur, one of the oldest of the Babylonian cities, near the entrance to the King's Library. As this city was destroyed more than six thousand years before Christ, it makes the age of this lamp at least eight thousand years. Excavations in Egypt, Asia Minor, and southern Europe, in the countries of the older civilizations, among the household utensils often yield lamps, or parts of lamps, which find their way into the museums.

The very earliest of these lamps are usually of clay, either sun-dried or kiln-burned, and of course are fragile and easily broken. Later they were cut from rock; and finally when the use of ores became known they were fashioned from iron, bronze and other metals, but invariably the shape was the same, no matter of what material made: a hollow receptacle for the oil, either open or covered, a handle for carrying it, on one side, and opposite it a little trough or gutter in which the wick rested. As civilization advanced the lamps assumed a more artistic aspect. The shapes became less clumsy, the general appearance more graceful and delicate ornamentation began to appear on those carved from stone or cast from bronze or other metals.

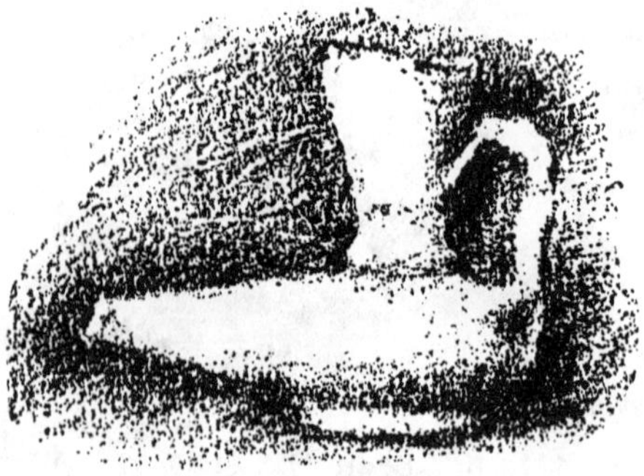

Both the Greeks and the Romans made lamps from alabaster and metals which show both in workmanship and design artistic ability of a very high order.

Lamps are frequently referred to in ancient writings. Homer, the Greek poet, writing about 950 B.C. speaks of the lamps and torches used in the temples, and Heroditus in 445 B.C. describes the procession of lamps, a festival held at Sais in Egypt, and remarks upon the vast number and variety of lamps there displayed.

An early mention in the Bible is found in the fifteenth chapter of Genesis — God is making his covenant with Abram and tells him to build an altar and place sacrifices thereon and then the record says:

> And it came to pass that when the sun went down and it was dark, behold a smoking furnace and a burning lamp [or a torch] that passed between those pieces.

Again there is more specific mention of lamps as we use the word in the account in the twenty-fifth chapter of Exodus of the directions for making the golden candlestick (or more properly a golden lamp stand) for the tabernacle. In the thirty-first verse we find:

And thou shalt make a candlestick of pure gold, of beaten work shall the candlestick be made; his shaft and his branches, his bowls, his knops and his flowers shall be made of the same — and six branches shall come out of the sides of it; three branches of the candlestick out of the one side thereof and three branches of the candlestick out of the other side.

Then in the thirty-seventh verse:

And thou shalt make the seven lamps thereof; and they shall light the lamps thereof; that they may give light over against it.

And in the twenty-seventh chapter, the twentieth verse we read:

And thou shalt command the children of Israel that they bring thee pure olive oil beaten for the light to cause the lamp to burn always.

And again in the thirty-seventh chapter, the twenty-third verse,—" And he made his seven lamps and his snuffers and his snuff dishes of pure gold ",— showing that ornamental lamps burning with a wick in olive oil were well known by Hebrew artisans at that early date.

In Greece and Rome at most of the out-of-door celebrations and arena games as well as the larger feasts indoors, the illumination was by torches in metal baskets of resinous woods, fats and other inflammable material, and one of the early Greek writers in speaking of the pale smoky flame from fats and oils says, " One could not enjoy the good things of the table until his indulgence in wine had made him indifferent to the stench of the smoking lamps."

A variety may be found in a very primitive and ancient form of torch or huge candle made up of long stalks of flax or rushes pressed together and saturated with grease or tallow. As this burns freely and rather rapidly, it is kept coiled up and pulled out as fast as it is consumed. These were used at the olden Hebrew weddings and other ceremonial occasions and were undoubtedly what was referred to by Jesus, when He said, " A bruised reed shall he not break, and smoking flax shall he not quench till he send forth judgment unto victory." These rush lights were also used extensively among the poorer people of Europe and also to a limited extent by the early Pilgrims in New England and were made in the same way — hollow reed, or rushes saturated with tallow or fat and made in long ribbons, burning them in rush light holders as shown in Plate 3.

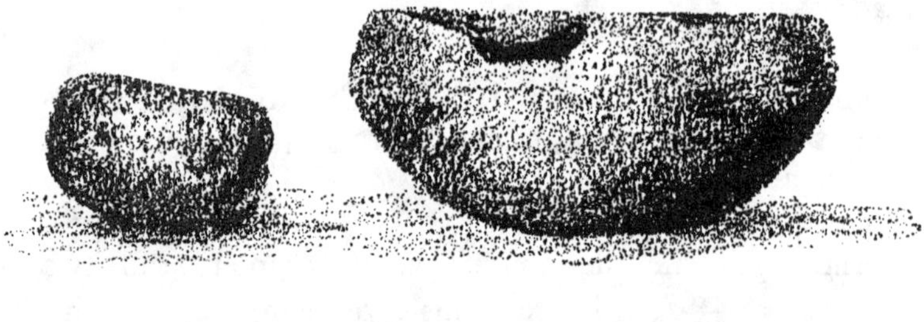

One curious fact is that the only aborigines of this continent known to have lamps were the Esquimaux, whose lamps of stone, clay, or bone were a very important and highly prized part of their household equipment. Oil of the seal, whale, and walrus was burned in these lamps, moss furnishing the wick,

PLATE 4. See pages 3, 16, 17

IRON "BETTYS" AND OTHER EARLY LAMPS
Dr. C. A. Q. Norton's Collection, Hartford

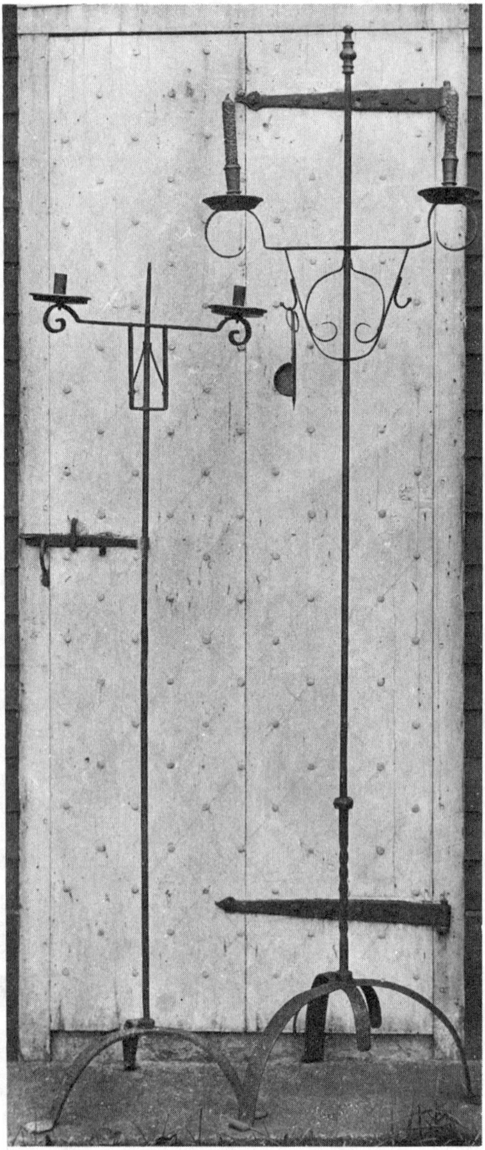

PLATE 5. *See pages 82, 87, 88*

TWO HAND WROUGHT IRON CANDLE STANDS, TAKEN IN FRONT OF THE DOOR OF THE IRON MASTER'S HOUSE, SAUGUS
Courtesy of C. Lawrence Cooney

and the Esquimaux often made long, hard journeys to the places where they could obtain the soapstone. So highly valued were they that no young man was considered ready to marry unless he could show at least one or more lamps, which became the dowry of the bride and in the family life were the particular pride and care of the women. But no trace of lamps of any kind has been found among the ruins left by the mound builders and other very early inhabitants of this country, and none was known by the Indians roaming the forests and hunting grounds when found by the first white men.

Plate 2 gives views of a very interesting collection of ancient lamps gathered together by the late Doctor C. A. Quincy Norton of Hartford, Connecticut, who became very much interested in the subject of lighting and spent a number of years traveling about the country, gathering specimens illustrating different periods in the gradual development, and particularly lamps having some historic association.

He planned to use his collection to illustrate a book on the evolution of lighting, with particular emphasis on the work of the colonists of America, which should be an exhaustive and authoritative treatise on the subject, but unfortunately he died before his book was completed and his vast store of information on the subject was lost to the world. After his death his collection was dispersed by auction sale in New York and several of the plates in this book are from the catalogue of that sale.

Perhaps his most attractive (to us at least) lamps are those associated with famous men and women — some of those are shown here in this book and will be referred to in later chapters.

His collection of ancient lamps was very interesting. In Plate 2, Numbers 1 and 2 are small lamps, some three inches in length made of sun-baked clay, and were found on the site of the buried city of Nippur in Babylonia. As this city was destroyed at least six thousand years before Christ, it means that the potter's hands who fashioned them worked some eight thousand or more years ago. Numbers 3, 4, 5, 6, and 7, while not so old, long outdate the Christian era and were found buried among the ruins of Rome and cities of Egypt and Palestine. Numbers 11, 14, 15, 16, and 17 are also clay lamps of a somewhat later period, most of them of Grecian origin and showing a decided development in form and decoration.

Numbers 21 and 22, while quite similar in shape, were found far apart. They show an open or saucer-shaped lamp of clay with a slight depression in one side for the wick. Number 21 came from Armenia and is supposed to be at least two thousand years old, while Number 22 was found in the north of Scotland and dates back to about the fifteenth century.

These open saucer lamps, either in pottery or iron, are occasionally found here, in New England or in the South, and are often locally known as " grease lamps " or sometimes called " slut lamps ", but as they were very crude the number used must have been limited and they were soon superseded by better and more efficient ones. Number 32 is a carved soapstone lamp from Japan and dates from the twelfth century.

It is interesting to note how closely the lines of these lamps follow one another though coming from places so widely separated.

Numbers 97, 109, 118 are all bronze lamps, probably of Grecian origin, while Number 343 is from Rome.

Number 132 is a very early Christian lamp, bronze, of undoubted Roman make and probably dates from the first or second century. It is in unusually fine condition for one so old.

These lamps, stretching over centuries, from many parts of the world, give us the starting point from which the active minds and brains of our own ancestors gradually evolved, slowly at first, then much more rapidly, keeping pace with the economic and intellectual development of the times, the various lighting devices which are the subject of the succeeding chapters.

CHAPTER II

EARLY COLONIAL LAMPS—IRON AND TIN

THE first Pilgrim lamp was of the type known to-day as the iron "Betty" as shown in the drawing. Captain John Carver, first Governor of Plymouth Colony, purchased in Holland just before he sailed a Dutch iron "Betty" lamp, the feeble light of which undoubtedly helped to make less gloomy that crowded cabin from which dates so much of our history.

Such small iron lamps, as may be seen, were very similar in shape to the old Greek, Roman and Assyrian ones and precisely the same in principle. The body was usually cast or wrought in one solid piece, with the nose or spout for the wick to lie in at one end, and a short, curved upright handle opposite. To this handle were often attached a short linked chain with an iron spindle and hooked end, and also a slender iron pick to free the wick when it became crusted with soot or carbon. The spindle was used either to hang up the lamp from the top of the chair where the reader sat or to fasten it in position by sticking the sharp end between the stones of the fireplace. Oil was obtained from the swarms of small fish found in great abundance all along the coast; but the light was very feeble, the wick constantly crusting over, and the odor of the burning fish oil anything but agreeable.

Another very common form of illumination in those early days was what is known as "Candle-Wood." Pieces of the resinous pitch pine, so common all along the wooded New England coast, were cut in length and size not unlike large candles and stuck between the stones of the crude fireplaces or in improvised holders. They burned freely, giving quite a bright flame with, however, considerable smoke; and since the only expense was the time and trouble of cutting and drying the wood, they were used very generally for many years. It was common at night to see the family gathered round the big stone fireplace, often in the only room of comfortable size in the crude log house. On the hearth a fire of huge logs briskly burned, and two or three of the resinous candle-wood torches — either stuck in the sides of the fireplace between the stones, or standing upright on the hearth — supplemented the light from the burning logs. By these mingled lights the good man could see to read the Bible, which he had brought with him from the old country; while the mother spun her flax or wool for the family clothing or industriously drove her shuttle back and forth in the big loom over in the corner; and while the children in their seats near the sides of the great fireplace studied from the few primitive books which they had, or did their daily stents in needlework.

Many families laid in each winter a large supply of this candlewood, which for many years in the poorer homes all over New England was the common illuminant for the long winter evenings.

One of the Pilgrim Fathers, writing in 1642, says of these candle-wood torches, "Out of these Pines is gotten the candle-wood that is so much spoken of, which may serve as a shift among the poorer folks; but I cannot commend it for singular good, because it droppeth a pitchy kind of substance where it stands." This form of lighting, however, seems to have been in general use for many years. It is said that Eliot, the apostle

PLATE 6. *See page 81*

FINELY WROUGHT IRON TABLE CANDLE STAND
Collection of C. Lawrence Cooney, Saugus

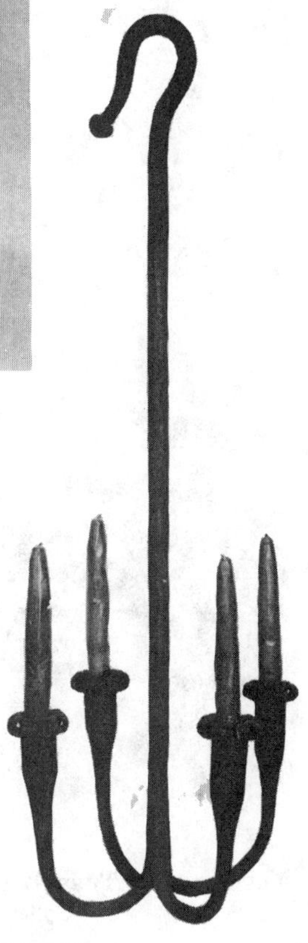

WROUGHT IRON HANGING CANDELABRUM FROM AN OLD VIRGINIA MANSION
Collection of Clarence W. Brazer, Chester, Pennsylvania

PLATE 7. *See page 90*

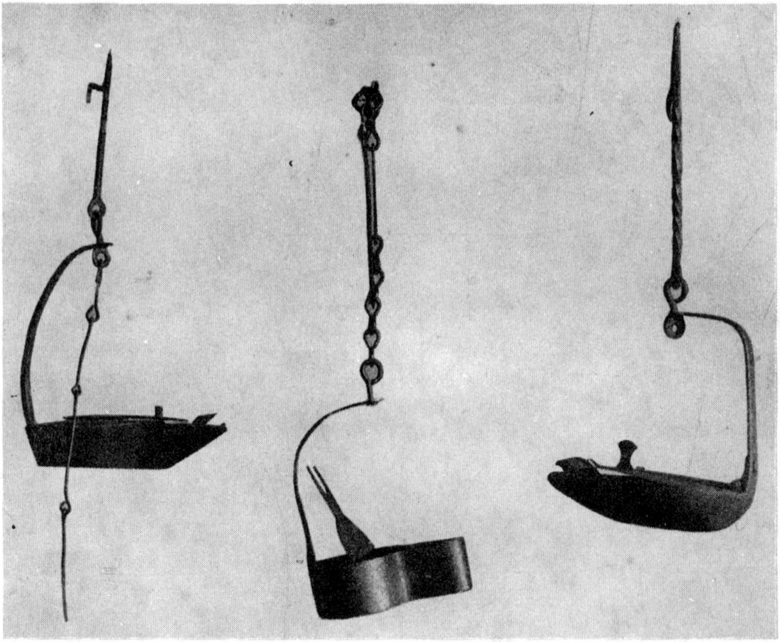

PLATE 8.

See pages 14, 16

IRON "BETTY" LAMPS

Author's Collection

PLATE 9.

See page 27

PAIR OF RARE TIN THREE-WICK GUEST ROOM LAMPS — ONE WITH SPICE HOLDER

Collection of C. L. Cooney, Saugus

to the Indians, translated the Bible into the Indian tongue by the light of these pine torches.

The very first Pilgrim lamps were the few brought over from England and the continent in the *Mayflower* and other ships, but the enterprise and spirit of independence so manifest in these sturdy pioneers soon asserted itself. Upon the discovery about 1630 of a deposit of bog iron some ten miles from Boston in that section of the country now within the limits of the town of Saugus, a primitive smelter was set up and the manufacture commenced of iron utensils such as pots, kettles, simple agricultural and carpenters' tools, and, doubtless, "Betty" lamps; for we find quite a variety of shapes in the various collections of these lamps which have been preserved.

The house of the master of this earliest of New England foundries, which is still standing, is well worth visiting. Originally built in 1639, it was discovered and acquired a few years since by Mr. Wallace Nutting, a gentleman intensely interested in everything pertaining to early New England. At the time he bought it, many of its original lines had been changed — its sturdy hand-hewn oak frames covered with laths and plaster, its fireplaces bricked up, its old stairs removed, and many other changes made. With the help of competent architects and interested antiquarians, he made a careful study of the house to determine the original lines. After slow, delicate labor to uncover the original wood and brick work and to replace parts destroyed, he had the satisfaction of restoring "Broadhearth", as he called it, to something probably very like its original appearance both inside and out, so that to-day it stands as one of the best examples of very early American houses in New England. Since many of those early houses were destroyed in the numerous encounters with the Indians, doubtless the preservation of "Broadhearth" is due to the fact that, when the deposit of bog iron was discovered, a smelter set up, and operations begun, the iron master surrounded his house, which was most pretentious for that early date, with the dwellings of a small army of workmen sufficiently strong to ward off the predatory attacks of roving Indian bands.

Mr. C. L. Cooney, a well-known collector and antiquarian of Boston, was its recent owner. He was fitting "Broad-hearth" out entirely with early New England furnishings from his large collection, aiming to preserve it as an educational specimen most valuable to the youth of to-day, but has recently died. An extended study of its interesting features, both outside and within, will well repay any one interested in the social history of New England.

Later than the development of Saugus iron, as ships brought supplies from England, tin was substituted for iron, since it is lighter, neater and more easily made. We find one pattern of lamp called the "Ipswich Betty" and another the "Newburyport Betty", from the settlements where they were made, both closely following the lines of the iron lamps. Some, instead of being made to hang like the iron "Betty", were attached to stands and were even made adjustable so that the light could be moved up or down at the will of the reader. In Plate 17, Number 396, Doctor Norton shows a tin "Betty" similar in shape to the iron one in the writer's collection (Plate 8).

But in all the lamps the same objectionable open wick, which gave little light but much smoke and smell, prevailed; and the constant crusting over of the wick made the incessant use of the pick a very troublesome necessity. To overcome this trouble in some measure, an unknown but ingenious mechanic entirely enclosed the wick in a circular tube. The body of the lamp with the round nose or wick spout still at the side as shown in Plates 10, 17, 29 and 51 was now made larger and deeper to hold more oil, and some lamps were furnished with two wicks, one on each side, thus doubling the light.

A rather curious feature of many of these lamps shows the habit of thrift even in so small a matter as the amount of oil —

a commodity although by no means scarce or expensive, at the same time not to be lightly wasted. This economical device was an extra spout immediately beneath the wick spout proper. This curved tin gutter was intended to save the oil, which, drawn up by the wick faster than it could burn, dripped down over the edge of the nose, was caught by the projecting rim beneath, and was carried down underneath the main body of the lamp itself to a separate receptacle where it would be collected for use again. Since these lamps, as well as the iron and tin "Bettys", are not at all common, they are well worth finding and collecting.

An early step from this stage of lamp design was the placing of the wick tube upright on the top of the lamp. This form continued to be made for a long time.

In the meantime, while these various changes had been taking place in the shape of the lamp itself, changes had also been made in the fluids used for fuel. At the very first the oil was tried out of the livers of the fish most conveniently at hand, with little or no attempt to refine it, but the very disagreeable odor and the insufficient amount of light given soon brought about a search for a more satisfactory illuminant.

In the early days, whales were very abundant all along the New England coast. I do not know who first discovered the fact that the sperm and right whales yielded in great quantity an oil which made an excellent illuminant, but, beginning earlier than 1680 and continuing for nearly a hundred years, whale fishing carried on from the shore in small boats became a common and quite important industry of many towns all along the New England coast. Along toward the middle of the eighteenth century the whales became so scarce that it was necessary to employ larger vessels and go much farther away for them. The whaling industry then became a very important one for a number of New England seaports and entered so much into every day life that at least one of the old fishing villages on Cape Cod in town meeting passed an ordinance that the heads of all whales captured by the townspeople should be given the minister. The little town of Nantucket, on the island of that name just off the southern coast of Massachusetts, from about 1700 to 1758, it is stated, " had more vessels employed in whaling than any other New England port." Later, however, New Bedford came to the front and held the supremacy for many years, until the discovery and introduction of kerosene as an illuminant lessened the demand for the sperm oil.

One interesting and significant feature of all " Betty " and " Phoebe " lamps is the similarity of design, a point illustrated clearly by Plate 4, showing iron lamps from Doctor Norton's collection. Numbers 72 and 73 vary from the usual " Betty " form in that each has a double base, doubtless to catch the drippings from the burning wick. This design is commonly called the " Phoebe " lamp. The two reproduced are old specimens from Normandy, whereas Number 60 is said to have been found in a mountain cave in Armenia and is thought to be even older. Number 168, an iron hanging lamp dating back more than three centuries, came from a small town in Italy. Although found in widely separated parts of the world, all these lamps are identical in size, shape, and burning arrangement.

The three New England " Betty " lamps in the author's collection, shown in Plate 8, though similar in size and general appearance, illustrate some differences. The perfect one, having the staple to hang it by as well as the wick pick, is almost identical in shape with the famous Governor Carver lamp, a drawing of which is on page 11. In this lamp an opening in the centre of the top is covered by a sliding iron plate. The lid of the iron lamp with a slightly rounded bottom covers the entire top and hinges at the base of the curved handle so that it lifts up and down instead of sliding sideways. The hanging staple in this lamp is much larger than that of the first lamp and the

PLATE 10. *See pages 14, 30, 31*

EARLY LAMPS IN COPPER, TIN, BRASS AND EARTHENWARE
Collection of Henry Ford, Dearborn, Michigan

PLATE 11. *See page 30*

EARLY LAMPS IN TIN, IRON AND PEWTER
Collection of Henry Ford, Michigan

PLATE 12. *See pages 87, 89*

Beautifully Wrought Iron Candle Stand with Extinguisher and Snuffers

Collection of Francis D. Brinton, West Chester, Pennsylvania

stem of it is twisted in a crude attempt at ornamentation. The third lamp, probably of a later date, is more carefully made. The bottom and top of the body, which is box-shaped, were cast separately and riveted together. The curved handle is also riveted on. The cover is unlike either of the other two in that it is hinged across the middle. All these lamps have circular openings cut out for the wick and each of the first two has a separate lip or spout, quite noticeable, for the wick to lie in. The chain and pick of this last lamp evidently do not belong to it.

Plate 4, Number 157 shows still another variation of the "Betty." This specimen, found in old Quebec, has, instead of the usual curved handle, a straight back with openings through which may run an upright rod controlled by a spring so that the lamp may be raised or lowered at the reader's convenience. But to a New Englander by far the most interesting lamp on this page is Number 100 in the centre of the lower row. Cast from heavy iron in the form of a cup and saucer with places for wicks in both the cup and base and with an iron handle to carry it by, this lamp is authentically reported to have been cast at the Saugus iron foundry and to have been used in 1692 during that strange and dark period in early New England history marked by "witchcraft" in Salem. The rude severity of this lamp well symbolizes the uncanny events of which it was a witness. In Plate 45 appears a somewhat similar grease lamp of cast iron, also connected with Salem witchcraft; for it is believed to have been used in the Salem prison during the trial and imprisonment of those accused. It stands about six inches high and holds in a little lip the wick of twisted rag.

Being myself a native of Salem and accustomed to see frequently Gallows Hill where the executions took place, I have taken some pains to acquaint myself with the history of that period and with the scenes brought vividly to mind by these lamps as connecting links between the present and that inglorious past.

There are several facts which should be taken into account when considering how such an hysteria or insanity could have spread so rapidly and taken such an extraordinary hold upon entire communities of sober, industrious, upright, God-fearing and intelligent people.

The colonists after undergoing in their home country persecutions, many of them most bitter, had established themselves in a new and strange land; surrounded by deep, heavy forests in which were wild animals and wilder and fiercer savage foes; obliged to endure untold hardships of privation, disease, hunger, biting cold, and ruthless attack; burdened with heavy taxes; thrown into dismay and uncertainty of their future by the loss of their charter; and their coast settlements invested by hostile sea-pirates and privateers so that commerce was nearly at a standstill. The colony was in just the mental condition to be swept by the fear of witchcraft, a belief in which was common in England and on the Continent for centuries. The mischief began early in 1692 in the family of the Reverend Mr. Parris, the minister in charge of the religious society in what was then Salem Village, now a part of Danvers. His daughter and niece, together with a young girl of the neighborhood named Ann Putnam — three children from ten to fifteen years old — began to act in a strange manner, putting themselves in odd postures, making queer gestures and noises, and attracting the attention of the family. There seemed to be no explanation and physicians were called in. One of them in an evil hour gave it as his opinion that the children were bewitched — that is, they were in the power of some one who had sold herself to the evil one or Satan. The belief that such bargains were possible was by no means uncommon in England and scattered examples of witchcraft had already been found in the new colony here. Some one or two other young girls of the neighborhood began to exhibit similar traits. The Reverend Parris called a council of the neighboring ministers to devote a day to religious services that the power of the evil one might be overcome. During these exercises the children had frequent and violent convulsive fits.

The news of this peculiar behavior spread rapidly and many came to witness the strange sights. When the public had been wrought up sufficiently to demand public investigation, the children, after having been asked repeatedly to name the person or persons attacking them, were forced to designate their supposed persecutors. The first accused or, as the phrase of those days was, "cried out upon", was an old West Indian[1] woman, a servant in the Parris family. An account reads: "By operating upon the old creature's fears and imagination, and, as there is some reason to apprehend, by using severe treatment toward her, she was made to confess that the charge was true and that she was in league with the devil."

We can easily imagine the effect of this confession on the public mind. The suspicious and credulous were confirmed in their belief, the more suggestible developed in their fright symptoms of nervous disorder that were interpreted as evidence that they were bewitched, and those with serious doubts were usually not courageous enough to stand against popular opinion, though some, notably the minister of the Old South Church in Boston, the Reverend Samuel Willard, and one or two of the judges expressed their disbelief and disapproval of the proceedings.

Accusations against others quickly followed, and those accused were at once thrown into prison so that the jails of Salem,

[1] An authority on colonial history made the claim recently that the Indian woman referred to was an "East" Indian, though without documentary evidence to prove the statement. All the old accounts and original manuscripts simply say "an Indian woman in Mr. Parris' family." Woodward in his "Witchcraft Delusion in New England" quotes this passage from Hanson's "History of Danvers" in a footnote: "An Indian woman named Titubba (Titiba or Titibe) said to have been a slave formerly in New Spain (West Indies) . . . When arrested and searched, the marks on her body produced by the sting of the Spaniard's whip were said to be made by the Devil."

Boston, Cambridge, and other towns were crowded with supposed witches.

Some unfortunately, to save their lives, confessed that the charges were true, which only added fuel to the fire now freely burning.

Every man's life was at the mercy of every other man, and many a private grudge was promptly indulged.

One account adds: "Fear sat on every countenance, terror and distress were in all hearts; silence pervaded the streets; many of the people left the country; all business was at a stand, and the feeling, dismal and horrible indeed, became general that the providence of God was removed from them and that they were given over to the dominion of Satan."

The arrests were not confined to the poor and unfortunate but included some in the highest walks, among them a Mrs. English, the wife of a Salem merchant of great wealth, whose accusers acted, it has been implied, through social jealousy. One of the judges was accused and also a member of the immediate family of Doctor Increase Mather, the famous divine, at that time president of Harvard College. Reverend George Burroughs of Wells was not only imprisoned, tried and convicted, but suffered death rather than increase the dangerous delusion by confessing himself guilty of the crime.

Considering the state of the public mind, it is greatly to the credit of the courts that, of the innumerable persons accused, only twenty met their deaths. Nineteen were hanged; one, Giles Corey, was pressed to death; but none was burned as many people believe to this day.

Not all of them came from Salem — though court was held there — but from Andover, Ipswich, Marblehead, Topsfield, and other towns. Most of the persons executed were of advanced age and some left large families of children. Some of the accused fled the country before they could be apprehended and a few escaped from jail. One young man effected his

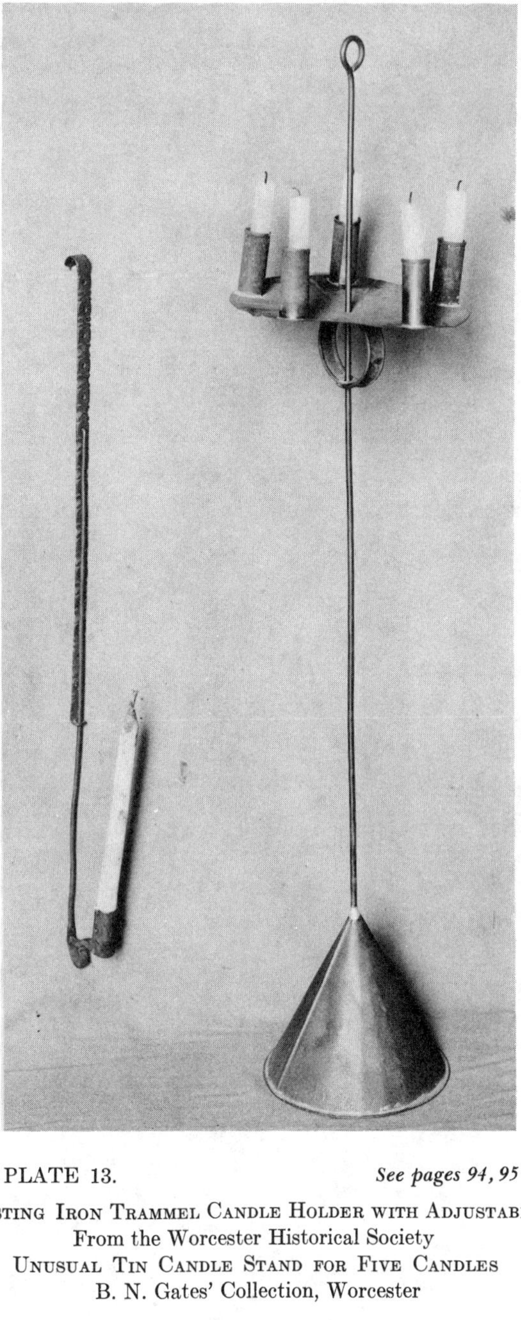

PLATE 13. *See pages 94, 95*

INTERESTING IRON TRAMMEL CANDLE HOLDER WITH ADJUSTABLE ARM
From the Worcester Historical Society
UNUSUAL TIN CANDLE STAND FOR FIVE CANDLES
B. N. Gates' Collection, Worcester

PLATE 14. *See pages 88, 89*

THREE VERY EARLY CANDLE STANDS — TWO OF WOOD, ONE OF IRON
Collection of Burton N. Gates, Worcester

mother's escape and fled with her on horseback to conceal her in a large swamp near what is now Danvers, where he fed her and cared for her until the danger was passed and it was safe to bring her home.

The wicked spell was, however, broken when Mrs. Hale, the wife of the minister of the First Church of Beverly, was accused. She was a woman of such noble character and distinguished virtues that she had endeared herself to the whole community, so that when she was made a victim it caused a storm of protest. Many were convinced that the accusers had deluded themselves, and from that moment the storm subsided as rapidly as it rose.

In addition to the twenty who lost their lives — Reverend George Burroughs of Wells, Samuel Wardwell of Andover, Wilmot Reed of Marblehead, Margaret Scott of Rowley, Susanna Martin of Amesbury, Elizabeth How of Ipswich, Sarah Wildes and Mary Easty of Topsfield, Martha Carrier and Mary Parker of Andover, John Proctor, John Willard, Sarah Good, Rebecca Nurse and Martha Corey of Salem Village, George Jacobs, Jr., Alice Parker, Ann Pudeater, Bridget Bishop (alias Oliver) and Giles Corey of Salem — eight women were in prison condemned to die, more than fifty others had escaped death only by confessing themselves guilty, one hundred and fifty more were in prison awaiting trial, and some two hundred more had been accused. All these in jail, including those condemned to death, were released. It is the opinion popularly accepted to-day that the children began in a spirit of mischief, perhaps with a fancied grudge against certain persons in view, and upon seeing the credulity of their parents and neighbors and that they were the center of so much attention, kept on in a spirit of bravado; but this explanation alone is wholly inadequate.

It is by no means certain that the children were shamming even at first. Hysteria and temporary insanity are not unknown in adolescent children to-day. In that day and in a community in its third generation of constant danger without and religious tension within, such nervous disorders were to be expected. Developed in one child, the symptoms would spread irresistibly by imitation to her playmates and would be exaggerated as they spread.

Supposing for a moment that the first symptoms were not hysterical but merely child's play, possibly some tricks of magic learned from the West Indian woman; what child of ten could fail to become hysterical when grave elders and authoritative doctors told her that she was certainly in the power of witches? The subsequent treatment of the children was enough to drive them to worse madness than pointing out the person they knew who was most like what they imagined a witch to be. The subsequent exhibition of the children to the most impressionable was enough to spread the hysteria. No one acquainted with the time and place can doubt that it was a fertile field for crowd insanity. No one who reads contemporary accounts can doubt that something very real and very serious ailed the victims. The cause is a different question.

In all fairness it must be remembered that as long as a popular belief in witchcraft prevailed, unscrupulous persons were likely to be found who made use of this belief by pretending to supernatural powers and by using the influence they thus obtained as best suited their purposes. Some of these "witches" were of course deluded by the theories of the day, their own thaumaturgy, and the behavior of their victims to suppose that they were actually in league with the powers of evil. And so they were as far as their purposes were malevolent. Incidentally the Calvinist doctrine of predestination to be damned tended to thrust the unbalanced toward diabolism. The law of to-day like the law of yesterday recognizes that those who pretend to exercise the power of magic should be punished, though the Biblical penalty is no longer the legal one. Whether any person or persons in Salem practiced witchcraft in this sense is probably open to doubt. That many were really suspected and that any who were guilty deserved punishment is not doubtful at all. The proceedings of the Salem court cannot be labeled hysterical and malicious any more than the danger to the community can be labeled child's play. Court records and contemporary history as well as the small number of executions in proportion to the number of indictments indicate cautious procedure. Furthermore, by excluding spectral evidence the Salem court established a precedent that was followed by European courts and did more than anything else to end prosecutions for witchcraft throughout the world.

It is worth recording that, after the reign of terror had passed, many who had been most active in their prosecutions repented of their folly and did all in their power to make amends to those who had been accused but afterward released.

Judge Sewall of Boston, one of the judges on the bench at the trials, during the remainder of his life annually spent a day of fasting, humiliation and prayer in his own home, and on the day set for the general fast, had read from the pulpit of the Old South Church where he worshipped (he himself stood during the reading) a confession of his error in these cases and prayed the forgiveness of God and the people for the part which he unwittingly had taken in the condemnation of the innocent. So ends a very sad chapter in Massachusetts history, caught sight of by the flicker of a long-extinguished lamp.

Iron lamps seem not to have remained long in favor; at any rate, genuine old specimens are quite rare and hard to find. They were soon superseded by tin lamps, made in infinite variety until well into the beginning of the nineteenth century. They were easily made, durable, efficient, and inexpensive. All of these qualities recommended them for common use so that even when, after a time, more elaborate glass lamps, candlesticks and candelabra came into favor, they never quite forced out the tin lamps for common use.

One very interesting thing about collecting lamps, especially tin, pewter, and glass, is the great variety in design and often ingenuity exhibited in their manufacture. Since they were made during a long period, something like two hundred years, it is often very difficult, sometimes impossible, to give an approximate idea of their age unless one is fortunate enough to be personally acquainted with the history of the particular specimen. As a general rule the first ones made naturally followed closely the lines of the "Betty" lamps.

One very odd and ingenious tin lamp in my possession is illustrated in Plate 29, the left-hand lamp in the top row. I have seen only a few like it and there is no mention of any such lamp in Doctor Norton's collection, so I judge it must be quite uncommon. The center cylinder, which has a tin handle and rests in a saucer-like base, is fitted with a threaded shaft running through, and protruding from, the top. This shaft has a tight, heavy piece of leather at the top of the cylinder, fitting snugly. At the bottom, and connecting with it, is a smaller cylinder, oval in form, which contains the wick — a flat wide one. The large cylinder was filled with oil, or perhaps some semiliquid fat like chicken grease; the top was then put on and the oil or fat, feeding down through the bottom into the side cylinder, was there picked up by the wick to feed the flame. If the oil did not feed freely enough, the top protruding from the large cylinder (the end of which was squared to fit a clock key) was turned, forcing the tight leather plunger or head down into the cylinder and consequently forcing the fat or oil through the bottom into the second cylinder, high enough for the wick to suck it up. In certain country districts where cheese was made, after the cheese had been put in the press there was a liquid residue containing much butter fat. This fat was carefully removed, clarified,

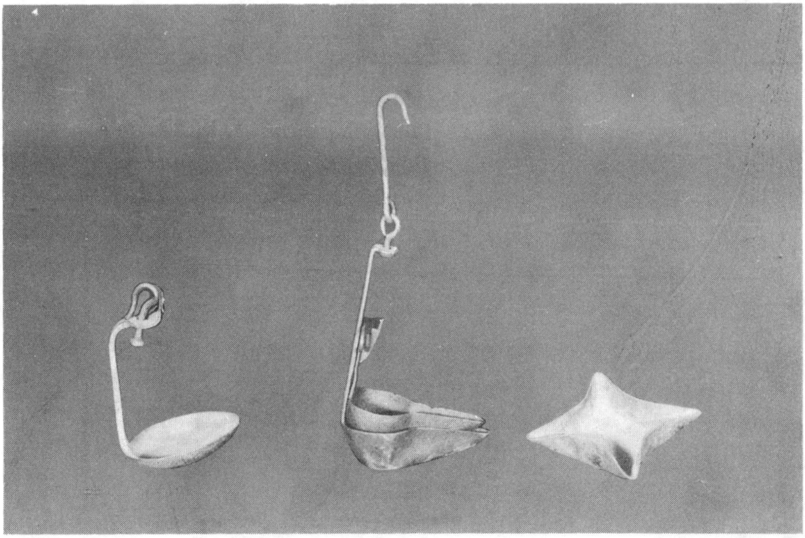

PLATE 15. *See pages 29, 30*

THREE PRIMITIVE IRON GREASE LAMPS
Collection of Henry Ford, Michigan

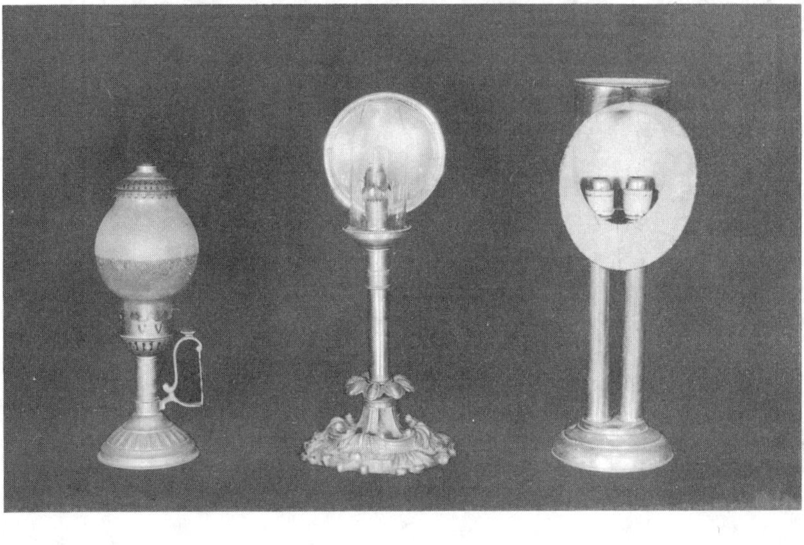

PLATE 16. *See page 103*

THREE CANDLE LAMPS
Collection of Henry Ford, Michigan

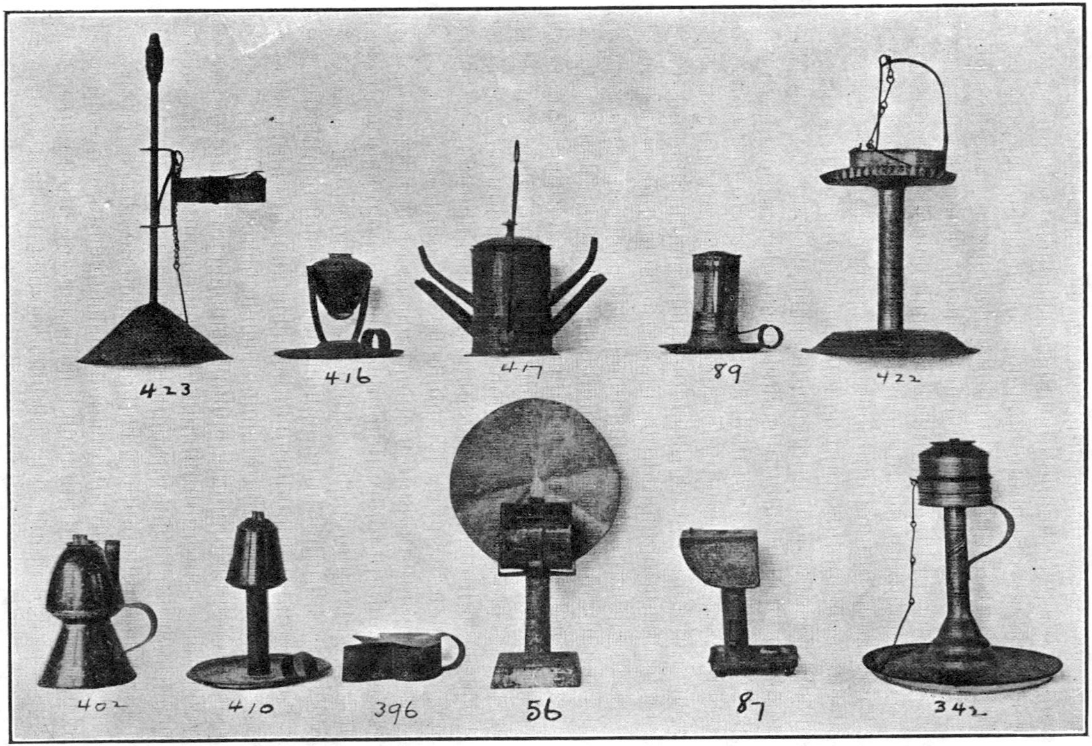

PLATE 17.
GROUP OF EARLY TIN LAMPS

See pages 14, 32, 33, 34, 35
Dr. C. A. Q. Norton, Hartford, Connecticut

and used in broad-wicked lamps called "whey butter lamps." It is quite possible that this lamp is one of them.

The two similar tin lamps, called sometimes shop lamps, one in the lower left-hand corner of Plate 51 and the other the right-hand one in the upper row of Plate 29 in the writer's possession, are early specimens and interesting in having drip pans to allow the superfluous oil to run into the separate removable compartments. One is a hanging lamp and the other sits in a tin plate with a turned up edge.

One occasionally runs across some piece which is quite strange and unusual. One afternoon while I was visiting Mr. C. L. Cooney, who was a very enthusiastic and well-informed collector, he showed me the curious lamp shown in Plate 57. This lamp is striking in design, workmanship, and material, because it is fashioned from copper — a rather rare metal in early lamps. The lamp is very old, but beautifully made. It consists of a long shallow box, divided by partitions into eight small compartments of equal size; over each compartment in the hinged cover is fitted a small wick tube holding a wick running down into the box beneath. The story is that this lamp was used by the early Jesuit missionaries among the Indians. These devout and self-sacrificing men, in order to teach the Indian converts the efficacy of prayer, divided these lamps into separate compartments, each of the same size, holding the same quantity of oil, thus signifying that every soul had the same value in God's sight. Each person was assigned a separate wick, the chiefs always the first and last fonts. Prayers were said while the lamps burned until each oil font was exhausted. This lamp, said to be the only one of its kind in existence, was formerly in the possession of Archbishop Burke of Albany, New York. In both design and material it is strikingly like the old Hanukkah lamps used by the Jews in their festival. Possibly the Jesuit missionaries came into possession of one of them and adapted it to their own needs in their work among the Indians. This rare and valuable piece links the present to that distant past when, for the faith, devout men both Catholic and Protestant, literally took their lives in their hands to plunge into that vast and uncharted wilderness inhabited by savage Indians, in order that the Gospel might be brought to them. Could this lamp talk, it would doubtless tell many tales of almost incredible hardships endured by these faithful Jesuits, and of beautiful self-sacrifice and devotion to the tenets of their Church. This rare lamp should some day come to its final resting place among the hallowed relics of the Roman Catholic Church.

In Plate 1 is a group of iron lamps on a table equally interesting and rare, the property of Mr. B. N. Gates of Worcester. It is an example of the trestle-table, or candle-stand, and probably dates from the seventeenth century, so it is quite in the period of the lamps it holds, wonderfully fine and perfect pieces. The first on the left is of course a " Betty " of wrought iron. The workmanship is noticeably good: it has a hinged cover, and though it has no pick like that on the lamp of similar design in the author's collection, the staple to suspend the lamp from the logs of the walls or the stones of the fireplace is of the exact length to use as a wick pick. Whether this peculiarity of design was intentional or only a coincidence, nevertheless it is an interesting fact.

The second specimen is an iron rush-light holder, descriptions of which will be taken up in the chapter devoted to candles and candlesticks. This holder also is a fine piece of iron work, probably made in England, although equally good work of a similar character was turned out from the forges of many New England blacksmith-shops.

The third lamp is as fine an instance as I have ever seen of the extremely rare double " Betty ", or, as it was often called, " Phoebe " lamp. The top part, or lamp proper, slides up and down on the flat iron upright and can be detached. In fact, when Mr. Gates bought it, it had been put on the handle, back side to, and also used as a lamp, making two suspended from the one handle. These lamps are much cruder and more simple than the regular " Bettys " and have no cover or wick trough, the twisted rag serving as a wick simply lying in the nose. There is nice work here in the end of the handle and in the slender iron rod with the shepherd's crook, which was used for suspending it from wall or chair back.

The last lamp on this Plate 1 is a more clumsily wrought iron " Betty " : its shape is not graceful and the curved handle is too short and light. The wooden turned stand of maple is the original and was found in either North or South Carolina.

A very curious and rare pair of tin lamps is shown in Plate 9 from Mr. C. L. Cooney's collection. Although there is nothing graceful or beautiful about them — in fact they resemble a steam boiler in miniature — they illustrate a rare type of early New England guest-room lamp. Alike, except for the flat tin plate suspended over one end of one of the lamps, they were used in the guest chamber, and, with the three wicks burning at the same time, must have given a fairly adequate amount of light. When the host wished to pay especial attention to the guest, he placed some spices or sweet smelling herbs on the shallow tin saucer directly over the flame from one of the lamps, so that the smoke from this incense might perfume the room and no doubt hide partly at least the smoke and odor from the burning whale oil.

Plate 25 is a photograph of a fascinating iron grease lamp in the collection of Doctor Robert E. Sievers of Bordentown, New Jersey. It has an open top with two well-marked lips, from which the wicks protruded. The lamp proper sits on a pedestal rising from a shallow saucer and is further supported by a round straight brace, from the bottom of the grease lamp to the edge of the base, which was used as a handle in carrying. A crudely made design of considerable ingenuity, it probably was the work of some early iron-moulder who evolved the idea from his own brain and cast a few for local distribution.

Such odd lamps as these add unusual variety to a collection and are consequently highly prized whenever found.

Another equally curious and very rare lamp, which is shown in Plate 23, really belongs to this group though its material is common earthenware or pottery. This lamp, the prized possession of a Pennsylvania collector, Mr. Francis D. Brinton of West Chester, was undoubtedly made in one of the Dutch potteries in that state. It is described as of a particularly rich and lustrous dark brown glaze, with a very luminous surface, as the photograph clearly shows. Its shape is particularly interesting. The top or lamp proper with its snugly fitting cover and neat knob follows closely the lines of a teapot, which, it is evident, suggested the design to its potter. The bottom is elongated quite a bit and terminates in a broad saucer with a sharply upturned edge. The handle is of wholesome size. It is of course a grease lamp, the wick coming out of the spout and the lamp being filled from the top like a teapot. It is in perfect condition except that the tip of the nose where the wick burned is much charred from the flame, the pottery composition being unable to withstand the constant burning as metal does. The splendid condition of the glaze speaks well for its good workmanship. The lamp now has a place of honor in a fine old house in Pennsylvania and is highly prized by its owner.

Another exceedingly interesting lamp is shown in Plate 18 from the collection of Mr. C. L. Cooney. I have never seen or heard of one like it, nor had Mr. Cooney in his long years as a collector and dealer seen another. It is a double "Betty" lamp, most beautifully hand wrought. Unfortunately the photograph does not give one a good idea of its beauty of work-

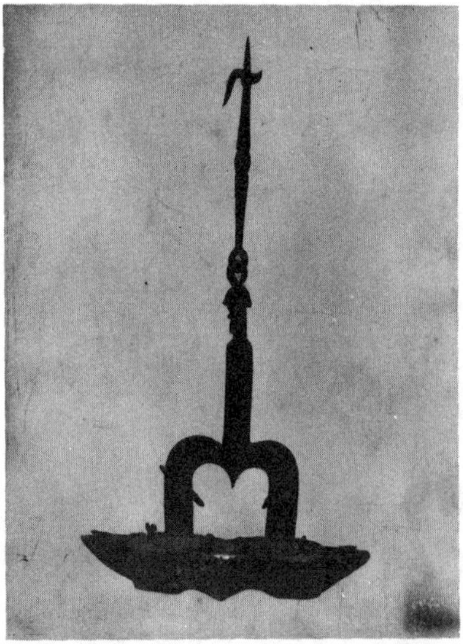

PLATE 18. *See page 28*

VERY RARE DOUBLE IRON "BETTY"
C. L. Cooney, Saugus

PLATE 19. *See page 52*

BRASS CAMPHENE LAMP, TINY WHALE-OIL LAMP AND EXTINGUISHER IN TIN
Horace R. Grant, Hartford, Connecticut

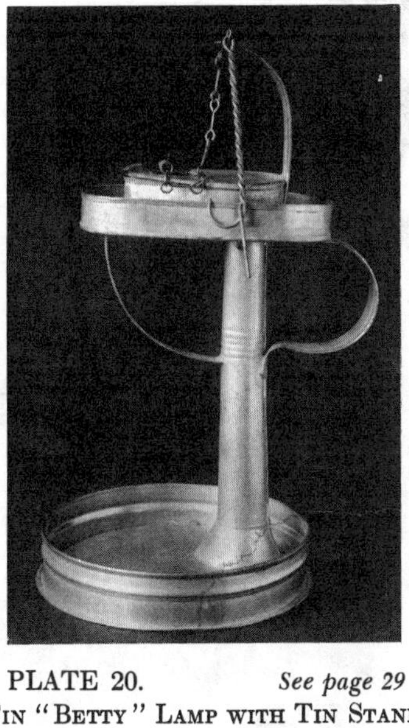

PLATE 20. *See page 29*

TIN "BETTY" LAMP WITH TIN STAND
Photograph by Miss Mary H. Northend

PLATE 21. *See page 52*

BRASS HANGING THREE-BURNER SHIP OR FACTORY LAMP
C. L. Cooney, Saugus

PLATE 22. *See page 81*

SHOWING THE USE OF THE SPUR AT THE TOP OF THE OLD IRON CANDLESTICKS TO HANG ON THE LADDER-BACK CHAIRS

Gates' Collection, Worcester

manship. It is hung from an iron staple like an ordinary "Betty", but the lamp itself consists of two iron bodies joined at the back, each having its separate oil receptacle, wick nozzle, and sliding cover. The effect of the whole is very artistic and graceful.

A fine specimen of the early tin "Betty" on its tin stand is shown in Plate 20. This tin "Ipswich Betty" is in excellent condition except that the original staple seems to have been lost and replaced at some later date with a poor substitute made of twisted wire. The most striking thing in this photograph is the very interesting tin "tidy-top" or stand on which the lamp proper rests. The deep, wide, flat base was kept filled with sand. The hollow tin upright is joined to the curved support for the tin top on one side and the tin handle for carrying on the other.

Although neither iron nor tin but pewter, the lamp shown in Plate 66 and very similar to one or two in Doctor Norton's collection really belongs in this chapter, for it is a very early variant of the "Betty." The shallow, cup-like font holds the oil in which floats the loosely woven wick of twisted cotton. The drip pan is half way down the long standard and the base is large and heavy enough to prevent its being easily tipped. Note the graceful handle and the pick hanging from the knob on the top. This lamp undoubtedly is of English or German make; for probably few if any lamps of this type were made here, although the design was in use about the time of the departure of the Pilgrims and for some years after. The few specimens were undoubtedly brought over by the earlier settlers, but they are almost impossible to find at the present time in American collections.

I have recently been forwarded some prints from Mr. Henry Ford, of Dearborn, Michigan, who has a collection of lighting devices particularly rich in odd, very early pieces. Plate 15 shows a group of three in iron of the earliest grease-lamp type. On the left is the prototype of the "Betty"—a shallow saucer slightly elongated on one side with a very crude hanging handle opposite — an attempt at a lamp much more crude than the very ancient ones in Plate 2. The one at the right is even more primitive, a shallow, round iron plate with the edges bent over to form four shallow gutters, in any one or all of which wicks may be placed, the ends floating in the oil or grease in the center.

The middle one is an early "Phoebe" lamp with its double lamp base. (An interesting group of very primitive iron lighting devices which were soon superseded by much more useful and dependable types but which possess a great interest to the collector.) As these were at their best makeshift devices, very few are found to-day. I am told that one is more apt to find them in the South where the scattered colored population continued to use them for many years.

Plate 10 and Plate 11 are from the same collection and show a varied group of early lamps, all of which are interesting and well worthy of close study by the collector. Made in a variety of material, they exhibit a greater variation in design. In Plate 11 the first in tin on the left is perhaps the more familiar, with its saucer base and upright with the flat-sided oil font on top. The next is an unusual lamp in iron, its flat-sided, open-top oil font swinging from side pivots and mounted on a slender, graceful iron stand rising from a broad flat base.

The third lamp in pewter is of a design more or less familiar to collectors of early lamps, but in this there seems to be a tube for an upright wick in the center of the open oil font instead of the usual arrangement of a wick lying in an open trough at the side.

The last lamp, also of pewter, is perhaps the most interesting of all. Of a very unusual shape, the wick tube coming from the side of the globular font holding the oil and the glass lens to magnify the flame, evidently indicating that it is a reading lamp, make a unique combination which I have never seen before.

The second group (Plate 10) is equally interesting though quite different from the first plate. Four lamps in four different materials, all of different designs, but all constructed upon the same simple principle. The taller at the left is made of copper, a rather rare metal in lamps of so early a date, and has the overflow trough quite separated from the main wick spout. The general design of the second is somewhat similar but carried out in tin. The wick tube at the side is long and has the drip gutter fitting very snugly. The third, of brass, is a kind of glorified "Betty" with its handle and hanging staple. The long curved wick spout with its enlarged lip at the end is a curious addition making it altogether an interesting piece. The fourth, however, is the gem of the lot, a fine specimen of that very rare article, an earthenware grease lamp. Of the very early open type, with the lip on the side for the twisted rag wick and its two-handled standard on the flat base, moulded of the dark brown pottery which the early Dutch settlers of Pennsylvania made so well, it is, in its perfect condition, a piece which any collector would be proud to own.

CHAPTER III

LATER TIN, PEWTER, AND BRASS LAMPS

I SAID in a previous chapter that iron lamps, being clumsy and heavy, were made for only a short time and were soon supplanted by lamps of tin and pewter. At first the tin lamps closely followed the lines of the iron ones. Gradually the colonies of settlers increased, more houses were built, and larger tracts of land brought under cultivation. The immediate needs of the colonists for food and shelter having been provided for, attention was given to the various conveniences of the home and then the real development of the lamp began.

In Plates 29 and 51 are shown two tin lamps from the author's collection with round wick spouts coming out of the sides. In Plate 17, from Doctor Norton's collection, the central lamp in the top row has a double wick and a handle for hanging. This type is sometimes known as a factory or shop lamp and is interesting because the drip pans are placed underneath the nozzles. On the same plate, Figures 422 and 423 show two tin lamps of the early "Betty" type, one of them with an upright standard upon which the lamp proper may slide, adjusting the light to the correct height for the reader's eyes. Number 423 was brought from England in 1630 by an ancestor of Doctor Norton's. The other, Number 422, is a fine "Ipswich Betty." Similar lamps were made by a tinsmith in Newburyport about 1680.

This specimen has the wick pick attached to it and stands on what was known as a tidy-top, a plate with fluted and upturned edges into which the lamp proper fitted. All stand on a tall base of tin which was commonly weighted with sand.

PLATE 23. *See page 28*

RARE PENNSYLVANIA POTTERY GREASE LAMP

Collection of Francis D. Brinton, West Chester, Pennsylvania

PLATE 24.

WALL SCONCE FOR SINGLE CANDLE WITH FIVE TIN REFLECTORS IN WOODEN FRAME

Collection of F. D. Brinton

PLATE 25. *See page 27*

EARLY IRON OPEN GREASE LAMP

Collection of Dr. Robert E. Sievers, Bordentown, New Jersey

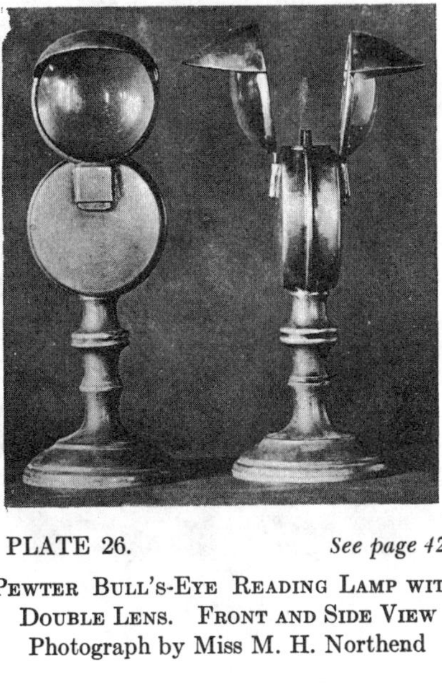

PLATE 26. *See page 42*

PEWTER BULL'S-EYE READING LAMP WITH DOUBLE LENS. FRONT AND SIDE VIEW

Photograph by Miss M. H. Northend

PLATE 27. GROUP OF PEWTER LAMPS
Dr. C. A. Q. Norton Collection

See pages 36, 38, 39, 40, 41

There are several other interesting lamps on this page, most of which are quite unusual and hard to find. In fact, good types of all old tin lamps are now rarely found and are soon snapped up by eager collectors. Number 416 on this plate is an old, tin, whaler's lamp, which must have acquired its sea legs many years ago, since it undoubtedly went on many a long voyage, and must have seen some interesting sights and could probably tell some thrilling tales of the sea. It swings on pivots at the sides and has a tin handle at the base. The shape of the font is interesting. This lamp was taken from the old ship *South America,* which the Government bought in 1861 and sunk at the entrance to Charleston Harbor, South Carolina, to prevent the use of the port by the Confederate blockade-runners.

Number 402 is called a petticoat-lamp. Another lamp of the same type owned by the author is illustrated in Plate 29. A different view of the same lamp in the lower right-hand corner of Plate 30 gives one a glimpse of the underside of the lamp, showing the peg socket underneath the petticoat. It is said that by this arrangement the lamp was secured on a side upright of the high ladder or bannister-back chair then in use, thus placing the light in such a position as to be most advantageous to the reader sitting in the chair.

Number 56 on Plate 17 was one of Doctor Norton's prized possessions; for it was representative of an interesting and unusual type. But association with its celebrated owner has made it more valuable. It was of a late model, made probably about the middle of the nineteenth century, and shows quite clearly that the fertile brains of many a lamp maker had studied and worked to evolve from the primitive type lamps of greater power and usefulness. One of the intensely interesting things about collecting lamps is the astonishing number of variations and improvements which have appeared from time to time; in fact, it is fairly difficult to get two lamps either in tin, pewter, or glass which match exactly. Number 56 has two broad, flat wicks in a drum-shaped font, which was filled with lard oil, a fuel oil used somewhat extensively in New England about 1850. This drum font, pivoted for ease in filling and cleaning, had a large adjustable tin reflector behind it. Supported on a substantial square base, this lamp must have furnished quite a respectable light. It was one of a pair which was used by Noah Webster while compiling his famous dictionary and lighted his arduous and painstaking work through many a midnight hour. It was secured from his old home in Amherst, Massachusetts, in 1852.

Number 87 on this same plate of Doctor Norton's is another odd and interesting specimen, again showing the often very ingenious changes which different makers employed in order to improve their wares. This is also a lamp for lard oil, and has a curious shaped, hinged oil font on an upright short base. It was found in the mansion of General Knox at Thomaston, Maine. General Knox was one of the outstanding men of Washington's time. Born in Boston and being of a patriotic nature he became interested in military affairs at the outset of the Colonies' struggle to shake off the yoke of England, and joined the militia. He became an officer of artillery, attracted the attention of General Washington by his competent work during the siege of Boston, and took part in many of the Revolutionary battles. Possessing Washington's friendship, he rose in the army to a position of importance and responsibility. He was a member of the court-martial which tried Major André; later was appointed the commander of West Point, and, under Washington's command, superintended the disbanding and dispersion of the Continental armies at the close of the war.

When Washington was elected the first President of the Republic, General Knox became his Secretary of War, which position he held for six years. He finally retired from public life and settled in Maine, where he did in 1806.

Number 89 on this Plate 17 of Doctor Norton's lamps is almost exactly like one in the writer's possession as illustrated in Plate 29. The lamp itself is quite shallow with a single wick; but over it, ingeniously hinged to the loop handle, is a top or chimney with a small mica or isinglass window in the front. The chimney protects from drafts the tiny flame that filters through the mica window. The writer has seen a lamp that differs from this in that it has three oval isinglass windows instead of the one square one and an arrangement for locking the chimney. In Plate 30 may be seen one of these lamps with the chimney turned back.

Collecting these early tin lamps is good sport, for they are not as common as their cheapness might seem to indicate. Varied in ingenious and interesting ways by craftsmen who often changed the pattern according to personal whim or fancy; cheapened by the neglect of collectors who have passed them by for wares more showy; tucked away in corners of little country antique shops — these lamps are game worth hunting. The successful hunter may walk out of the shop after bagging such a lamp with a very pleasant thrill of pride, particularly if the price is low.

During those first bitter years, when so many succumbed to privations and disease in the Plymouth colony that, in order to hide from the Indians how decimated the little band had become, they buried their dead secretly and planted corn over the graves, all the energy of the colonies was given to providing the barest necessities. As the settlements became larger and more successful in fighting the climate and the Indians, more attention was paid to refinements such as were enjoyed in the mother country. The household utensils at first were of the crudest and simplest. One or two iron pots swinging on a crane in the big open fireplace, and a few wooden plates or trenchers upon which the family meal was served, comprised the simple equipment of the ordinary home. The more well-to-do had in addition a few pewter plates or platters which they had brought with them from England. As supplies arrived and the colonists found themselves in better condition financially, pewter gradually came to take the place of the rude home-made wooden dishes. It was not until many years later that the manufacture of earthenware and porcelain dishes commenced in England, so that pewter was the general table ware. Pewter is an alloy of lead, tin, copper, and sometimes antimony and zinc; its main body being lead — the more lead the poorer the pewter, the more tin the better and brighter. It is a soft metal, easily scratched, bent and broken, so that a dish or platter often became badly worn or marred, and was sent to the pewterer's to be recast. It was quite natural, therefore, that since this metal was convenient and well adapted for the purpose, the manufacture of lamps of pewter should commence and continue for many years. At first the pewter lamps closely followed the lines of the tin ones, with the oil font below and the wick at the top coming through a small circular spout; although now and then one may be found made like the "Bettys." By this time the open spout such as that of the "Betty" had been generally abandoned and the wicks were now encased in snugly fitting tubes. Often these tubes and the top which screwed into the lamp itself were made of brass, better fitted to stand the wear of being unscrewed every time the lamp was filled; for almost all the early pewter lamps were filled from the same opening in the top into which the wick went.

These pewter lamps, though more easily found than the very early tin ones, offer by their infinite variety of size, shape, and workmanship, a very fascinating field to the collector, as witnessed by several plates in this book. Plates 27 and 33 show more than a dozen from Doctor Norton's collection, no two of which are alike; for they represent probably more than a century and a half. The writer's pewter lamps in Plate 35, though somewhat similar in shape, show quite a variation, es-

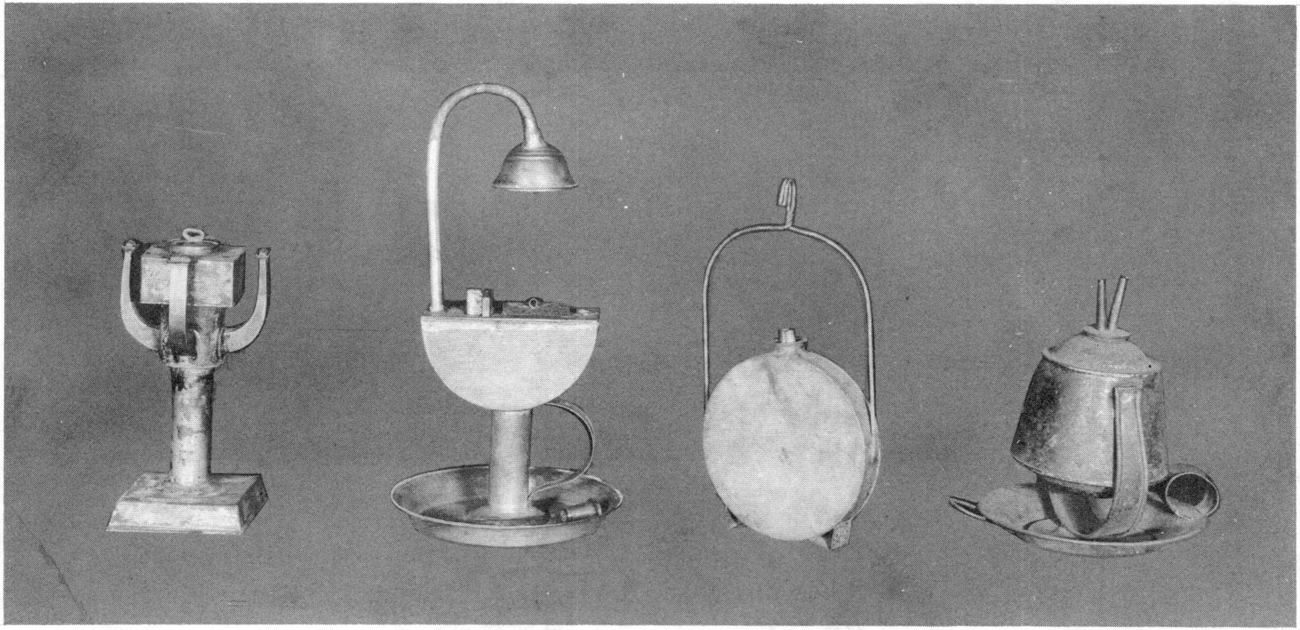

PLATE 28.

EARLY TIN LAMPS IN UNUSUAL DESIGNS
Collection of Henry Ford, Dearborn, Michigan

See pages 53. 54

PLATE 29.

GROUP OF TIN LAMPS
Author's Collection

See pages 14, 24, 25, 32, 33, 35, 51

pecially in size — the smallest one in the center of the top row being only an inch and a quarter in height, while the interesting three-wick one beside it is six and a half inches high.

Quite a few of these pewter lamps as well as some of the tin ones have two, and occasionally three, wicks. This change from the single wick is said to have been the invention of Benjamin Franklin, who became interested in lighting at a very early age. In the Boston shop of his father, Josiah Franklin, a tallow chandler, Ben, at the age of ten, commenced his notable career by cutting wicks. As he grew older, he noticed that the wicks of the lamps in his and his neighbors' homes soon became encrusted with soot or carbon from the faulty or imperfect combustion and constantly needed "picking up" in order to give even a dim light.

The thought came to him that two wicks, side by side, would create a stronger current of air and more oxygen would come in contact with the wick, thus insuring freer burning and more and stronger light. He at once experimented and found that this was a fact. Thereafter most of the lamps were made with two wicks instead of the single wick, and a few were made with three, but singularly enough three were found not to work so well, the twin wicks giving the best results.

Just as there was a great variation in the composition of the pewter from which the lamps were fashioned, equally varied were the lamps. In Plate 35 from the writer's collection the large center lamp at the bottom and the smaller one next on the right both take a very high polish, quite like silver, and are probably almost pure tin; but most of the pewter lamps were like the platters, mostly lead and not taking a high polish.

The pewterers' guild was very large and influential in England. Strict watch was kept over its members and many rules were laid down as to standards of workmanship, material, etc. Each master pewterer was required to register his private mark, or " touch " as it was called, and this " touch " was stamped on each piece with other marks indicating the quality of the metal, place of manufacture, etc. An X on the bottom of a plate indicated that it was of the first quality called " hard mettle ware." Any unscrupulous maker endeavoring fraudulently to stamp his wares as of better quality than they really were, was severely dealt with. That it is rare to find a lamp with any pewterer's mark on it may indicate that many of the pieces were recast from discarded plates, platters, etc.

It is much more interesting in collecting to get, if possible, the history of a piece. Doctor Norton, with his wide acquaintance, in the course of his extensive travels all over the United States in pursuit of his favorite hobby, was enabled to pick up many lamps of more than ordinary interest. Illustrations of some of them will be found in Plate 27. Number 385 in the top row is a small pewter lamp with a camphene burner. Camphene, a burning fluid, was a product of refined turpentine which came into quite general use about 1845 to 1850. Unlike whale or lard oil, it was highly explosive. To prevent therefore any danger of the flame's getting down into the oil font, the wick tubes were made longer, as in this lamp and Number 413 in the same plate.

The interesting thing about lamp Number 385 is that it was formerly the property of Franklin Pierce, the fourteenth President of the United States. President Pierce, though one of the lesser known presidents, was a man of strong character and considerable personal charm.

At his birthplace, the little town of Hillsboro in New Hampshire, his former home, now occupied, I am told, by one of his nephews, contains many interesting objects connected with his public life. His father was a prominent man: Governor of the State, and one of the Continentals who fought the British in the famous battle of Bunker Hill. His son, who was also interested in military affairs, when the war with Mexico broke out, took an active part as colonel of a regiment. Since Hillsboro was on the direct stage line between Boston and Concord, his father entertained many notables at their home and young Franklin had the opportunity of meeting many of the most prominent of the Colonies' patriots.

He entered Bowdoin College at the age of 16 and was graduated with honors. He proceeded to imitate his father's career as a politician. Being a great favorite all through that section of the State, he was elected to Congress when only twenty-nine years of age and four years later entered the Senate, as the youngest member. Among his most intimate friends was Nathaniel Hawthorne, whose friendship he kept unbroken during his lifetime. He was present when Hawthorne died. The two men outwardly had little in common: Pierce — genial, making friends easily, enjoying the attentions which a public life at that time commanded; Hawthorne — retiring, shunning the public eye, sad, almost morbid at times; yet the strong friendship was only broken by death. In the old homestead at Hillsboro are preserved among many other mementos a number of letters from Hawthorne. It is not at all improbable that some of these letters of Hawthorne's may have been perused by the light of this little oil lamp. Other letters in this collection are from another close friend of President Pierce, Jefferson Davis, afterward President of the Southern Confederacy, whom President Pierce appointed Secretary of War and who served during his administration. The friendship was formed while Franklin Pierce was a young member of the Senate. This little lamp then has seen some of the most stirring history of our country in the making, and is one of those small but significant links which bind the historic past to the turbulent and perplexing present.

Number 409 on Plate 27 of Doctor Norton's is an interesting deviation from the ordinary burner. If one observes closely he will note three projections on the top. The two outer tubes are for the wicks, whale oil being burned in this lamp, but the longer center tube is for the purpose of carrying the heated air from the burners to the oil in the font beneath, thus keeping it in a liquid state during the winter. The mind which devised this ingenious arrangement thought enough of it to have it patented but deponent saith not whether the device actually worked.

Number 414, the pewter lamp with the peculiar egg-shaped font, is another with historical associations. This lamp was the property of John C. Calhoun of South Carolina and was used by him during his residence in Washington from 1845 to 1850 while he was Senator. Many of his famous speeches in the Senate chamber were probably written by the light from the broad wick of this lamp.

Number 392 is one of the few lamps marked with the pewterer's name. This one was made and stamped by Boardman Brothers who had a factory in Hartford, Connecticut. It is a double-wick, whale-oil lamp.

Number 420, with the single whale-oil burner, a modest little affair, was the property of Doctor Josiah Bartlett of Amesbury, one of the less known signers of the Declaration of Independence. Doctor Josiah Bartlett, born in Amesbury, Massachusetts, was elected a member of the Continental Congress and helped form the new Constitution. Afterward he became President of the New Hampshire colony and in 1793 its first Governor when it was admitted as a separate State. He died in 1795.

Number 170 is a marked English pewter lamp, made somewhere about 1700. Its form is interesting: the lamp itself on the top of a standard some eight inches in height is similar to a " Betty ", a shape unusual in pewter; about half way down the standard is the drip pan and the handle for carrying connects the two; and the whole stands on a large circular base. The hall marks, the usual pewter marks, are found on the han-

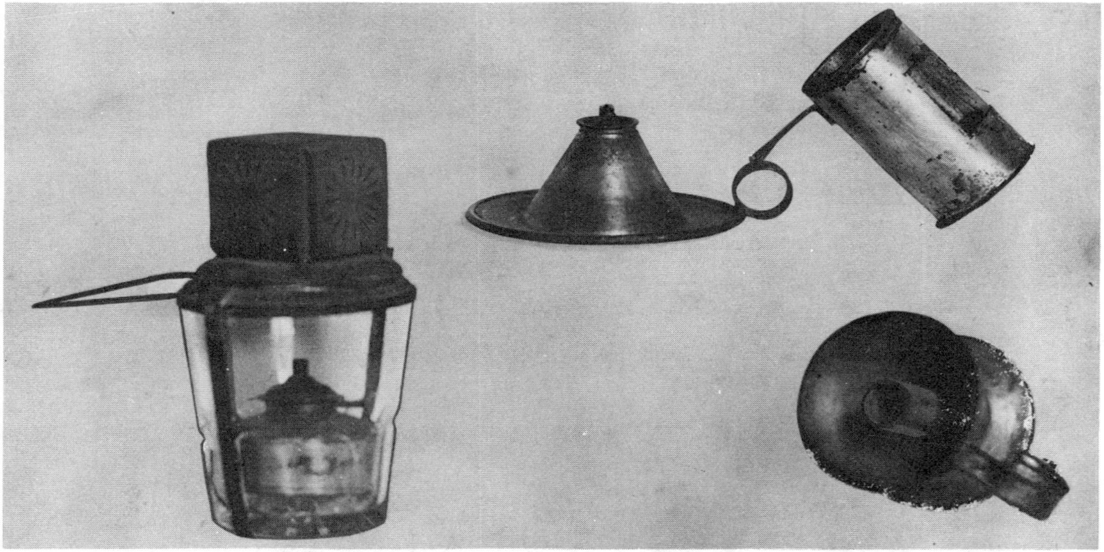

PLATE 30. *See pages 33, 35, 51, 130*

PATENT WHALE-OIL TUMBLER LAMP AND DIFFERENT VIEWS OF TWO LAMPS IN PREVIOUS PLATE

Author's Collection

PLATE 31. PAINTED AND JAPANNED TIN HAND LAMPS *See page 53*

Collection of Henry Ford, Michigan

PLATE 32. *See page 53*

SMALL TIN HAND LAMPS

Collection of Henry Ford, Michigan

dle. Though this is not a Colonial piece, its rare shape makes it attractive.

Number 171 is very similar to 170, except that the drip pan is omitted. This lamp also has the very rare hall marks, and, from its similarity to Number 170, was probably made about the same time and possibly by the same pewterer.

Number 401 is a pewter lard-oil lamp. An unusual feature of this lamp is that it has a wheel to regulate the broad flat wick. This lamp dates from about 1840 and came from the house of General Robert E. Lee at Arlington, Virginia. The wide range of these lamps, geographically, is a most encouraging thing for collectors; because it shows that a persevering search in almost any part of the country is likely to yield rich returns; in fact, one of the pleasantest features of this antique hunt is that one's reward is usually found in the most unexpected places.

The last lamp on this page, Number 341 down in the lower right-hand corner, a modest pewter lamp with a brass camphene burner, was used by Captain John Ericsson, the famous inventor of the more famous *Monitor,* in his office. I wonder if the shape of the lamp suggested to his fertile mind the idea which he afterward developed in his famous little boat, "a cheese box on a raft" as it was called, which fought so valiantly for the Union.

An interesting type of pewter lamp, Number 140 in Plate 33, is an improved reading lamp. This one happens to be of English manufacture, Doctor Norton says, and was made, he estimates, about 1760. It burns whale oil in its drum-shaped oil font, but the peculiar feature is the two bull's-eyes of glass, one on each side of the flame, with a pewter shade over it, to catch and concentrate the feeble rays upon the reader's page beside it.

These bull's-eye lamps were made here and are usually found with only one lens. Since they are not at all common, a lamp of this kind, in good condition, is considered a find. These pewter bull's-eye reading lamps were evidently one of the most popular improvements; for they seem to have been in quite general use and some ten or twenty years ago were found in almost every antique shop. Of late years they have almost entirely disappeared, so that if one wants to study them, he must look for them in the cabinets of private collectors. I was fortunate in securing photographs of two or three. Plate 26 gives both a side and front view of a double bull's-eye pewter lamp very similar in shape and size to Doctor Norton's but differing slightly in the turnings of the base. There is also shown in Plate 42 from Mr. Henry Ford's collection a fine double-wick and double-lens pewter reading lamp.

In the beautifully clear group of Mr. Gates' pewter lamps in Plate 37, the central one is a single bull's-eye with a double whale-oil burner and is a particularly pretty and graceful design. This lamp is probably the oldest of the lamps in this group.

Number 172 in Plate 33, though very unpretentious in its general appearance, is closely connected with some of the most stirring events of the history of our infant republic. This lamp was secured by Doctor Norton in the homestead of Josiah Quincy of Braintree, now in the town of Quincy, Massachusetts, and the family tradition is that it was made in the workshop of the famous Paul Revere at Boston. The accuracy of this tradition is open to doubt as there appears to be no authentic record of Revere having worked in pewter. Pewter lamps however were in use at this time and it is quite possible that he, or one of his workmen, might have made this one as a gift. Doctor Norton evidently accepted the story as he dated this lamp prior to 1770.

Paul Revere was a very versatile man. Not only was he a celebrated silver and gold smith, but he was an artist of more than mediocre ability, engraving many of his own drawings on copper. Later in life he established the first plant in America for refining copper in which he rolled the plates for the frigate *Constitution* and other vessels building for the government; he also cast many church bells, manufactured gunpowder and cast cannon for the Continental army and kept a general store. He will doubtless be best known to posterity by his famous ride to warn the patriots, John Hancock and Samuel Adams, whom General Gage, England's representative then living in Boston, had ordered arrested for high treason. Hearing that they were visiting friends in Lexington, General Gage decided that it would be a good opportunity to seize them there without starting the tumult which their arrest in Boston would doubtless precipitate. On the night of April 18th, 1775, he therefore quietly despatched some eight hundred of his British troops with great secrecy to proceed to Lexington and arrest the men and incidentally seize and destroy some military stores which he had learned the patriots had collected and secreted in Concord, a few miles beyond. But the patriots, in some manner, learned of the expedition. Longfellow in his famous poem tells the rest of the story, but historians say that Mr. Longfellow is not quite accurate in his account, for Revere's two companions deserve fully as much credit as did Revere. In fact, Revere was captured by the British before he reached Concord. However this may be, Paul Revere was a staunch patriot and very ready to undertake any mission no matter how dangerous or arduous which might help the cause of the Colonies for independence. I have in my possession an old Boston newspaper, the "Columbian Centinel" printed July 16, 1800, in which is a notice from the Board of Health of Boston regarding the quarantining of vessels entering the harbor and signed "P. Revere, President", showing that he took an active and prominent part in the town's affairs for many years.

Recently a friend of mine who is a collector of old bottles, particularly the tiny hand-blown vials which were used by apothecaries and housekeepers years ago and which usually have a very lovely decided greenish tinge to the glass, was talking with an old lady from whom she had received some of the slender delicate ones. This old lady said she recalled distinctly, as a young girl, helping her mother clean and fill the small whale-oil lamps, which were used in their home. She particularly remembered one of these small glass bottles which hung at the end of a shelf, suspended by a string, and which was kept filled with turpentine. Near it on the shelf was a small piece of wire with a wisp of cotton on the end and after the lamps had been filled, cleaned and the wicks "picked up" and freed of the encrusted soot of the night's burning, it was her duty, with the tiny wire, to carefully allow a drop of turpentine to fall on the tip of the cleaned and ready wick. "Only one drop," she said, "and great care must be used not to allow the turpentine to touch anything else." This I presume was to keep the wicks in condition to light readily when needed.

I do not know if this was a universal custom — I had never heard anything of the kind before — but it was an interesting sidelight on the necessity for care to get even the little light which these lamps gave under the best of conditions.

One of the pewter lamps shown on Plate 33 and numbered 173, Doctor Norton says, is one of the most interesting in his entire collection. Although not strictly speaking a Colonial lamp (its home having been in Germany) it is unique, and the fact that it was probably used about the time of the departure of the Pilgrims from Holland, gives it a place in these pages. Since one of these lamps is shown in an old Dutch print dated 1610, we may assume that they were in use then in Holland and may have been familiar to the Leyden Pilgrim Colony. This pewter lamp, like the "Betty" in shape and design, stands about sixteen inches high on a base of pewter. Its especially interesting feature, however, is the glass font on top

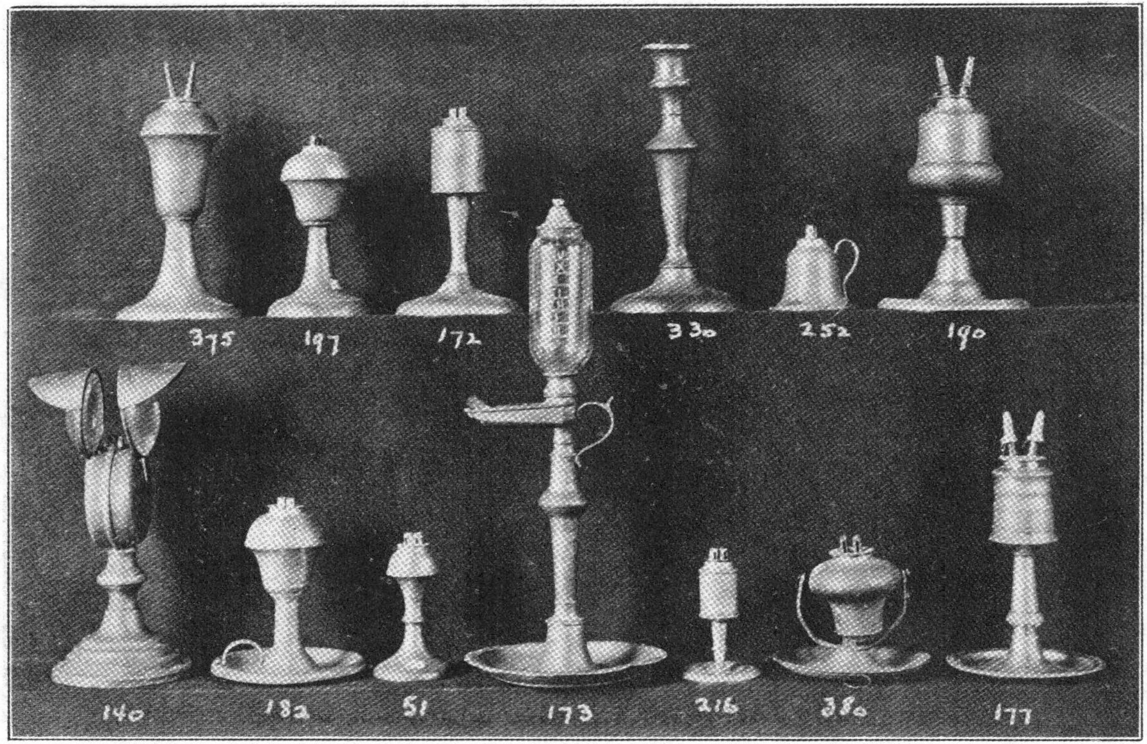

PLATE 33. WHALE-OIL AND CAMPHENE PEWTER LAMPS
Dr. C. A. Q. Norton Collection

See pages 36, 41, 42, 44, 45, 46, 92

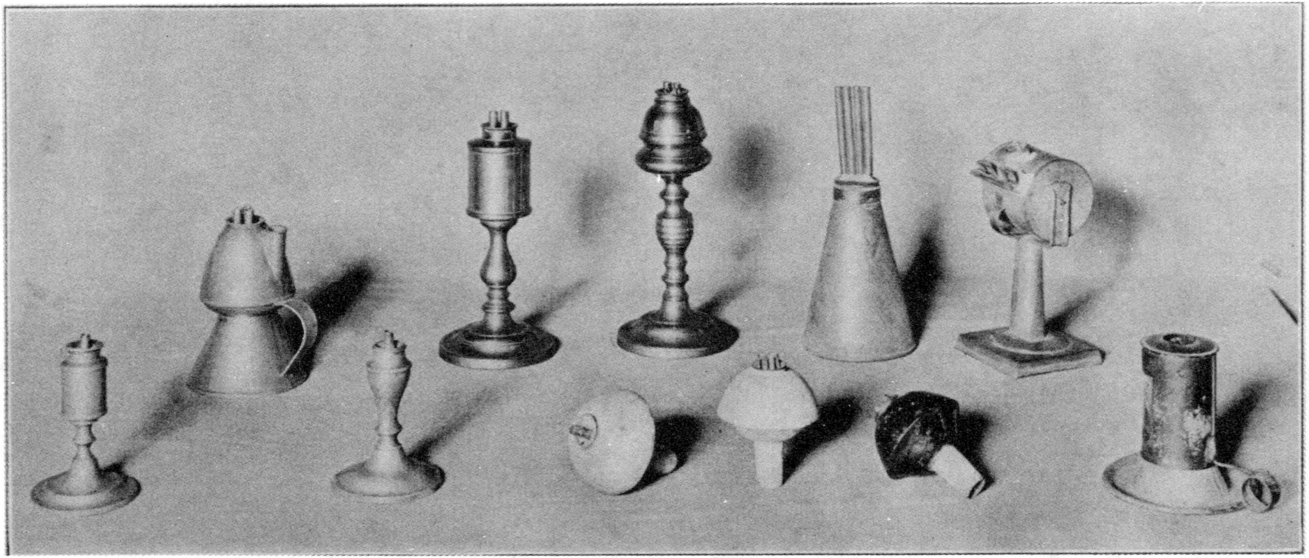

PLATE 34.

See pages 50, 51

Group of Unusual Lamps in Tin, Pewter, Brass and Iron
Collection of B. N. Gates, Worcester.

which holds the oil and upon whose sides in Roman numerals are marked the hours, the gradual lowering of the oil as it is burned up in the lamp marking the time. These "time-lamps" as they were called were not only not unknown in the Colonies but were even made here, to a very limited extent, upon the model shown in this Continental one. They are rarely or never found now. I have never seen one at a dealers, but have a friend, Mr. V. M. Hillyer of Baltimore, long a collector of lamps, who has one or more of American make.

Numbers 177 and 190 on Plate 33 from Doctor Norton's collection are both pewter lamps of American make and show very fine workmanship, dating somewhere between 1825 and 1850. The tall wick burners indicate that the lamps were fitted to burn camphene as is also Number 375 on the same plate. This last lamp is further protected from the dangers of camphene explosions by a wire gauze wick holder inside the long acorn-shaped font.

Number 252 in Plate 33, the little hand lamp with inverted bell-shaped base and double whale-oil burner, is a good specimen of what was sometimes called a "squat" lamp. It is identical in shape and size to the "tavern" lamp of pewter, block tin, or glass, specimens of which may be found in Plate 35 and in Plate 79 from the collections of Mr. Gates and the writer.

It is reported that these lamps received their name from the fact that they were commonly used in taverns. When the guest wished to retire for the night he was handed one of these little lamps to light his way; and if, as was frequently the case, he had been drinking somewhat heavily, no harm would result if he dropped the lamp while navigating a difficult course up to his bedroom; or if again he forgot to blow out the light, its small supply of oil would soon do that for him. But perhaps these little lamps were more generally known as "spark" or "sparking" lamps. When the young woman of the household heard the footsteps of her favored swain approaching on his courting or "sparking" night, she would light one of these little lamps. The flame from it was not embarrassingly brilliant and when it flickered and went out for lack of oil, that was a gentle but well understood hint that it was time for the young man to find his hat, say good-night on the door stoop and start for home!

Number 380 in the bottom row of Plate 33 of Doctor Norton's is called a marine lamp. The font is swung on pivots so that no matter what the rolling of the vessel the lamp remains upright. This lamp has a ring in the side of the saucer-like base by which it may be hung from a convenient hook, the lamp itself remaining upright while the pewter base acted as a kind of reflector. This specimen was taken from the old U. S. S. *Vermont.*

Very similar swinging pewter lamps, sometimes known as chamber lamps, may be seen in Plate 37 of Mr. Gates' collection. The two front lamps on the right of this plate are splendid examples of workmanship. The long wick stems indicate that they were probably made for camphene burning. They have the same little ring on the edge of the saucer for hanging on the wall and a round handle on the opposite edge. The shapes of these two lamps are good and they have the original extinguishers attached by tiny chains. This whole group is a particularly good one as all the lamps are in perfect condition, of extra good workmanship, and without the dents and bruises which mar so many specimens, the soft pewter lending itself so easily to marrings from rough handling. The other two camphene lamps in the front row have very similar handles, and the second one perhaps has a more unusual shape than the inverted bell at the extreme right. This lamp is remarkable also for the fact that it is a marked piece, stamped with the maker's name, Morey and Ober, Boston. It is one of the few marked pewter lamps of American manufacture.

The first tall lamp in the back row of Plate 37 with the broad flat wick is intended for the heavier lard oil and shows a fine piece of turning. The tall one on the right is unusual in its shape, its simplicity of line giving it a very dignified appearance. This lamp is also stamped with the maker's name, T. M. Brickley, Troy, N. Y. Since it is unusual to find an early American pewter lamp or candlestick with the maker's name on it, these two marked pieces in this small collection are a good indication of the high degree of excellence of this well selected group. It is a collection of pewter of which any owner may be justly proud and exemplifies the advice which so many young collectors disregard: "Work for quality rather than quantity, for a few well-chosen, perfect specimens are much more worth while than five times that number of battered, incomplete and commonplace lamps." It is quite as much an art to know what to discard as what to gather together, and every discard helps some one else's collection just that much.

In the margin is a drawing of a small, simple, tin whale-oil lamp which is authentically reported to have been owned and used by Abraham Lincoln in his law office during his early days. In 1866 Lincoln's log cabin was exhibited in New York City. Doctor Norton was one of the lecturers who daily gave addresses there on the great Emancipator. At the conclusion of the exhibition in payment for his services he was allowed to take several of the relics which had been on view there, and one of them was this tin lamp.

Brass lamps, which came later than the tin and pewter ones, seem not to have been made in such abundance as brass candlesticks, for they are comparatively hard to find. It may have been because glass lamps were then coming into general use and were being sold much cheaper that the demand for brass lamps was negligible. Doctor Norton in Plate 36 has a few very good ones from his own collection, which perhaps typify fairly well the usual designs for them. Number 338 is a tall, double-wick, whale-oil lamp, the base of which suggests strongly a candlestick design, the oil font that of a tin or pewter lamp. This lamp Doctor Norton dates about 1820.

Number 326 is a pretty hand lamp, which was secured in Deerfield, New Hampshire, from the birthplace of General Benjamin F. Butler, that brilliant but eccentric lawyer, military man and politician, whose stormy career made him some close friends but many bitter enemies.

Beginning his business life as a lawyer, he gained much prominence particularly as a criminal lawyer, and was always an active politician. He ran for Governor of Massachusetts just before the commencement of the Civil War, but was defeated. Having risen to the rank of Brigadier-General of Militia, he was appointed commander of the 8th Massachusetts Regiment with which he saw considerable service. After the surrender of New Orleans to Admiral Farragut's forces, he was appointed military governor of the city. At the close of the war he re-entered Congress, was again defeated for Governor, but not discouraged, ran again in 1882 and was elected. He was a candidate for the Presidency in 1884 on a Greenback ticket, but was overwhelmingly defeated.

General Butler was a striking figure about town. Short and quite stout with a large head, his was a personality to be noticed in any assembly, particularly as a marked droop to his eyelids gave his face a peculiar appearance. He was always very particular about his clothes and was rarely seen on the street without a fresh flower in his buttonhole.

An able lawyer, he conducted many celebrated criminal cases. I recall when I was a boy going to the courthouse in Salem where he was the lawyer in a suit, as I remember it, to break the will of an aged farmer who had died leaving considerable

PLATE 35.

GROUP OF PEWTER LAMPS
Author's Collection

See pages 36, 37, 45

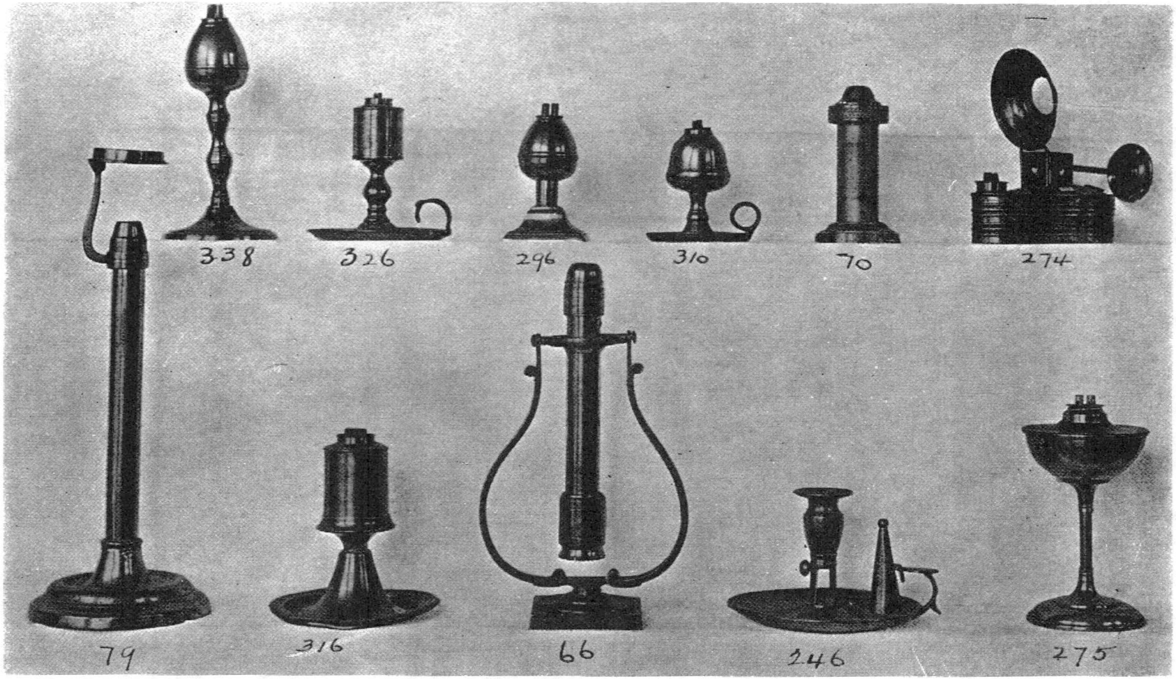

PLATE 36.

See pages 48, 49, 90, 91

BRASS LAMPS AND CANDLESTICKS
Dr. C. A. Q. Norton's Collection

property, but in his will cutting off a number of relatives. They took the matter to court and tried to have the will set aside on the ground that the old farmer was insane when he made it.

As General Butler appeared for the defense, I can recall him now, his short rotund figure fastidiously dressed, the customary flower in his coat, and — as was his usual custom in court — an unlighted cigar in his mouth, which he chewed from time to time.

When I was there, he had a witness, an old neighbor, on the stand who was testifying that he had seen the old farmer sit reading the *Salem Observer*, a newspaper which had been published in Salem for many years, but which had always strongly opposed General Butler in all his political aspirations. When Butler was through with his witness (who was testifying to the sanity of the deceased) he remarked apropos of his being seen reading this paper: "That's the first evidence of insanity which has been introduced in this case," a remark which brought much laughter from the audience.

Numbers 296 and 310 in this Plate 36 are good examples of hand or chamber lamps as they were variously called, 310 being from the house of Doctor Jacob Quincy of the famous Quincy family, great-grandfather of Doctor Norton. Number 274 is a large brass binnacle lamp — with double whale-oil burner, reflector, and extra-sized font — which was used on the U. S. S. *Georgia*, Government transport and hospital ship during the Civil War.

Many of Doctor Norton's lamps were directly associated with this war, doubtless because Doctor Norton's position as an enlisted man in the 1st Maine Cavalry and later on the staff of the Surgeon-General brought him in direct contact with many of the leading men in this great conflict and gave him opportunities to acquire many lamps with interesting histories.

The broad flat wick of Number 316 indicates that it was intended for lard oil. Number 275 with its wine-glass shaped oil font and slender stemmed base was secured at the homestead of General Neal Dow, that famous and fiery advocate of temperance from Maine, so well known to my readers of the older generations.

The lard-oil lamps which may be distinguished by their broad flat wicks are not nearly so common as the whale-oil ones.

A very good specimen of a japanned tin hand lamp may be seen in Plate 48 from the Worcester Historical Society's collection and another unusually good lamp of this kind from the collection of Mrs. A. A. Dana of West Orange, New Jersey, is shown in Plate 109. It is, I think, complete; the tin reflector at the back, which is usually missing from lamps of this type, is an uncommonly fine shaped one at that. The square tin base is out of the ordinary. One can see quite clearly in this excellent print the curved brass spring close to the middle of the oil font in front. It held the drum-shaped font when pulled down to allow the wicks to lie in the oil even when it had been nearly all consumed.

Another lamp of this same type in Mr. Gates' collection is the one on the extreme right of the back row in Plate 34, which gives an excellent side view showing the brass spring holding the oil font with the wicks well down the side as they would be when the oil was low.

This plate also shows the side supports which hold the drum and the filling place; but the tin reflector is missing. These two lamps, though quite similar to one from Doctor Norton's collection spoken of earlier in this chapter, are good specimens of a type which is rarely met with now; for since lard oil was used as an illuminant to a limited extent as compared with whale oil and camphene, fewer lamps were made for its use, and consequently fewer are found to-day.

The collection of Mr. Gates in Plate 34 is an unusual one in that the specimens are all in such good condition. The lamp in the lower right-hand corner is similar to one in the writer's collection, which is spoken of before and shown both open and closed. (See Plates 29 and 30.)

The first lamp on the back row of Plate 34 at the left is a particularly fine specimen of the "petticoat" lamp; an exceptionally large tin one in perfect condition, showing a double wick and separate filling hole. The next two in the back row are fine brass lamps, much later of course, but beautifully turned. One may hunt for months before finding two brass lamps approaching these in design and condition.

The next one with its funnel-shaped base and four long brass wick spouts is a mystery. Neither its owner nor the writer has ever seen another like it and its purpose is obscure. Just why this shape or what its use is unknown. I hope that this note will reach the eye of some collector who has a similar piece and who knows something of its purpose and history.

In the front row, the first two are beautiful little single-burner pewter lamps. I think they might properly be classed with the tavern or "spark" lamps, though they have no ring handles, but their single wicks and small size indicate their classifcation there.

The three remaining lamps in this plate, Number 34, all alike except that two are painted white and one japanned, are specimens of the very rare tin "peg" lamps. Peg lamps, which were usually of glass (so called because the bottom part was shaped to fit into the top of a candlestick), will be taken up in a later chapter. The interesting thing about these lamps is that they are authentically reported to have been used in the Massachusetts State House on Beacon Hill, Boston, about the time of the War of 1812. They have, as you see, very small oil fonts and double whale-oil burners, so that it must have taken a great many of them to light even dimly one of those great rooms.

Hanging over the heavy iron-bound door of the Iron Master's house in Saugus is a quaint brass lamp (Plate 21). Originally I think its home was on a vessel, but later it was used in a store or shop, perhaps hung as now over a door. It has three long, straight, wick spouts coming out of its sides, each fitted with an extra spout beneath to catch the drippings and carry them back into the lamp. The wicks would be of large size and would undoubtedly give a heavy flame with considerable smoke. This is the only brass lamp I have seen of this description and the only three-wicked one — most of the others being one or two-wicked and of tin.

Mr. Horace R. Grant, a collector in Hartford, Connecticut, has sent a photograph of two quaint lamps (see Plate 19). The one on the left is as beautiful an example as I have seen of a double-wick, camphene-burning, brass lamp; the turnings and proportions of the base, standard and top being particularly good. Beside it is a miniature, japanned tin, whale-oil lamp, hardly taller than the tin candle extinguisher at its right.

A particularly good specimen of a real " tavern " or " sparking " lamp is the one which Mr. Cooney allowed me to photograph in Plate 53. It is of pewter, in perfect condition, about three inches high, with a brass, single-wick oil-cap, and an interesting curved flat handle of pewter. It is easy to imagine many a traveller with this little lamp in his hand mounting the steep stairs of some wayside inn, after a hearty supper and a round or two of mulled wine or ale or some real good old flip in front of the huge chimney with its cheery roaring fire of huge hickory or oak logs; for this was exactly the sort of lamp which the olden taverns furnished to their guests.

A striking combination of a tin stand with a small glass lamp (very possibly a peg lamp) is to be seen in Plate 44. The shade, painted like the base with its ring handle, is neatly attached and the single-burner, camphene lamp is evidently intended for a student or reading lamp, one of those odd varia-

PLATE 37.

See pages 42, 46, 47

Fine Collection of Pewter Lamps
Burton N. Gates, Worcester

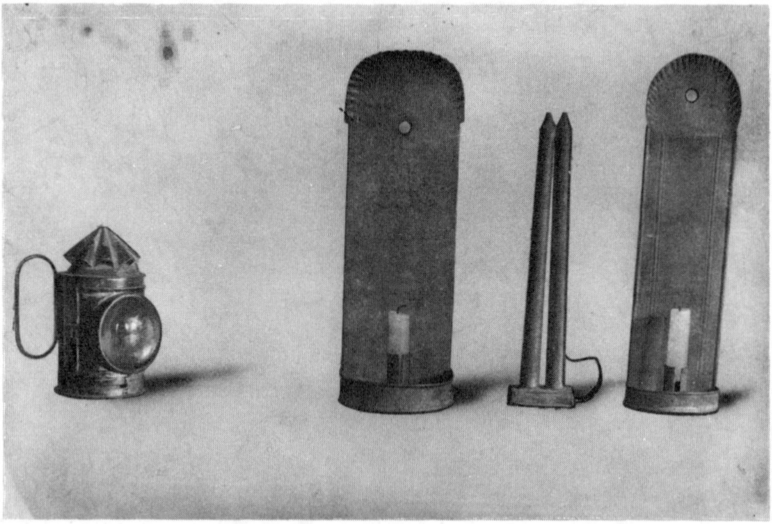

PLATE 38 *See pages 61, 94*

BULL'S-EYE WATCHMAN'S LANTERN, EARLY TIN CANDLE SCONCES AND CANDLE MOULD — Author's Collection

PLATE 39. FOLDING BRASS CANDLESTICKS *See page 99*

The two circular bases screw together with the removable candle holders inside

tions from the accepted type which one is constantly finding.

An attractive group of the japanned and painted or stencilled tin hand lamps may be seen in Plate 31 from the collection of Mr. Henry Ford of Michigan. The first is probably the oldest, a single-burner whale-oil lamp with the familiar acorn top having a separate filling place at the side. This one has the ring handle on the base.

The next lamp, also for whale oil, has a very flat saucer with a loop handle. The last two, which are very similar, have the broad flat wick tubes for lard oil and loop handles.

Plate 32 shows some smaller hand lamps also in tin, from the same collector. The second specimen is a good type of the "petticoat" lamp with its single wick for whale oil and its separate filling tube at the side directly over the handle. The next is a choice specimen of the double-wick, funnel-shaped hand lamp, while the last is a curious cup-shaped lamp with three long wick tubes projecting from the cover.

To me the most interesting of the plates from the collection of Mr. Henry Ford is Number 28 which shows four very unusual tin lamps. Mr. Ford seems to have been particularly fortunate in securing some very unique specimens in tin, and the group here shown is a most fascinating one. In fact, so unusual are all four that it is quite impossible to select one as of greater interest than the others.

The design of the lamp on the left, with its sturdy squared base from which rises the stout column supporting the box-like oil font is most uncommon. The curved arms, which protect but do not seem to offer any support for the oil font, are also most unusual.

The design of the next is perhaps even more striking. Here upon a deep and broad saucer base rises a short but substantial column which supports the oil font. This font, which strikingly resembles a round top, drop-leaf table in miniature, has at one end the capped hole for filling, while opposite is a long curved arm terminating in an inverted bell, probably for taking care of the smoke. Across the top is a broad flat wick indicating the use of lard oil as an illuminant.

The third lamp of this extraordinary group is shaped like a round canteen with flat sides. At the bottom two V-shaped pieces of tin allow it to stand upright, while a twisted wire over the top is for convenience in hanging. A single wick tube projects from the top, forming a lamp of most original design.

The last lamp is of a pattern more commonly found in pewter than in tin. The large font swings freely on a gracefully curved arm which rests in the center of the saucer-base. This base has a ring handle at one side for convenience in carrying, while on the opposite edge is a wire loop for hanging the lamp upon a wall, its freely swinging oil font enabling it to maintain an upright position. This has two long camphene wick tubes.

Plate 42, also from Mr. Henry Ford's collection, shows four good pewter lamps. The first looks as if it might have been altered at a later date to burn kerosene. The shape of the base is good and the old glass chimney is quite in harmony of design with the rest of the lamp. The high polish of the second lamp would indicate britannia metal or possibly brass, but its unique feature is the arm at the side of the oil font holding the double-wick oil burner.

The remaining two are good specimens of the more common types of pewter lamps, in perfect condition, the long-capped wick tubes indicating the use of the dangerous camphene, while the last is a particularly good specimen of the double-lens reading lamp. Both the single and the double lens type are now increasingly difficult to find and one may consider himself fortunate to acquire one of as good a design in such perfect condition.

CHAPTER IV

LANTERNS

A BRANCH of lamp collecting which offers a fascinating field for the collector is that of old lanterns. Since the variety here is very marked, it is impossible, in one short chapter, to begin to cover the field.

Plate 46 shows some which Doctor Norton collected and which, perhaps, are typical of the many variations of size, shape, and design which are embraced under this one head.

It is evident that lanterns were not used to any extent until many years after the first settlement of the Massachusetts Bay Colony; in fact, it is rather difficult to assign a much earlier date than the first quarter of the eighteenth century, although undoubtedly here and there some may have been made and used before then.

The "two-story" iron lantern in the second row, Number 37 of this plate, is an interesting historical one. It was captured during that famous expedition, in 1745, against the strongly defended fortress of Louisburg, when a little army of less than four thousand New Englanders, most of them from Massachusetts, trained little or not at all and officered by men of no military experience,— in fact, their commander William Pepperell was a merchant,— set sail for the coast of Cape Breton, and, after a siege of six weeks, with the assistance of a small fleet of British vessels which blockaded Louisburg harbor, captured it from the French.

Some of these early lanterns used candles, others had small oil lamps. Most of them used glass for their windows, but occasionally one finds an old lantern with the window made of thinly scraped horn, a substitute of doubtful value which shows, notwithstanding, the ingenuity of those early workmen when proper material was not to be had. Such a one is Number 361 in the second row. This tall dark lantern is made of copper with a handle and, behind the horn window, a socket for a candle. It was used on the U. S. S. *Enterprise* during the War of 1812. Another intensely interesting specimen of these very early horn lanterns is the large one shown in Plate 43. This lantern, the property of Mr. Horace R. Grant, a collector in Hartford, Connecticut, was of English make, is said to have been in the possession of the Lee family of Guilford, Connecticut, for over two hundred years, and therefore would date close to the beginning of the eighteenth century. It is a piece worth studying because it has more than one horn window and because the several dormer-window shaped ventilators in the top are quaint.

Lanterns, or lanthornes as they were called in the olden days in England, with windows of thinly scraped cow's horn, are extremely rare here. I have never found one in any antique dealer's, and I infer that since most of the specimens found in collections are of English manufacture, very few were made in the Colonies.

Numbers 223 and 169 of Doctor Norton's collection in Plate 46 are tin lanterns using candles for lights. The top of the octagonal one is particularly interesting. This lantern was used in the first fire house in Portsmouth, New Hampshire. Number 169 is unusual in that it is semi-circular in shape with a small door in the back; this is a shop lantern which, it is said, was used in a store house during the time of the American Revolution.

PLATE 40.

See pages 69, 96, 130

GROUP OF UNUSUAL LIGHTING DEVICES
From the Worcester Historical Society

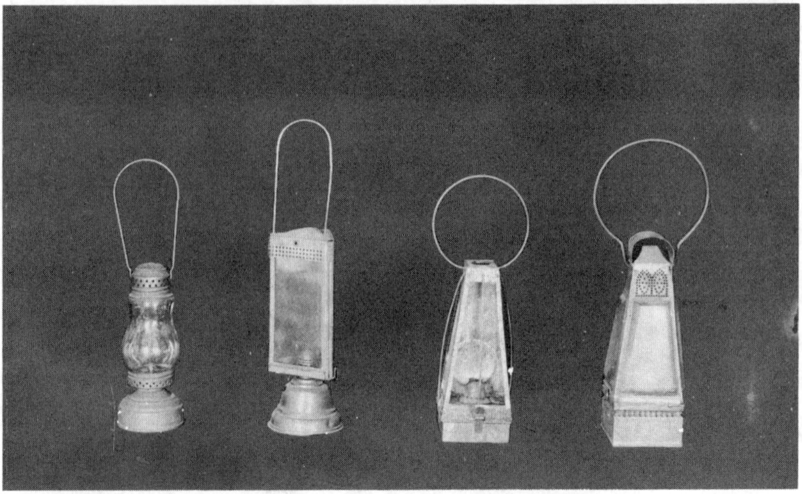

PLATE 41.

See page 69

Four Lanterns of Unusual Designs
Collection of Henry Ford, Michigan

PLATE 42.

See pages 42, 54

Group of Pewter Lamps
Collection of Henry Ford, Michigan

The drawing on this page is of a lantern, one of a pair, which was used on the first through railroad trains between New Haven, Connecticut, and Springfield, Massachusetts, in 1844.

Supplied by a single candle, the dim light on either side of the coach (for those early railroad cars were really stage coaches fastened together and running on light rails) must have made night travelling anything but a pleasure.

Both 261 and 277 in Plate 46 are not unusual types of lanterns, tin top and base and heavy glass sides, but are of interest from their associations.

Doctor Norton in an interesting article on "Lanterns in Early America", published in the *Connecticut Magazine* for June, 1904, gives us a story of how he found the old tin hand lantern for three candles, a drawing of which is shown on this page, in the house in Torrington, Connecticut, where John Brown, the hero of Osawatomie and the great-hearted champion of the black man, was born in 1800. The house was found in a very dilapidated condition, but I think has since been bought by an association which has restored it with the intention of making it a permanent memorial to him.

In the old kitchen, in the big chimney, with its great fireplace, was a huge old oven, nearly filled with ashes and bits of broken stone, the accumulations of years. Wishing to secure some memento, Doctor Norton started searching in the old oven and after taking out great quantities of this debris, he discovered the tin lantern pictured here, which had evidently lain there for many years and is probably contemporary with the boyhood of this grand old man.

It is a hand lantern, semi-circular in shape, with a front which was intended for a square of glass held in place by grooves. The handle at the back cannot be seen, but the three candlesticks and the rows of rudely made holes at the top and bottom for the admission of air and the escape of smoke can be plainly seen.

John Brown, who hated slavery and all its evils, devoted his days to, and in the end laid down his life for, the cause, going to his execution with such calm contentment and royal bearing as to impress his captors, apparently serene in the belief that he was but an instrument in God's hands.

Peace to his soul! While his body was scarcely in the ground hundreds of thousands responded to the call which was so urgent to his heart. The cause for which he gladly sacrificed everything finally prevailed and that stain upon our national life was wiped out forever.

Number 261 of Doctor Norton's in Plate 46, a small tin lantern with straight glass sides, is of interest to all lovers of Charles Dickens, for it stood on a shelf in the little cabin of the steamboat which made daily trips between Springfield and Hartford on the Connecticut River and on which Dickens was a passenger in 1842 when he was preparing his "American Notes." The glass cylinder, very thick, requires no protecting wires. The lantern was secured to the wall by a strip of brass. Dickens' description of the little steamboat is very amusing and I should advise my readers to get down their Dickens and look it up.

He says, " It certainly was not called a small steamboat without reason. I omitted to ask the question, but I should think it must have been of about a half pony power. I am afraid to tell how many feet short this vessel was, or how many feet narrow; to apply the words length and width to such measurement would be a contradiction in terms. But I may state that we all kept in the middle of the deck lest the boat should unexpectedly tip over; and that the machinery, by some surprising process of condensation, worked between it and the keel; the whole forming a warm sandwich about three feet thick." However, Dickens made the trip in perfect safety and this little lantern with its whale-oil burner no doubt helped to light his way.

Number 277 from Doctor Norton's collection in Plate 46 is a watchman's lantern, or was used for this purpose by men guarding the U. S. Treasury building in Washington about 1860 or 1861. It is rather an odd shape for this purpose, but has a D-shaped handle which does not show in the plate. The metal top and bottom are of copper. There was a tradition among the older employees of this department that a gross of these lanterns was imported from England in 1845 for the use of the government watchmen.

With our brilliantly lighted city streets of to-day, it seems almost unbelievable that only about two hundred years ago, after the sun had gone down, large cities with miles of streets and thousands of homes inhabited by industrious and prosperous citizens were left in total darkness, relieved only here and there by a feeble glimmer from some lantern or torch at the gate, or beside the door, of the house of a citizen, public spirited enough to be willing to help the faltering footsteps of his neighbors.

In Boston it was somewhere about 1690 to 1700 that the town placed iron fire baskets on the corners of a few of its most frequented streets to be kept filled and burning by the night watchmen going their rounds. For some time before a larger iron basket on a tall pole had been erected on the top of one of Boston's highest hills and used as a signal to the inhabitants of this and surrounding towns in any case of emergency like an attack by hostile Indians or other foes, fires, etc.; hence the name of Beacon Hill.

It was not until many years later in 1772 that a meeting of the citizens was held to discuss means for more adequately lighting the streets after nightfall. A committee was appointed, of which John Hancock was a member, and after considerable discussion it was decided to send to England for several hundred lanterns suitable for street lighting purposes, as the record runs, "lamps suitable for properly lighting ye streets and lanes of ye town." As far as I am aware, none of these earliest street lanterns is known to exist at the present time, but they were undoubtedly tin or iron lanterns with glass sides, probably fitted with small whale-oil lamps.

These lanterns were not paid for from the town's treasury, but a public subscription was taken to defray the expense. Unfortunately the ship which was bringing them over from England was wrecked off Cape Cod, for, in a letter from a Boston man at that time he says, "It is unlucky that Loring had ye lamps on board for our streets. I am sorry if they are lost as we shall be deprived of their benefit this winter in consequence of it."

However, some if not all the lanterns seem to have been salvaged; for in the diary of one Thomas Newell under date of January 8, 1774, is the record, "Began to make tops (sides?) of ye glass lamps for ye town." A little later he must have completed his work for the record shows that on the evening of March 2nd, 1774, a number of the lanterns were hung and lighted for the first time and that a large concourse of the townspeople turned out to see the great improvement. So satisfactory were they evidently that a little later two citizens were appointed from each ward to decide upon fitting locations for the remainder of the lamps. That was only one hundred and fifty years ago!

For many years the streets at night were patrolled by night

PLATE 43. *See page 56*

Old English Tin Horn Lanthorne
Collection of Horace R. Grant, Hartford, Connecticut

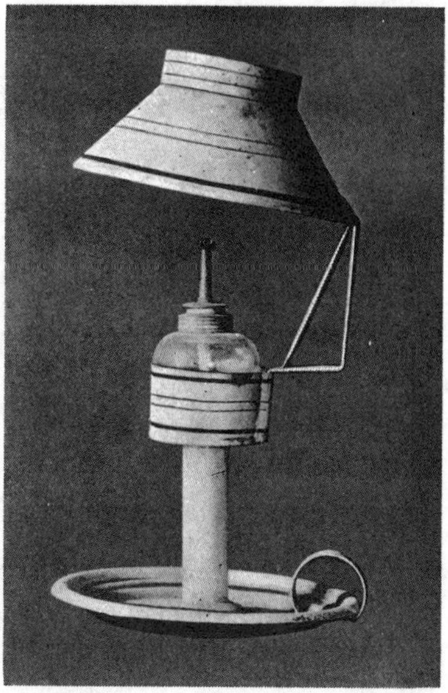

PLATE 44. *See page 52*

Painted Tin and Glass Whale-Oil Hand Lamp
Photograph by Miss Northend

PLATE 45. *See page 17*

Cast Iron Grease Lamp, Said to Have Been Used to Light the Witchcraft Prisoners in Salem Jail
Photograph by Miss Northend

PLATE 46. *See pages 55, 56, 57, 58, 59, 61, 63*

TYPES OF OLD LANTERNS
Dr. Norton Collection

watchmen who usually carried small hand lanterns and with their cry of the hour and "All's well" told the inhabitants that they were performing their duty. These watchmen's lanterns are sometimes found. The small triangular lantern in Plate 51 from the author's collection is undoubtedly one of them. The bull's-eye lantern in the writer's collection in Plate 38 is a watchman's lantern of a later date.

Number 262 of Doctor Norton's in Plate 46 is interesting as the very crude ancestor of our modern, slide-frame, farm lantern. This one, as you will note from the cut, burns a candle for light, protected from drafts by a glass chimney. This particular one, Doctor Norton says, was used in the shipyard by Ericsson while the original *Monitor* was being built.

Another lantern connected with the naval history of our own Civil War is Number 240 on this plate. This is a heavy tin lantern called a "Magazine Safety." Note the large, thick bull's eye fitted to the projecting tube. A broad-wick, copper, lard-oil lamp furnishes the light. The bail on top is of brass. This ship's lantern was taken from the U. S. S. *Kearsarge* after her famous victory over the C. S. *Alabama*. Number 285 is an odd combination of glass and pierced tin, semi-circular in shape, the top and back pierced, whereas the straight front has a glass panel. It is fitted with a single-burner, whale-oil lamp. This lantern was really quite an elegant affair, for it was silver plated inside and the lamp was of copper instead of the usual tin. In 1829 it hung in the gentlemen's cabin of the *Oliver Ellsworth*, which is believed to have been the first boat to make the regular trips between Hartford and New York. Number 283 on this same Plate 46 of Doctor Norton's is a rare type of square lantern, its glass sides protected with iron bands. Standing about nine inches high and provided with a heavy ring for carrying or hanging, it was originally fitted with a double-wick oil burner.

The pierced lanterns from Mr. Gates' collection, several of

which are shown in Plate 47 are an interesting variation from the types previously mentioned. They are often spoken of as Paul Revere lanterns, why I do not know, for it is extremely doubtful if such lanterns were ever used by that active patriot. The tall one in the center should be especially noted. Aside from its size, which is unusual, the piercings, which any Mason will at once recognize, makes it of great interest because it is the only one, to my knowledge, with these Masonic emblems worked into the design, although there may be similar ones in private hands.

Many of these lanterns are pierced in intricate and beautiful designs so that, when illuminated with the candle light inside, the pattern is marked in light with a charming lace-like effect. The amount of real illumination, however, which they give is very small and they were probably used largely when one was obliged to be abroad evenings and carried close to the ground so that one could avoid puddles and rough places.

These pierced lanterns should, however, be collected with considerable caution as they are comparatively easy to counterfeit, for acid treatments and burial in moist earth will give a new lamp a very creditable appearance of age and rust which will deceive the unwary. Since they are found in considerable numbers in many shops, I suspect that they are not always what they pretend to be. If possible, deal with reliable people and check up all information relating to previous owners and history of the lantern. If the dealer is honest, he will gladly help you with what knowledge he has to authenticate your purchases. As I have just remarked, the common name for these pierced tin lanterns is " Paul Revere " lanterns. Just why this type was selected as the lantern which the patriots hung out from the balcony of the old North Church I do not know, but popular tradition seems to have selected this particular type, and, in the absence of any definite proof to the contrary, will probably stick to its belief. I have, however, stood on the bridge between Boston and Charlestown with the tower of Christ Church (the old North Church) in plain view on my right, and the shores of Charlestown on the left, and tried to imagine one of these lanterns, with a candle or small whale-oil lamp glimmering inside, hung out from the corner of the balcony round the spire. By the wildest stretch of the imagination, I cannot conceive of the slightest ray of light showing to any one "booted and spurred and ready to ride" looking for a signal across the bay; so I infer that if the signal was really given by lantern it must have been by some other kind.

In the Marine Museum in Salem, which was founded by the old sea captains and merchants in the East India trade, is a wooden ship lantern standing some two feet high, a huge, clumsy affair burning a candle in it for light. It was used before 1750 by Captain Samuel Page of Danvers.

By far the most interesting lantern of Doctor Norton's on Plate 46 is the hanging one in the center of the top row, numbered 297. This hexagonal lantern, with iron frame and cathedral glass panels, lighted by a candle inside, though attractive in itself, is much more so from an historical standpoint; for this lantern hung in the upper hall of the famous Hancock mansion on Beacon Street, Boston, next to the State House, when from 1770 to 1780 the house was occupied by Governor Hancock and his charming wife.

I doubt if the destruction of any of the many notable houses of New England has been more regretted than that of this Hancock mansion. Of an elegant and distinguished appearance, it stood for years a fitting companion to the imposing Bulfinch State House, but was finally demolished before the citizens of Boston awoke to its architectural and historic value.

Its best memorials to-day are the designs used by several of the Staffordshire potters, showing the Boston State House flanked on either side by the Beacon Street residences of distinguished Bostonians. These designs, printed in the fine old blue and used on dinner sets, found ready sale in New England, but pieces of it to-day are rather rare and command good prices.

One design shows the front of the State House and a bit of Boston Common, on which cows are feeding. Another shows an old, one-horse, two-wheeled chaise and also the houses of the aristocratic neighbors of the governor: Honorable John Phillips, the father of Wendell Phillips; Doctor John Joy who lived on the corner of the present Joy Street; and, on the opposite side of the State House, the stately homes of Joseph Coolidge and Thomas Amory. The latter mansion was rented in 1825 to General Lafayette and his suite. Next to them was the house occupied for many years by Governor Christopher Gore, and next below, the home of Josiah Quincy, Jr.

One of the Staffordshire potters, J. & J. Jackson, with works at Burslem, England, made a series of American views among which was one of the John Hancock house. All these plates are now very scarce and command a high price whenever offered for sale.

This Hancock mansion was built in 1737 by John Hancock's uncle, Thomas Hancock, from whom it came to John by inheritance. The building itself was of stone, set back from the street and approached by a paved walk. In the north wing was a hall sixty feet long. In this wing many distinguished guests were received during Governor Hancock's occupancy, so that this historic lantern has lighted the steps for such prominent men as Generals D'Estaing, Lafayette and Washington, and Lords Stanley and Wortley, Labouchere and Bougainville. In the last years of its existence (near the close of the Civil War) it was filled with valuable relics, pictures, and furniture. It is a burning disgrace to the citizens of Boston that they should have allowed the destruction of such a noble monument to one of Massachusetts' most distinguished men.

The Hancock lantern came to Doctor Norton as a family inheritance, since he was a direct descendant of the famous

PLATE 47. FOUR OLD TIN LANTERNS (Note the Masonic one)
B. N. Gates' Collection

See pages 62, 68

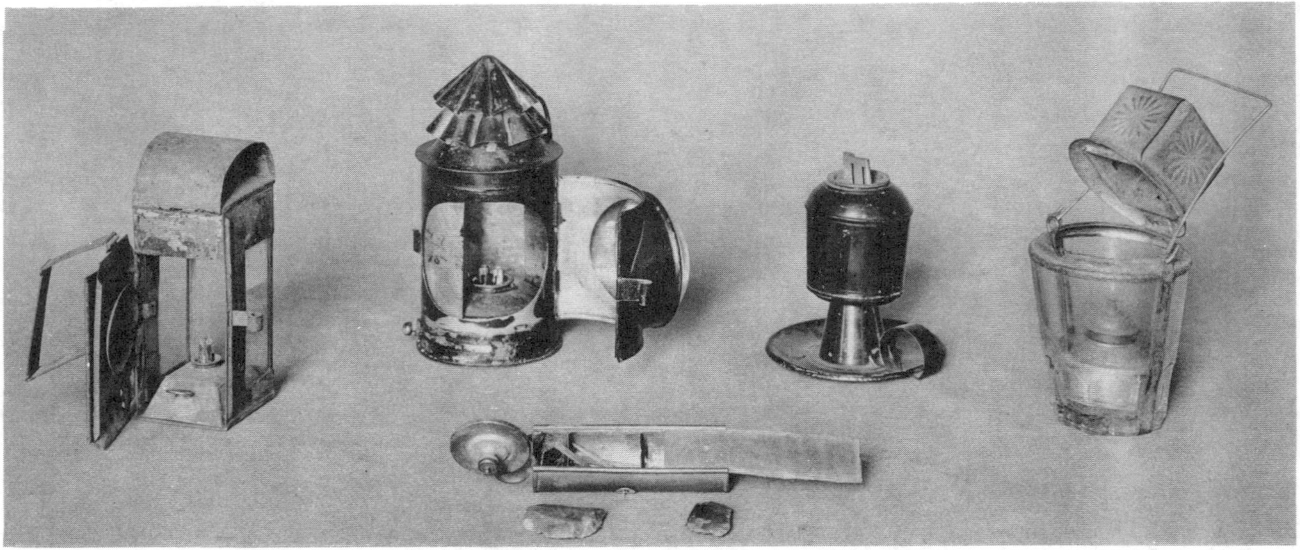

PLATE 48.

INTERESTING GROUP OF LIGHTING DEVICES
Worcester Historical Society

See pages 50, 70

Quincy family, as did also a pair of brass mantel lamps which were presented to Dorothy Quincy by her father on her marriage to John Hancock.

Probably no figure stands out more prominently during the stirring days before and after the war which gained for the American Colonies their independence than does John Hancock.

Of most distinguished appearance, standing fully six feet tall, and broad shouldered, he was usually dressed in the height of fashion, appearing one evening at a secret meeting of patriots in an apple green coat with silver buttons, knee breeches of silver net tied at the knee with ribbons to match in color his coat, white silk stockings and pumps with large silver buckles, while his shirt at wrist and throat was adorned with fine rich lace. His fine clothes, however, did not prevent him from taking active part in all the secret meetings and various plots of the American patriots who were seeking by every means possible to throw off the burdensome yoke of England. At this time, John Hancock had paid ardent court to one of Boston's distinguished beauties, Dorothy Quincy, the daughter of Judge Edmund Quincy, with such success that in spite of the attractions of many other suitors, Dorothy had bestowed her heart and hand upon the young patriot and great preparations were being made for such a socially distinguished wedding. Judge Quincy, fittingly to celebrate the event, had ordered wall paper from Paris to be hung upon the walls of the parlor of the Quincy family mansion, which was built on a grant of five hundred acres at Braintree, now Quincy, Massachusetts. Miss Mary Northend, in her entertaining book, " Historic Homes of New England ", gives us a vivid glimpse of this love affair of John Hancock and " Dorothy Q." The wedding plans were rudely disarranged, however, by the Revolution, which broke out at this time. A price was set on the heads of some of the most ardent patriots by the British officials. John Hancock and Samuel Adams were forced to flee for safety to

Lexington because General Gage, commanding the British troops in Boston, had received orders to arrest them and ship them to England to be tried for high treason. But Adams and Hancock slipped quietly away before the British troops arrived there and took refuge in Woburn.

While John Hancock was staying in Lexington, he was visited by his aunt, Madame Hancock, accompanied by his sweetheart, Dorothy Quincy, and when the warning came of the approach of the hated redcoats, Dorothy was for returning to her father's house, but Hancock, knowing the hatred of the Tories for all the prominent patriots, of whom Dorothy's father was one, insisted that the two women should seek safety with them in Woburn. Dorothy, wishing to have her own way and assert her independence of her patriot lover, insisted upon returning to Boston and a lovers' quarrel was the result. Finally Hancock and Adams were forced to escape to Woburn, taking with them Madame Hancock and Dorothy, who continued on to Fairfield, Connecticut, where they took up their residence in the family of Thaddeus Burr. There Aaron Burr met and fell in love with Dorothy, and became so marked in his attentions that Madame Hancock became alarmed on behalf of her absent nephew and despatched a note to him explaining the situation.

John Hancock, thereupon, being too wise to reproach Dorothy for her fickleness, sent her a handsome present and a request for the hair chain which she had promised him. She, however, being apparently a maid who preferred to have her own way, at any rate while she remained single, continued her flirtation with the young and fascinating Army Lieutenant to such purpose that Madame Hancock sent a peremptory note demanding the immediate presence of John at Fairfield. Congress, of which he was an influential member, being in recess, he came in person and soon succeeded in regaining his place in the affections of the fair but fickle Dorothy, so that soon after she became his wife and the mistress of the great mansion, where as the first lady of the Commonwealth she entertained in a truly regal manner. So this old lantern must have witnessed many merry gatherings of distinguished men and beautiful women within the walls lighted by its feeble beams.

Since there is a great variety of such lanterns, I have devoted a number of plates to them that my readers may get somewhat familiar with them. They offer a splendid field for the amateur just starting because they are comparatively easy to find, usually priced at a few dollars, and, if in fairly good condition, will give their owner the satisfactory feeling of having acquired something that really counts in a new collection. They are quite decorative and my private opinion is that in a few years the ones with the good old glass in the odd shapes which they used will have generally disappeared from the markets, and when found will command much higher prices than at the present time.

The three plates representing lanterns from the collection of Mr. Gates of Worcester show a well-selected variety, each lantern being a good representative of its particular kind.

Plate 54 perhaps shows the most unusual ones. The central one has, as the cut plainly shows, four places for candles. The front is one large glass pane. The semi-circular back, which is of bright tin to act as a reflector, has a small door in the center through which the candles may be lighted and snuffed. The outside is japanned and provided with a stout handle and a ventilator in the top to allow the smoke and hot air to escape. This lantern was undoubtedly used to light a store, or, as Mr. Gates thinks, may have been used to illuminate a show case or window. The square one at the left has three sides of glass and the fourth of tin which opens. The small reflector against it enlarges the flame from the camphene burning lamp within. The brass extinguisher on the top of the wick holder, with a ring through its top instead of the customary chain, is an innovation quite uncommon, as is also the arrangement of the top of the lamp and handle.

The other one is six sided, much rarer than the round or square lamp, and is lighted by a candle. It has both a handle at the back and a ring on top for carrying. The ventilator on top, from which the ring hangs, is also of a very unusual type. Odd variations like these make a collection of much more interest than a large number of the commoner types.

Plate 55 shows three of the more common type, but in excellent condition, the first one having a good ribbed glass. The next one, with the glass protected by a wire guard, is a conductor's lantern and was used on the old Fitchburg & Worcester Railroad. With a reading glass one can distinguish the initials F & W cut in the glass. The third is a lantern manufactured at the works of the New England Glass Co. (spoken of in Chapter VI) stamped with their name and "Pat. Oct. 24, 1854." The last one on the right is of a somewhat earlier and cruder type, with a handle at the back and folding tin doors opening in front of the flame over a mica window — a great rarity in this type.

The other plate, Number 47 of Mr. Gates', gives us views of two good square lanterns for candles, protected by wire guards but of quite dissimilar designs. Of the two pierced ones, the first is an excellent lantern of an unusually good design and exceptional workmanship, while the larger one is chiefly interesting from its Masonic emblems, spoken of elsewhere in this chapter.

The writer has two of these tin lanterns with the original glass, shown in Plate 51, neither of which is unusual, both for whale-oil lamps. The little triangular watchman's lantern in this plate is, however, odd in its small size: it is only about four inches high, with two sides of glass and the back of tin. It is lighted by a small, three-cornered oil lamp attached to the

PLATE 49. *See page 69*

ROUND WHALE-OIL LANTERNS
Collection of Henry Ford, Dearborn, Michigan

PLATE 50 *See page 69*

CANDLE LANTERNS IN BRASS AND TIN
Collection of Henry Ford, Dearborn, Michigan

PLATE 51. *See pages 14, 25, 32, 61, 68*

THREE TIN LANTERNS AND EARLY TIN WHALE-OIL LAMP

Author's Collection

PLATE 52. *See page 99*

CANDLESTICK WITH MICA CHIMNEY

Photograph by Miss Northend

PLATE 53. *See page 52*

FINE TYPE PEWTER SPARK OR TAVERN LAMP

Collection of C. L. Cooney

bottom, which is hinged at the back and drops down, fastening by a spring at the side.

To one collecting lanterns, an endless variety is a constant incentive to add still more. Even of railroad lanterns there is quite a variety and a fairly sizable collection might be made from these alone. In Plate 49 from the collection of Mr. Henry Ford of Michigan, the two at the right are very evidently of this classification — one having the initials of the road ground on the glass and both with double whale-oil burners. The smaller one with the octagonal glass and the single-tube burner is more familiar, but the queer shaped one at the left with the hook on top is not familiar to me and may be a type of miner's lamp of the old whale-oil burning kind, though I am not sure.

Plate 50 shows four good candle lanterns also from Mr. Ford's collection. The oldest one in the group, I should judge, is the tin lantern at the right with its glass sides protected by the crude wire guards. The remaining ones are of brass and the two in the center have mica windows.

In Plate 41 Mr. Ford gives a view of four lanterns of perhaps a little later type. The one with the triangular top is unusual while the two tin lanterns at the right with the tapering square tops are of designs not commonly found.

Unusual lanterns of good design like these are certainly a source of satisfaction to their owner and bear me out in my statement that perhaps no branch of lamp collecting yields richer or more satisfactory returns than does this one of lanterns.

In the rooms of the Worcester Historical Society are a number of interesting lighting devices which they have kindly allowed me to photograph. In Plate 40 is a quaint old lantern, a combination of wooden sides with glass windows and a perforated tin top with a door opening on wire hinges. It is lighted by a candle which may be seen inside in an old turned-up edge, tin candlestick and is carried by a leather strap over the top. This lantern is probably of quite early make. Another is shown in Plate 48, the first on the left, a small, square, tin lantern with glass front and sides and a solid back upon which a tin reflector is hung to increase the light from the small sperm-oil lamp. Note the shape of the lamp and the ring to pull it out by. Also note a quite unusual feature, one I have never seen before — a folding tin handle on the back of the door which shuts up perfectly flat when not in use.

The second lantern in this plate, though not so unusual, is a good example of a tin, watchman's, or dark, lantern. The curved door with its heavy bull's eye of glass is open to show the small two-wick, sperm-oil lamp in the base. The tin slide, which shuts off the light and is controlled by the knob at the bottom, is shown partly closed.

A lantern with an unusual glass is shown in Plate 65. Since most of the lanterns had plain glass globes, it is rather uncommon to find one with a glass like this with its three rows of "nail-heads" around it. This is not a very old lantern, as its lamp indicates.

Lanterns were of very ancient origin. In China they have been in common use for thousands of years, their origin being lost in the dim mists before the beginning of authentic history. It is stated that in some of her ancient books, the use of paper lanterns in temple worship is mentioned as early as five thousand years before Christ. In the first month of the new year is held in China the "Feast of Lanterns", one of their great national festivals, in which the streets of the cities and towns are lined with innumerable lanterns of every conceivable size, shape and color, some of paper but many of beautiful silks, painted and decorated, with elaborately carved and gilded frames, some of them very costly. The following Chinese legend is given as the origin of this Festival:

An only daughter of a famous and powerful mandarin,

while walking on the edge of a pond on her father's estate, had the misfortune to fall into the water and was supposed to have drowned. Her father, with his neighbors, went to look for his beloved child. Happily she was found and rescued from her dangerous position and restored to her parent. To celebrate the recovery of his daughter, the grateful father held a festival annually on the spot where she was found, and, because lanterns played such an important part in her recovery, he had the whole park brilliantly illuminated.

From this beginning the "Feast of Lanterns" grew and in time became a national festival.

In the elaborate carvings upon the inner walls of the rock-hewn tombs wherein were laid the mummies of Egypt's rulers hundreds of years before the Christian era, may be seen the representation of a soldier carrying a long rod from the end of which is suspended a lantern not unlike the so-called "Paul Revere" or perforated tin lanterns shown on these pages.

In the Bible, so far as I am aware, lanterns are mentioned but once. In the New Testament, John 18: 3, we read, "Judas then, having received a band of men and officers from the chief priests and Pharisees, cometh thither with lanterns, and torches, and weapons," showing that the use of lanterns was well known in those days and probably among other nations as well, for they are spoken of by early Greek and Roman writers. Our modern word is a derivation of the old English word "lanthorn", referring no doubt to the thin plates of scraped cow's horn which often formed the sides of those very early English ones. That they were in common use in Europe at an early date is proved by many old writers and by old engravings.

In 1416 the Lord Mayor of London, "ordained, that lanterns with lights be hanged out on winter evenings, betwixt Hallowtide and Candlemasse."

Allusions to lanterns in Shakespeare are quite common and

in Queen Anne's time, lighting with lanterns seems to have been very general in London.

There is an old English print made shortly after the famous gunpowder plot of Guy Fawkes in 1604 which shows him at the moment of his discovery in the vaults beneath the House of Parliament. He is there depicted with a small dark lantern in his hand very similar to some of the very early lanterns shown in this book.

It is very evident, then, that the shapes and general characteristics of our early Colonial lanterns were copied from those in use on the Continent.

After the War for Independence was over and the colonists had recovered from its effect upon their business, the daily currents of affairs had resumed their regular flow, and the wealth of the communities increased; there was an increased demand for luxuries from those who could afford them. Many articles were imported from England and the Continent, which were either not made here or of which the workmanship was not to be compared to the more finished and artistic products of England, France, Italy and other countries of Europe. Nearly every vessel entering our ports from abroad brought quantities of china, glassware, silver, materials for all kinds of clothing, linens, silks, and many other things. The newspapers from about 1785 to 1810 printed many advertisements which make fascinating reading to-day. It was very common to advertise the arrival of a vessel and give a list of her cargo for sale. Some of the articles there mentioned would be totally unknown to the young people of to-day.

The wealthier people demanded more and better lighting for their large fine houses and began to give thought and attention to a subject which up to now had been almost neglected, the lighting of the different halls of their mansions.

I have already spoken of the lantern which lighted the hall of the Governor Hancock house in Boston. It was customary

PLATE 54.

THREE ODD SHAPED LANTERNS
B. N. Gates' Collection, Worcester

See pages 67, 68

PLATE 55.

See page 68

FOUR OLD LANTERNS (ONE USED ON FIRST WORCESTER RAILROAD)
B. N. Gates' Collection, Worcester

to have one hung from the ceiling in the front hall near the foot of the winding flight of stairs which led to the floor above.

In addition most of the larger houses had other lanterns, perhaps not so elaborate, in the other halls. Tradition has it that there were three lanterns in the lower hall of the Hancock mansion.

The home of the famous Lord Timothy Dexter in Newburyport is said to have been lighted by many beautiful lamps and lanterns. No less than four hanging lanterns of most elegant design are said to have been used in lighting his dining room.

Many of these lanterns, as well as the more elaborate chandeliers and candelabra spoken of in another chapter, were imported from England and France, where work of this kind was in a much more advanced state than in this country.

The earlier hall lanterns burned candles, but in the later ones whale-oil lamps were used. Beautiful work was put into the hanging frames of brass or bronze and particularly into the glass for the lanterns or the fanciful shaped globes, elaborately cut and etched and often of colored glass.

Careless handling, of course, was fatal; and for that reason one rarely finds a good old hanging lamp with the original glass unbroken.

In Plate 113 you have a fine example of one of those hall lanterns. I do not know surely, but from its appearance should judge it to be an imported one. Note the grace of the whole design. The three bronze chains support the delicately curved arms from the upper rim. The same design is repeated on the lamp holder at the base of the ruby glass globe, upon which is ground a bold design, showing the clear glass beneath. Over the top is a clear glass smoke protector.

Two others from Mr. Gates' collection are given in Plate 112, both excellent specimens, the smaller at the left having a plain glass which held a candle for light, the ornamentation being in the band holding the globe and the candle holder to match. The larger one, with a globe of similar shape but cut, has a metal band to hold it at the extreme top. Both are in perfect condition.

Plate 89 shows a hall at " Indian Hill " the fine old mansion at West Newbury, Massachusetts, near Byfield, formerly owned and occupied by the late Ben Perley Poore, an enthusiastic collector of antiques. This hall is not in the original house which dates from 1680, but is part of a wing lately built. Into it has gone old lumber and parts of other old houses, so that it well preserves the lines and atmosphere of the rest of the house. Mr. Poore hung an old lantern here and Miss Northend has kindly allowed me to use this photograph that my readers may see an old hall lantern in its proper environment.

CHAPTER V

CANDLES AND CANDLE HOLDERS

THE first cattle imported from England were three cows in 1630, but cattle were not common for twenty or thirty years more. Consequently there was little fat or tallow for the making of candles; and the fat of the deer and bear which roamed the woods in large numbers at that time was frequently used.

A cheap form of candle was the pith of the common reed known as cat-o'-nine-tails (so common in all New England swamps) when dipped in tallow or similar fats. These candles, known as "rush-lights", were burned in peculiar holders made so that the unburned portion could be curled up, straightening it out as it was consumed.

Other substitutes for tallow were found in the wax from the honeycombs of the swarms of wild bees, found in crevices of the rocks and in decayed tree trunks all through the New England forests, and also quite extensively in the fruit of the bayberry, growing on low bushes along the edges of the salt water in the sand dunes. Spermaceti, a fatty substance found in the head of the sperm whale, made most excellent candles, giving about double the light of the tallow dips, and was also used for many years.

In 1730 a few of the streets of Boston were lighted by little square tin lanterns enclosing spermaceti candles.

Candles were a luxury for many years. In 1634 no candles could be purchased for less than fourpence, a sum which was considered the height of extravagance in those days.

Although most families used their oil lamps on all ordinary occasions, they almost all kept a good supply of candles on hand for all special affairs and it was one of the duties of the thrifty housewife each fall to make up and store away a large enough supply to carry them through until another fall.

Two distinct ways of candle making were used, dipping and moulding. Dipping, the earlier method, was the more interesting and required no little skill on the part of the maker.

In the fall when the cattle were killed to supply the winter's meat, great iron kettles were hung from the long cranes over the fire in the kitchen fireplace, filled with tallow, or whatever fat was to be used, and boiling water. The fat rising to the top was carefully skimmed off and, after this process was repeated several times to clear the tallow of all impurities, was put back over the fire where it would keep at as even a temperature as possible.

Two long poles were then placed parallel to each other across the backs of chairs with smaller sticks crosswise from which hung the candle wicks. These shorter sticks with the cotton wicks hanging down at regular intervals would then be taken, one at a time, quickly dipped in the kettle of hot fat, and hung up to dry across the two long poles. By the time the housewife had reached the last stickful of wicks, the first ones would be sufficiently cooled for a second dipping and so the process was repeated; each dipping adding another coating of wax over the previous one, until the candles were of the desired thickness. The skill came in keeping the kettle of fat at just the right temperature to add a bit to the candles at each dipping. If too hot it would tend to melt off what had been previously put on and no gain in size would be made, and if too cool it would lump and give the candle an uneven surface which would prevent its proper burning.

The good house-mothers took as much pride in their candles as did our own grandmothers in their skill in making the tooth-

PLATE 56

See pages 82, 83, 94, 96

ODD-SHAPED TIN WALL SCONCE, TIN TINDER BOX WITH CANDLE HOLDER ON COVER AND IRON PISTOL TINDER
Collection ot C. L. Cooney

PLATE 57.

See page 25

OLD LAMP IN COPPER, USED BY EARLY JESUIT MISSIONARIES TO THE INDIANS
Collection of C. L. Cooney

PLATE 58.

See pages 82, 83

VARIETIES OF TINDER BOXES, FLINTS AND STEELS
Collection of V. M. Hillyer, Baltimore

some pies and rich cakes for which New England cooks were justly noted.

As you can imagine, this candle making was an exceedingly slow and tiresome task; the candles had to be cooled very slowly or they would be apt to crack, and the fire and pots watched constantly, but it was no uncommon thing for a skilled worker to turn out two hundred finished candles in a day.

For the second process, which came into use a little later, tin and sometimes pewter moulds were used (as shown in Plates 59 and 60). These moulds ranged from single candles to as many as six or eight dozen or even more in a mould, and the process, of course, was much simpler and more rapid. Still care and some degree of skill had to be used in keeping the candle wicking taut and straight as it hung down inside the mould. Plate 59 shows a group of candle moulds from the collection of Mr. V. M. Hillyer of Baltimore. The larger wooden stand at the right containing two dozen pewter moulds is a particularly rare piece. In Mr. Hillyer's description of this photograph he says, "Candle moulds usually had from two to two dozen barrels and were made of either tin or pewter. The twelve barrel mould was perhaps the commonest, although six and eight were not unusual. The single barrel pewter mould illustrated is probably one of a bank like the large one of twenty-four barrels shown standing at the right. The mould in the right foreground shows how the wicks were supported before the tallow was poured. An original poured tallow candle in the single barrel mould shows the loop that was of necessity always found in such candles."

Another interesting group of smaller tin candle moulds is seen on Plate 60 from Mr. Gates' collection. Hanging on the wall is a four-candle tin mould (the tin moulds commonly used came in one, two, four, six, eight, twelve and sometimes twenty-four and higher candle combinations, though four, six and twelve seem to have been in most common use) showing the finished candles in place just as moulded, the stick at the top holding the wick loops while the tops are projecting from the ends of the moulds at the bottom. The four-candle mould at the right is filled but shows some of the candles partly drawn out; the loops here are more plainly seen. All of these candle moulds are in excellent condition and this plate will give one a good idea of the candle-making process. The writer has a tall two-candle mould and several of twelve and twenty-four candle capacity. Candle moulds a few years ago were very plentiful and lightly valued, but the demands of collectors have become so insistent lately as to practically sweep the market bare.

The bayberries furnished the material for the choicest candles, and since it took a large quantity of berries for each candle made, they were highly prized and kept for very important occasions. The bayberry is a very small, silvery-gray berry, growing in thick clusters on the brittle stems of a low-growing bush found close to the seashore. It has to be boiled and skimmed several times before the fat is a delicate, semi-transparent light green indicating that it is sufficiently refined. These candles burn quite freely and give off a delicate fragrance.

As the demand for candles increased, in time men made a business of travelling from house to house around the country, stopping a day or two in each place long enough to make up the winter's supply and they were usually warmly welcomed because they supplied the family not only with candles but also with all the news and gossip of the countryside, a matter of no small importance when newspapers were unknown.

With the use of candles came the making of an infinite variety of holders, so that a collector may have a very busy and interesting time if he simply wishes to confine himself to candlesticks and candle holders. He may find them in iron, tin, pewter, wood, brass, glass, silver and earthenware, with a bewildering variation in form, size, design, etc., in each kind. Some are common enough to be found in almost any little country antique store, while others are so rarely met with that it often takes years of patient search before one is rewarded.

I am fortunate enough to number among my friends Mr. Burton N. Gates of Worcester, a gentleman who has been for many years a collector of that fascinating ware made in the town of Bennington.

In 1793 two brothers from Connecticut by the name of Norton started a pottery in Bennington, Vermont, for the manufacture of common earthenware household utensils from the red earth found in that vicinity. In 1800 they commenced the making of stoneware. Just how long they continued or how successful they were, I am unable to say, but in 1846 three young men formed a partnership under the firm name of Fenton, Hall, and Norton and commenced the making of yellow, white and Rockingham wares in the old stoneware pottery of the Nortons. This enterprise seems to have met with success from the start. In 1849 new buildings were erected and occupied.

The membership of the firm changed several times, one or another of the partners dropping out and others coming in, but Mr. Fenton remained and seems to have been the guiding spirit of the enterprise. The name of United States Pottery, Bennington, Vermont, was now adopted and the products were generally known under this name. They made several different wares, but the white Parian marble and the mottled Rockingham or Flint Enameled ware as it was called seems to have been the most popular. This latter ware, a patent for which was issued to Mr. Fenton, is what is commonly known to collectors to-day as Bennington, and this is the ware of which the collection of candlesticks shown by Mr. Gates is made. The mottled coloring of browns, yellows, soft greens with touches here and there of dull blues and reds produced a very lovely and striking effect, which seems to have exactly suited the tastes of the public; for these wares became very popular, so that by 1853 the pottery was employing one hundred hands. This coloring was produced by different metallic oxydes applied on the glaze, which latter served as a medium to float them about upon the surface while in a state of fusion, this producing the variegated tints and moss-like effect.

Many other potteries, seeing the success of this ware, tried to imitate it, as several examples in his collection of Mr. Gates will show, but any one at all familiar with the genuine Bennington can tell it at a glance.

The factory, however, was short-lived, closing its doors in 1858 when Mr. Fenton moved West. To-day there is probably no American ware more eagerly sought or more ardently admired than Bennington. Many collectors specialize in it, and so keen is the rivalry whenever a really good piece comes on the market as to often run the price up to three figures.

This wonderful collection of Bennington candlesticks in rich and distinctive colorings of mottled cream, brown, yellow, and dull green glaze, the distinctive mark of this ware, is all in perfect condition. The collection shown in Plate 71 is the reward of many years of patient and diligent seeking, the value of which can only be approximated when one considers how rarely to-day can be found even a single one and that usually damaged. In this collection the pair of candlesticks just at the left of the center, with the pierced bases, are spurious, made to imitate Bennington by E. & W. Bennett, potters of Baltimore. The single stick at the right of the center is also an imitation and was made by a potter in Trenton, New Jersey. All the others are genuine Benningtons and the central piece, which is a lamp base, is marked. This is the only lamp, so far as I am aware, in any collection to-day, marked with the Bennington stamp. These candlesticks are only a small part

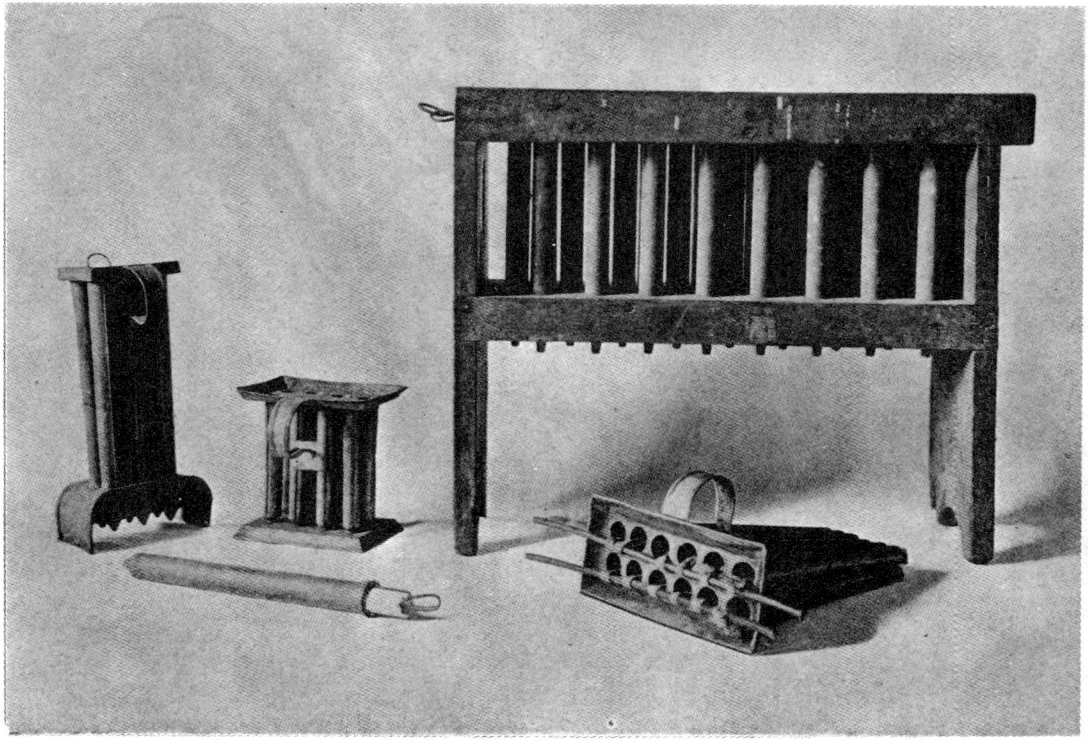

PLATE 59. GROUP OF CANDLE MOULDS IN TIN AND PEWTER
Collection of V. M. Hillyer, Baltimore

See page 77

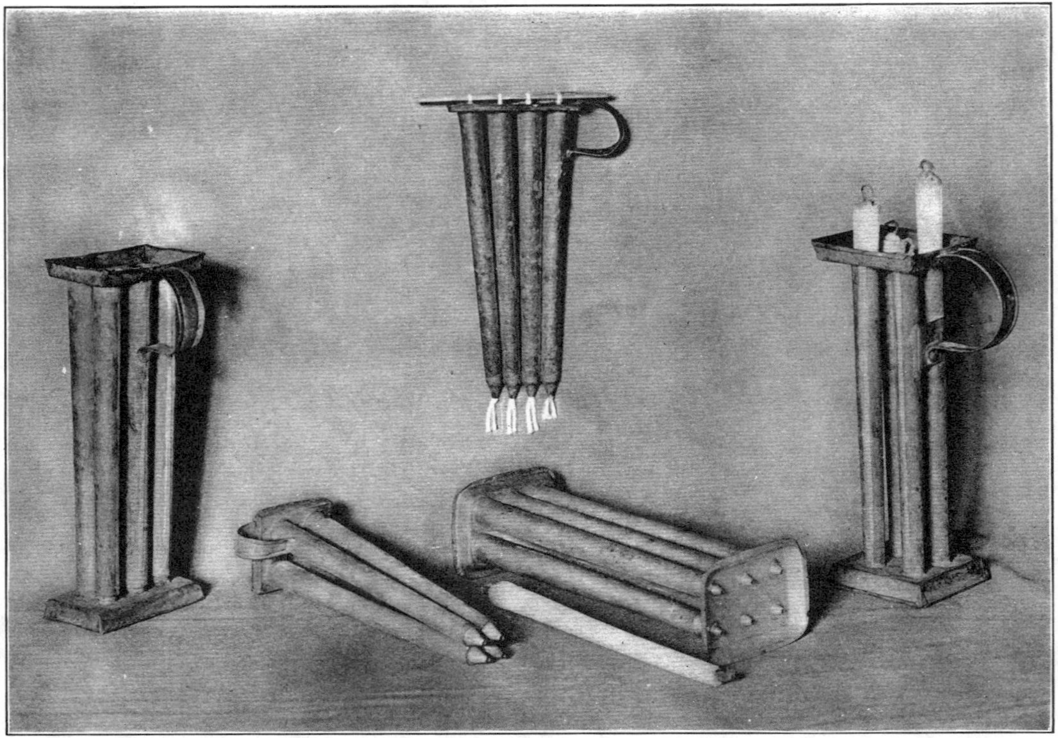

PLATE 60. GROUP OF TIN CANDLE MOULDS (two filled with candles)
B. N. Gates' Collection

See page 77

of the collection of Bennington which he has been gathering for many years and which now includes specimens of almost all the many forms of pitchers, bowls, household utensils of all kinds, mantel ornaments, picture frames, small statuettes, etc., which were turned out by those Vermont potteries.

Other potteries, less celebrated than Bennington, occasionally made candlesticks and some were brought from England, but metal and glass candlesticks were the more commonly used.

Of the iron ones, which were of early make and quite soon superseded by tin and brass, few remain to-day. Although they are crude and far from ornamental, they are of interest to the collector who wishes to make his record as complete as possible and should be sought for.

They were usually in the form of a small cylinder attached to a broad base and sometimes had a slide in the cylinder which enabled the candle to be pushed up as it was burned. One of the special features found on some of these early iron candlesticks is a lip of iron at the top of the stick where the candle enters the socket. This is for the purpose of hanging on the high ladder-back or similar type chair so that the light coming over the shoulder may guide the fingers of the knitter or illumine the pages of the book of the reader sitting in the chair.

Mr. B. N. Gates has placed one of these on the back of a chair to illustrate the method of using, in Plate 22, though a higher chair with more slats should have been used.

Candlestands in iron were often wrought by the skilled hands of the early blacksmiths, showing in most cases a strong feeling for line and proportion and often delicately and skillfully wrought. Plate 6 from the collection of Mr. C. L. Cooney shows a well designed table stand for two candles, the graceful arms and legs and the twisted stems being very well done. Note particularly the curved top to lift it by and the very graceful legs, also the spiral twists in both the central upright and the two candle branches.

In Plate 5 are two taller stands, also from Mr. Cooney's collection, for use beside the big fireplaces. These are also well worth close inspection for the workmanship is of a high order.

One of the most vexatious things about the early lamps and candles were the means for lighting them. As friction matches were not invented until 1827 and did not come into general use until some years later, and even then were rather clumsy affairs and by no means certain, the use of flint and steel and tinder boxes was universal.

Of course by far the easiest way, when there was a fire on the hearth, was to light a sliver of resinous wood from the glowing coals. Very carefully was the fire covered at night with ashes so that live coals in the morning might be easily fanned into a cheerful blaze. But there were times when it was necessary to get a light when a fire was not available and then the tinder box was resorted to. In Plates 56 and 58 may be seen a tin tinder box with a stand on the lid for a candle. These boxes were filled with charred linen cloth or some substance which would catch fire easily, called tinder, and then a bit of rough flint with a sharp edge was struck sharply against a piece of iron causing sparks to fall into the box igniting the tinder.

A very early flint, steel and tinder box which has seen much actual service is shown in Plate 74. This was a pocket outfit, the flint with the flat piece of steel resting on it at the right and the tinder box which consisted of a hollow wooden tube for carrying the tinder, with a cork stopper at the left. The cork has been taken out to show several bits of the charred rags which were used as tinder.

A small piece of wood coated with sulphur was then thrust into the burning tinder and from this primitive match the candle or lamp was lighted. It often took some time to get a light to the exhaustion of one's patience and temper.

A unique variation of a flint and steel is shown in Plate 56 from Mr. C. L. Cooney's collection. This was for use in the well-to-do homes and is exactly the same in principle and almost identical in appearance to the old flint-lock musket or pistol. Instead of the hole into the barrel where the spark from the flint and steel would ignite the powder, there was a tiny square tinder box into which the spark fell when the trigger was pulled, and, after several attempts usually, the tinder would catch fire and then the candle, which was often attached to the side of the pistol tinder box, could be lighted.

In Plate 58 may be seen a very extraordinary collection of tinder boxes used in Colonial America and all probably of home manufacture with the exception of the box-like arrangement in the lower row which seems to be of Spanish origin.

This wonderful collection is reproduced here by courtesy of its owner, Mr. V. M. Hillyer of Baltimore, who describes them as follows:

"The two tinder boxes at the lower left of the illustration are the common types used in Colonial days — one with and one without a candle socket on the cover. Both had an inner top and of course contained tinder, flint and steel.

"The smaller box to the right of the two mentioned is a pocket tinder box. The steel is fastened to the front edge. The flint is shown just before it.

"The next box to the right is a combination ink well, sand-cup, and flint lock pistol type of tinder box, a very rare specimen damascened with gold inlay. The two pistol tinders — both with candle sockets, though the one in foreground is hidden behind — are less rare — but these are unusually good specimens and still in perfect working order. The trigger was pulled, the flint-headed hammer struck the steel, at the same time lifting the lid of a little pocket containing tinder, which was ignited. The light was then carried by sulphur-tipped splints to the candle at the side.

"The large filigree 'Steel' hanging to the upper left of the illustration was hung by the fireside for common household use and purposely made of this size and weight (it weighs nearly two pounds) to prevent its being inadvertently put in one's pocket and carried off.

"The pocket 'Steel' hanging next, to the right, is fitted also with a corkscrew and whistle. The indentation on the edge of the steel has been worn down by innumerable strikings.

"The cylindrical tinder box next is a pocket form, while the one to the right is a de luxe affair of silver, which was carried like a watch by some Colonial dandy. The name plate bearing his initials has a double edge of steel for striking, the flint is suspended by another part of the chain and the tinder of braided rags is carried through a hexagonal barrel."

Since some of my readers may have become by this time so interested in candles and candle making as to want to try the experiment of their manufacture for themselves, I append the following careful directions, copied from "The Domestic Encyclopaedia" in five volumes by "A. F. M. Willick, M. D. — First American edition, with additions applicable to the present situation of the U. S. by James Mease, M. D." and published in Philadelphia in 1804 — nearly a century and a quarter ago!

"CANDLES . . . There are two species of tallow candles, the one dipped, and the other moulded; the first are those in common use; the invention of the second is attributed to LeBrege, of Paris. Good tallow candles ought to be made with equal parts of sheep and ox-tallow; care being taken to avoid any mixture of hog's lard, which occasions a thick black smoke, attended with a disagreeable smell, and also causes the candles to run.

"When the tallow has been weighed and mixed in the true proportions, it is cut very small, that it may be more speedily dissolved; for otherwise it would be liable to burn or become

PLATE 61.

See page 97

INTERESTING GROUP OF CANDLESTICKS IN IRON, TIN, PEWTER AND BRASS
B. N. Gates' Collection, Worcester

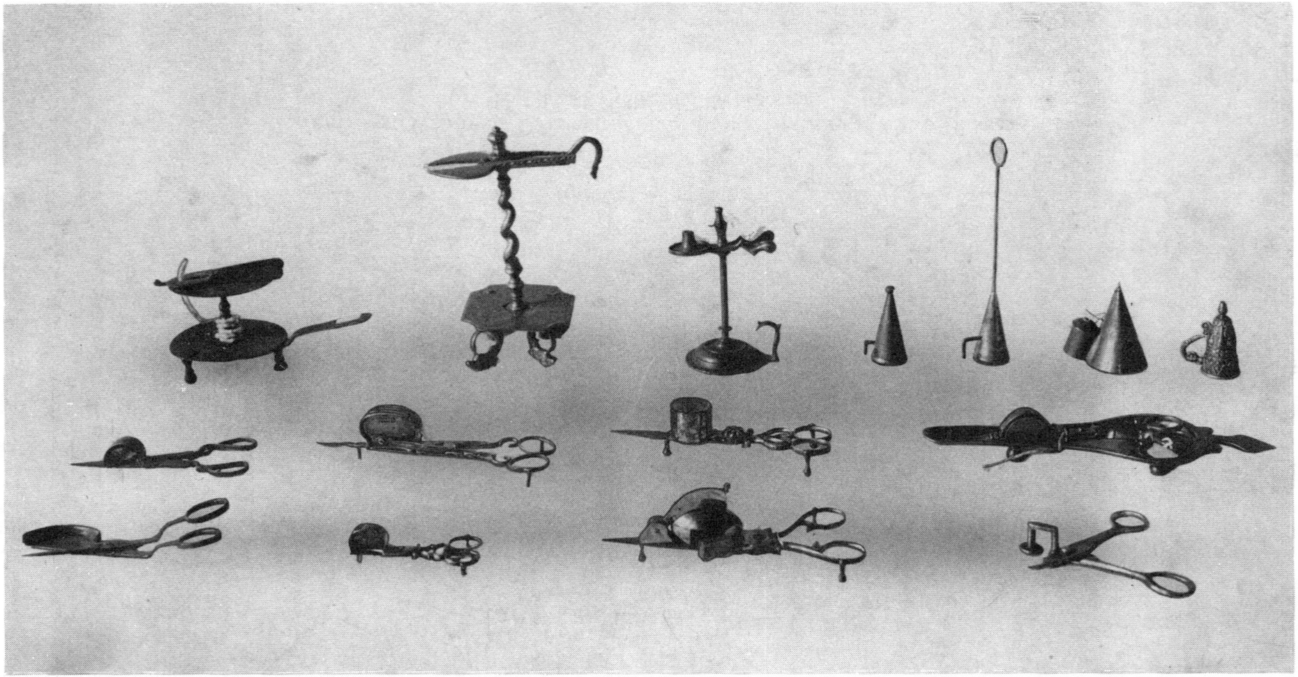

PLATE 62. GROUP OF SNUFFERS, EXTINGUISHERS AND TAPER STICKS
Collection of V. M. Hillyer, Baltimore

See page 101

black, if left too long over the fire. As soon as it is completely melted and skimmed a certain quantity of water, proportionate to that of the tallow, is poured in for precipitating the impure particles to the bottom of the vessel. This, however, should not be done till after the first three dips; as the water, by penetrating the wicks, would make the candles crackle in burning, and thereby render them useless. To purify the tallow still more, it is strained through a coarse horse-hair sieve into a tub; where after remaining three hours, it becomes fit for use.

"Wax candles are of various kinds and forms; they are made of cotton or flaxen wicks, slightly twisted, and covered with white or colored wax. This operation is performed either by hand or with a ladle. In order to soften the wax it is worked repeatedly in a deep narrow cauldron of hot water. Then taken out in small pieces, and gradually disposed round the wick, which is fixed on a hook in the wall, beginning with the larger end, and diminishing in proportion as the neck approaches; to prevent the wax from adhering to the hands, they are rubbed with oil of olives, lard or other unctuous substance. When it is intended to make a wax candle with a ladle, the wicks being prepared as above mentioned, a dozen of them are fixed at equal distances around an iron circle, which is suspended over a tinned copper vessel containing melted wax; a large ladleful of which is poured gently and repeatedly on the tops of the wick till the candle has acquired a proper size, when they are taken down, kept warm, and smoothed upon a walnut-tree table with a long square instrument of box, which is continuously moistened with hot water, to prevent the adhesion of the wax. In other respects this mode of making wax candles corresponds with that of manufacturing them with the hand.

"From the very great utility of candles, they early became the object of adulteration; hence it is provided by various acts of parliament, that all adulterated candles shall be forfeited; and if any tallow-chandlers, or melters make use of melting-houses without giving due notice to the excise-officers, they shall be subject to a penalty of £100.

" Although candles are preferable to lamps, as their light is less injurious both to the eyes and lungs, and as they do not produce so great a volume of smoke, yet a clean chamber-lamp which emits as little smoke and smell as possible is far superior even to wax candles; for 1. as all candles burn downwards, the eye necessarily becomes more fatigued, and strained during the later hours of candle light; 2. because they yield an irregular light which occasions the additional trouble of snuffing them; and lastly because, if the air be agitated ever so little, or if the candles are made of bad materials, they injure the eye by their flaring light.

" A method of making this useful article with wooden wicks is practiced at Munich in Bavaria; and as it promises to be of great utility, we lay the following account before our economical readers.

" The wood generally used for this purpose is that of the fir tree, when one year old; though pine, willow or other kinds are frequently employed; the young shoots must first be deprived of their bark by scraping; which operation ought to be repeated after they become dry, till they be reduced to the size of a small straw. These rods are next to be rubbed over with tallow or wax, so as to be covered with a thin coating of either of these substances; after which they should be rolled on a smooth table in fine carded cotton, of the same length of the candle-mould; care being taken of an uniform thickness around the wick, excepting at the upper extremity, where it may be made somewhat thicker. By this preparation, the wicks will acquire the size of a small quill, when they must be placed in moulds in the usual manner, and good, fresh tallow, which has previously been melted with a little water, be poured around them. The candles then manufactured emit nearly the same volume of light as those made of wax; they burn considerably longer than the common tallow candles; never crackle or run; and as they do not flare, are less prejudicial to the eyes of those persons who are accustomed to long continued lucubrations. . . . Professor Hernstadt of Berlin finds by experiment . . . that pure white wax candles are, with regard to the time they last, the most economical; that tallow candles, provided the wicks be in proportion to the tallow, burn the slower the smaller they are. . . . He also finds that spermaceti candles are subject to the greatest waste of any and emit more smoke than tallow candles, although their vapor causes no disagreeable smoke like them."

In an old newspaper in the author's possession, the *Columbian Centinel*, published in Boston, Massachusetts, and bearing the date of July 16th, 1800, is an advertisement of Rawson and Davenport, 13 Orange Street, of "100 boxes of dipped tallow candles."

Just imagine the long weary hours of hard work which went into the making of those hundred boxes!

One of the earliest forms of candlesticks is called a "Pricket." It consists of an iron pin or spike upon which the candle is impaled and this pin is upheld on a base of various forms, usually a three- or four-legged rude iron stand. These seem to have been in common use in England and other Continental countries and the first designs made by the blacksmiths here were modelled after the European ones. Later iron stands were made taller with usually two or more candles in holders instead of on pins to stand upon a table or the floor. A piece like that shown in Plates 5 and 12 is a great find (if genuine) and the fortunate owner will usually not part with it except at a large figure. An especially well-made piece in good condition often fetches between one and two hundred dollars or more.

Since, however, they are very scarce and worth so much, it is a great temptation for unscrupulous dealers (of whom I am very sorry to say there are some) to counterfeit. This is done by skilled iron workers so that in purchasing a piece of this sort, one should use the greatest care, deal only with a man in whom one has the utmost confidence, and then it would be well to have the piece passed on by some expert. The two examples shown in Plate 5, from Mr. Cooney's collection, are both good pieces of early American iron work and are undoubtedly genuine; the one at the left is fine in its restrained simplicity of design and proportion. The two candle holders at the extreme ends of the iron arm with its graceful curves turn on the round upright. The square braces which hold this arm are unusual and interesting. The taller on the right is rather more ornate but hardly of so pleasing a design. The curves are not so good and the curved brace is not nearly so well done. The top of the central spindle is ornamented by a turned piece in brass and there is also a twist in the lower part of the shank. The feet are similar in both, but the one on the right, you will note, has the three feet made separately and carried past the center, an oddity which one seldom sees. Observe also the iron candle snuffers hanging from the hook.

The central stand, from Mr. Gates' collection in Plate 14, is probably earlier. The sockets for the candles are placed on the cross bar itself, which widens out at this point for the purpose, and the brace to hold the arm is well designed; its three legs are entirely different from the two stands in Plate 5 and are especially good. This also has the iron snuffers hanging from the hook under the arm. This piece was found in New York State.

Wooden candle holders similar to the remaining ones, also from Mr. Gates' collection, in this plate are very rarely met with, are extremely interesting, and command extraordinarily high prices. For these reasons they should be bought with the greatest care because there is every inducement to "fake" pieces of this sort.

PLATE 63. *See page 98*

Unusual Candle Sconce with Pewter Reflectors
Collection of Mrs. Henry A. Murray, New York City

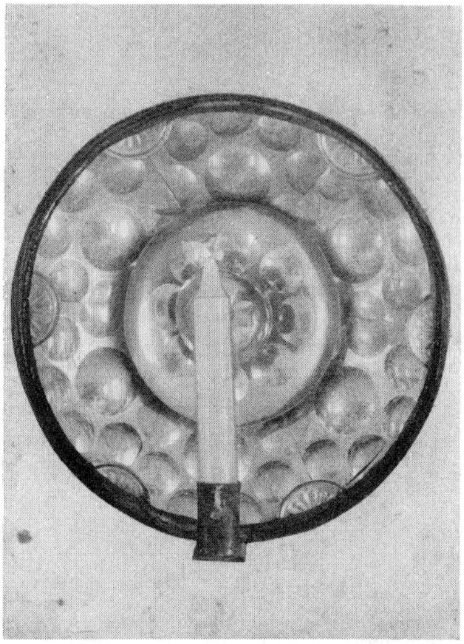

PLATE 64. *See page 98*

Tin Wall Sconce with Odd Glass Reflector
Photograph by Miss Northend

PLATE 65. *See page 70*

Tin Lard-Oil Lantern with "Nail- Head" Glass
Photograph by Miss Northend

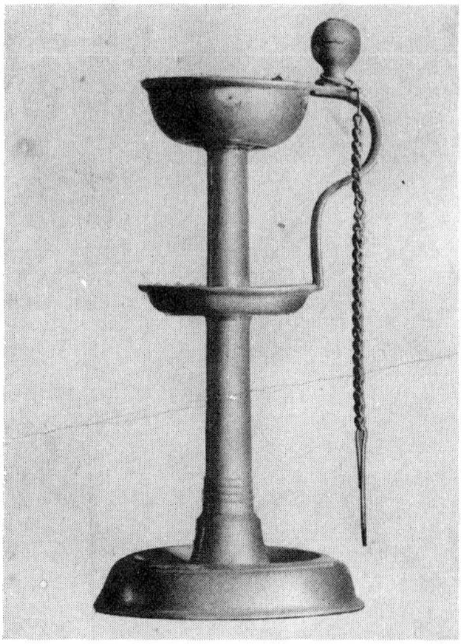

PLATE 66. *See page 29*

Old Pewter "Betty" Lamp of Unusual Shape
Photograph by Miss Northend

PLATE 67. *See page 103*

PAIR OF CANDLE SHADES OR "HURRICANE GLASSES"
Collection of Henry Ford, Dearborn, Michigan

These pieces, which are almost always of home manufacture, whittled out often in the long winter evenings, are perhaps more ingenious than strictly beautiful, though they usually have a rugged grace of their own. The figure on the left is made for two candles and is all original except that the wedge to hold the candle-arm was missing and had to be replaced. The slab at the base, into which the upright was fitted, shows the marks of the early hand saw. Mr. Gates found this piece within a year in an antique shop in Boston, showing that genuine old pieces still find their way to the markets and have not all been gathered into collections.

When Mr. Gates found this holder the candle-arm had slipped down to the bottom and it was something of a puzzle to know by what means it was held in place as there were no holes for pegs in the upright standard, which would seem to be the simplest way to hold the candle-arm. By studying carefully, however, the shape of the opening he decided that a wedge such as he has constructed was used. This proved the right solution, for faint marks up and down indicate different points where the wedge was formerly driven in to hold the candles.

The remaining wooden stand is also very crudely made, but the extension arm, very evidently whittled out with a jackknife, like the candle holder, is so ingenious but simple as to make this stand interesting. Note the heavy, hand-hewn slab at the base. This piece also was found in New York State.

Plate 12 gives a view of perhaps the most graceful of all the tall holders. The design is particularly good and is carried out in iron with the ball at the top and the two candle-holders of brass. The stand is also fully equipped with a fine old pair of snuffers and an extinguisher, hanging on their respective hooks. This stand is the property of a Pennsylvania collector, Mr. Francis D. Brinton of West Chester.

A very early piece of wrought iron work is shown in Plate 7. This chandelier for four candles was made to hang from the great hand-hewn beams running across the top of the living or dining room and was used in the famous old Westover Mansion on the James River in Virginia. It is now in the collection of Mr. Brazer, an architect of Chester, Pennsylvania. There is fine work in the large hook at the top and in the terminals of the candle-arms.

As I stated previously in this chapter, few candlesticks were fashioned from iron. These were followed by similar shapes in tin, a more convenient metal. But tin did not lend itself readily to ornamentation although convenient and acceptable for ordinary usage; so the demand for something better soon brought about the general use of brass for candlesticks and, to a more limited extent, pewter. Since brass took a high degree of polish and could be easily worked into graceful designs, brass candlesticks came into great favor, and, since they were almost indestructible, are to-day among the most easily found of the early lighting devices. The plates show a few of the many designs which were used. In Plate 36 Doctor Norton shows a rather unusual type of chamber candlestick in brass, Number 246 on the bottom row.

This candlestick, it may be seen, has a brass knob which slides up and down to regulate the height of the candle. It is also fitted with an extinguisher. Some of the taller sticks, such as Number 79 on this same plate, had a spring in the bottom of the central shaft upon which the candle rested and which was held in place by the top, which screwed on, leaving an opening for the wick. The spring by its gentle pressure beneath kept the candle so that the burning wick was always at the top of the stand, no matter what the length of the candle. A variant of this is found in Number 66 on the same page. Its lyre-shaped pivots on a square base enable the candle to keep an upright position. As indicated by its design, this piece was for use on naval vessels and has quite an interesting history.

When that famous battle took place off the coast of Massachusetts in 1812 between our frigate *Constitution*, under the command of brave Captain Hull, and the British man-of-war *Guerrière*, commanded by the boastful Captain Dacres, in which, in less than an hour, the British ship, riddled with shot and in a sinking condition from the well directed fire of her rival, was obliged to surrender, Captain Hull sent a prize crew aboard under Lieutenant Hoffman.

He soon discovered four feet of water in her hold and that she would be unable to keep long afloat and was ordered to blow her up.

Before setting her on fire he had the personal effects of the British officers removed to his own vessel, and, desiring to preserve some memento of the engagement, he took from the cabin of the British commander this candlestick which bore on one side of its base the " Broad Arrow ", the official stamp of the British Navy, and afterward had stamped on the opposite side *U. S. S. Constitution* and the date of the fight " August 19, 1812."

Number 70 in this Plate 36 of Doctor Norton's is another of the candle holders in which a concealed spring keeps the candle always at the top of the stick. This one, designed for a short candle, is stamped " Palmer & Co. patent ", was taken from Fort Sumter in 1865, and was probably there during the famous bombardment at the commencement of the Civil War.

The first candlestick, Number 85, of the brass ones shown in Plate 70, which dates, Doctor Norton says, from about 1829, was taken from the home of Oliver Wendell Holmes. Number 248, though not of American make, is of the general type used here and is of a particularly graceful design in bronze and brass. This was brought home and used by an American sea captain from the Island of St. Helena, which he visited in

1824. He obtained it from the lodge in which resided Napoleon's chaplain in 1818. The three central sticks in the bottom row of this plate are all similar in design. Number 44, a candlestick of French make and of the Louis XIV style, came from Portland, Maine, from the home of Mr. Clapp, Member of Congress in 1848. The central one, Number 81, is probably of American make and was owned by Elbridge Gerry, one of the signers of the Declaration of Independence, who, besides his active participation in the Continental Congress, afterward represented Massachusetts, was appointed commissioner to France, elected Governor of Massachusetts in 1810, and Vice-President of the United States in 1813.

The oblong-based candlestick with the brass extinguisher, Number 54, in Plate 70, came from the Directors' Room of the Mobile State Bank, one of the important banks of the South and the depository for the Confederate Government.

One of the few pewter sticks is Number 330 in Plate 33. It came from the birthplace of Hannibal Hamlin in China, Maine, and was given to Doctor Norton by Mr. Hamlin himself while he was U. S. Senator, after having served his term with Abraham Lincoln as Vice-President from 1860 to 1864 during the gloomiest and most bitter years of the great Civil War.

In the beginning of this chapter I mentioned the rush lights, a very early and elemental form of candle, which, however, was much in use among the peasantry of Europe at the time of the Pilgrims' embarkation.

The holders for these rush lights were crude affairs and were copied from the forms with which the Pilgrims were familiar in the mother country. They were probably not used to any great extent and were in the nature of a makeshift until regular candles could be obtained or simple oil lamps. Consequently, genuine rush-light holders are rarely found and usu-

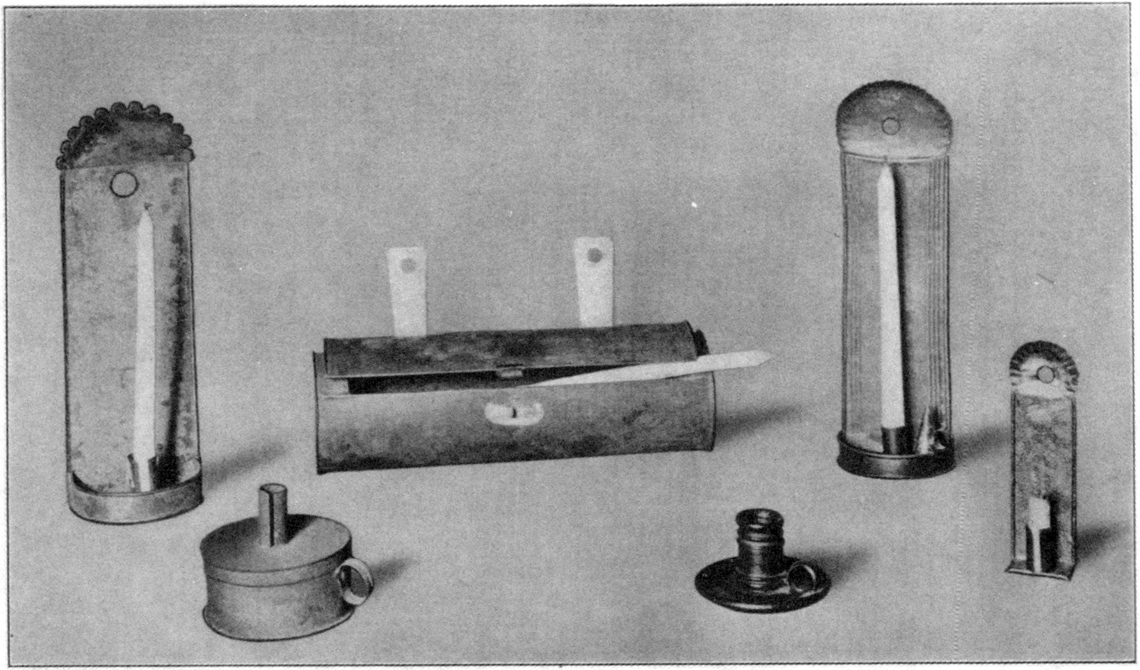

PLATE 68. *See pages 94, 95, 96*

THREE TIN WALL CANDLE HOLDERS, OLD TIN CANDLE BOX WITH ORIGINAL MOULDED CANDLES, RARE CLAY CANDLESTICK AND TIN TINDER BOX

B. N. Gates' Collection, Worcester

PLATE 69. GROUP OF UNUSUAL TIN WALL SCONCES
B. N. Gates' Collection, Worcester

See page 95

ally command high prices (that is, high to the casual collector, who merely looks at the crudity of the object without properly understanding its value as defined by its rareness).

The collection of Mr. V. M. Hillyer is therefore of unusual interest to the reader, because it gathers in one group many of the extremely rare types as shown in Plate 3. I will give you Mr. Hillyer's own description of these very fine primitive light holders.

"Rushes or the pith of cane or similar reeds or grasses were soaked in fat or grease and burned for light. The iron ladle in the centre is a 'rush-dipper' or 'rush-pot' used for soaking rushes in the fat. The rushes when lighted were held by tongs or clips of which a variety of specimens are here shown. The first to the left is a simple pair of tongs with a chisel-like tongue at the base so that it could be driven into a crack in the wall, into a beam or into the floor and so hold the rush light in any position. The second and third examples are similar holders with wooden bases. The fourth example, which is later, has a socket for a candle in case this more expensive article could be obtained. In the fifth example the jaws are controlled by a double spring grip.

"The first on the back row at the left is a standing or floor rush-light holder with slide for adjusting the light to a desired height. It has both the rush-holder and candle-socket. The second at the back has a horizontal support to be driven into the ceiling beams and could be adjusted horizontally as well as vertically. The third at the back is one of the earliest forms of standing candle holders, with a crude folded socket for a single candle. The corkscrew or 'helix' candlestick at the extreme right lower corner was an improved form with an ingeniously arranged 'elevator' that wound up the helix to keep the candle raised as it burned."

A similar rush-light holder with a wooden block base and with the candle socket also, is shown in Plate 109 from Mr.

Cooney's collection. This is a little better piece of workmanship since the twisted stems indicate a slight attempt at ornamentation. Mr. Cooney placed a wax taper (the nearest modern substitute for a rush light) in the iron jaw to give one the idea of its method of operation.

Another very interesting early iron candle holder is the one owned by the Worcester Historical Society and shown in Plate 13. It is intended to be hung from a beam or beside the fireplace and is adjustable by a very simple device, as may be readily seen. The fine work on the main stem being exceptional, it of course is an extremely rare piece.

Very early, however, tin seems to have been especially favored for candle holders. The collector who specializes in tin holders has a wide field for his search and I can assure him the game is sufficiently scarce and wary to make it an extremely interesting sporting proposition, if he is to be at all successful, necessitating patient searching and a well-filled pocketbook for ammunition.

Probably one of the very early forms is that known as the "sconce" in which the candle is placed a bit in front of a piece of tin, which acts as a reflector as well as a draft protector for the candle flame. The first ones were crude affairs. The author shows two in Plate 38 and there is a very early one with a square top and no attempt at ornamentation at all in Plate 56 from Mr. Cooney's collection, probably the earliest one shown.

In Plate 68 there are two for tall candles from the fine collection owned by Mr. Gates — the one on the left showing a very simple attempt at decoration in the scallops around the top. Note how crudely the candle holder at the base is made. The one on the right has the top slightly crimped and incurved with a bit of decoration up and down the sides. The candle holder is much better made. The little one at the right is interesting as being the smallest of this type that I have seen.

The turned up base holding the candle is also an oddity. This size is extremely rare in this type.

The collection of seven tin sconces in Plate 69 represents years of search on Mr. Gates' part before he could get together such an unusual collection. With the exception of the extraordinary pair in the center — a matched pair with a fancy reflector in perfect condition being very hard to find to-day — these show as great a variety in the form of the reflectors as in the candle holders themselves — no two being at all alike. They are well worth studying, for Mr. Luce with his camera has given such a very clear, fine picture that all details are brought out much better than by mere description. The one at the extreme right with the wooden block for a base has a slightly concave circular back covered with tiny pieces of looking glass fitted together with infinite skill, multiplying the light of the candle many times. These glass reflectors are extremely scarce. Usually the glass is in much larger sections and not nearly so carefully put together as this remarkable piece. This plate I consider one of the gems of the book and my thanks are due Mr. Gates for allowing me to use its subjects.

Another candle holder of great interest is the tall tin one on Plate 13, also from Mr. Gates' collection. This, as you will see by the print, is an iron rod standing some five feet high on a large funnel shaped tin base and supporting a flat round tin plate holding five candles. Note the round tin brace under the plate where the central rod goes through.

In Plate 68, showing the candle sconces, is seen in the center a candle box, which was hung upon the wall to contain an extra supply of candles. It was of tin and the later ones were sometimes painted, but this one is probably fairly early. When Mr. Gates got it, it still held a supply of moulded candles, one of which in the picture is left sticking out under the lid.

On the left in this group is a tinder box, one of the more

common tin variety with its crude candle holder on the top of the cover and the flint, steel, and tinder inside.

While these tinder boxes are not so scarce as the sconces mentioned above, it may and probably will necessitate some searching before a good specimen can be found. Another, from Mr. Cooney's collection, slightly different in shape, and shallower, may be seen in Plate 56, and on the left of this plate one of the rare pistol tinders, described by Mr. Hillyer in his collection. This one is all of iron and is a rather heavy, clumsy device although in perfect working condition. The author was fortunate enough to find one some short time ago (the first that he has ever seen for sale), very similar except that the handle was carved wood and the two flat legs in front a little longer and not so clumsy. When found, it was perfect except that the trigger was missing. I took it to an old gun-smith who made a specialty of repairing old flint locks and other ancient arms and he cut out and fitted a trigger so that now it works perfectly — that is, I imagine one could get fire if his patience lasted long enough. Getting fire from flint and steel was a solemn, arduous business, not to be undertaken lightly or without due preparation of material and patience, particularly the latter.

The other modest little piece in Plate 68 of Mr. Gates' is an extremely rare earthenware chamber candlestick in perfect condition. This was made in Sterling, Massachusetts, of the common red clay found in that vicinity, at one of the little local potteries which years ago were found in many rural communities making the crudest and commonest jugs, pots, and the like. It probably was made about 1840. Since this early local pottery was easily broken and not valued much, a piece like this, in perfect condition, is not to be duplicated in years of search.

A very quaint and unusual specimen, the property of the Worcester Historical Society, is shown in Plate 40. This they

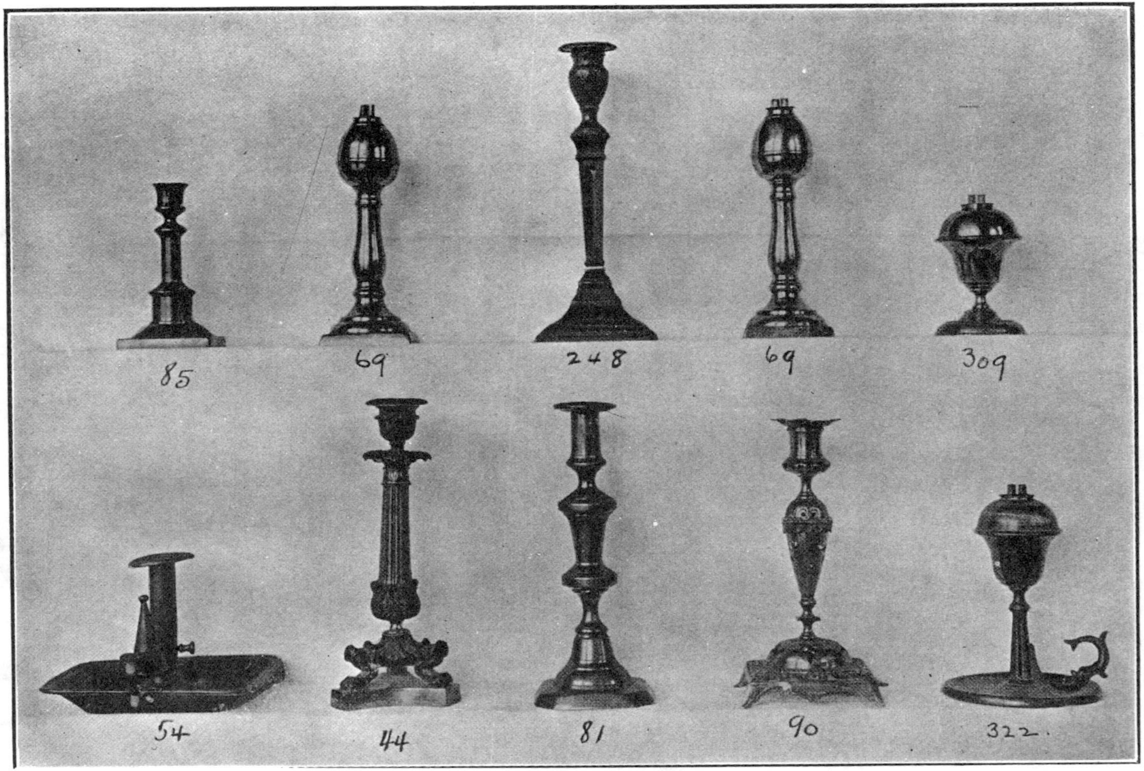

PLATE 70. BRASS CANDLESTICKS AND LAMPS Dr. Norton's Collection See pages 91, 92

PLATE 71. COLLECTION OF BENNINGTON WARE — CANDLESTICKS AND ONE RARE LAMP BASE IN CENTRE
Collection of B. N. Gates, Worcester

See page 80

call an upright candle student lamp. The stand and the shade are made of tin and very well done, both the shade and the candle holder being adjustable on the square center rod which terminates in a brass ring for carrying. The rod starts from a deep tin saucer base, which is weighted with sand so that it is not easily tipped over. The curved arm which supports the candle holder is very prettily made. This lamp was used by Elijah Demond while he was a student at Dartmouth College and Andover Seminary in 1816 to 1820. He graduated from the Seminary, was ordained a minister, and settled over the church in Holliston, Massachusetts, about 1832. He died in Westboro, Massachusetts, in July, 1877.

Plate 61 shows Mr. Gates' very choice collection of candlesticks, in a variety of material as well as shapes.

The first one on the extreme left is probably the oldest of the lot. It is of iron and was locally sometimes called a "pork-barrel" candlestick, from the fact that the lip of iron protruding from the top of the stick was found very convenient, when the housewife went down into the cellar for a piece of salt pork, to hang the candle on the edge of the pickle barrel while she was selecting just the piece she wanted. These sticks were also known in country districts as "hog scrapers." In the winter or fall when the hogs were killed and salted down for the winter's supply of meat, after they had been scalded, these strong iron candlesticks were found very convenient for removing the bristles. This stick has the iron slide and is further ornamented with a brass ring about half way up the cylinder.

The stick at the extreme right with the square base and the one in the center with the very large and deep base are both of tin and I should judge came next in point of age. They are both out of the ordinary in shape and illustrate quite well the interesting variations which one is apt to find at any time.

I cannot imagine why the center stick had such a tremendously big base, for it seems out of all proportion and must have been made so for some special purpose.

The second and third sticks and the last but one with the square base and handle are made of brass. The tallest is one of those patent sticks with a concealed spring inside which gently presses the candle up against the top. The top is removed, the candle inserted, pressing down the spring, and the cap fastened back in place, leaving the top of the candle protruding from the hole.

The smaller brass saucer stick has an odd handle like a saucepan. The large brass stick with the ring handle and quaint four-sided, turned-up base and candle holder with slide, is called a "loom" stick — just why I do not know, for I cannot see any particular reason why this type should light a weaver busy at her loom better than any other stick. The remaining two are a beautiful pair of pewter — perfectly matched and of most attractive design — all together a choice collection in four metals.

There has just been sent to me from a collector of New York City, Mrs. Henry A. Murray, a photograph of a most unusual candle sconce which you will see in Plate 63. In a very shallow box are three large pewter reflectors of curious design, made, so I am informed, by pouring the melted pewter over cut and polished glass. The rest of the space is filled by eight smaller pewter disks, which are there evidently more for ornament than for any use. This box hangs flat against the wall. Fastened at the bottom is an ordinary tin candle holder with a crimped saucer base and a similar piece of tin over the top. A very curious and original design in a sconce.

If one is collecting sconces, odd, unusual ones are the rule rather than the exception, and it is quite difficult to get two which are approximately alike, the variety is so great.

Plate 64 shows a tin sconce with a most fascinating reflector in an unusual design. Though I am not sure (never having seen the original from which this was made) I should say the reflector was of pressed or perhaps cut glass silvered. It would give a pretty series of reflections of the flame from the single candle in the simple tin holder in front.

Coming back to the more recent candlesticks, one or two oddities may be seen in Plates 52 and 39. The first shows a hand candlestick of either tin or brass with quaintly hammered designs; a broad flat saucer, from one side of which stands the candle holder with its mica chimney to steady the flame against drafts, and next to it in the saucer a small covered box evidently intended for lucifers as the early matches were called. Though not old, an attractive piece for a collector.

Plate 39 is a pair of brass folding candlesticks owned by Mrs. A. C. Marble of Worcester. The two candle holders with attached rings for carrying may be unscrewed and put inside one of the saucer bases while the other base screws on it like a cover, thus making a neat, flat, round package which may easily be carried in the pocket. I am told these sticks were made for the use of officers in our Civil War.

In the chapter on glass lamps you will read a bit about the glass making industry which flourished on Cape Cod. The products of the Sandwich Glass Works are eagerly sought by collectors to-day.

Besides glass dishes of all kinds, they made great quantities of lamps and some glass candlesticks though not in nearly the quantity of their lamps. These candlesticks, particularly the very early moulded ones, are well worth collecting because they are graceful in design, the glass itself is of a bright silvery texture, and their rarity makes their successful hunting sufficiently difficult to be interesting. In Plate 75 is shown a group of Sandwich candlesticks which have been gathered together by Mr. B. N. Gates of Worcester. You may notice when you come to the glass lamps that some of the bases are similar.

This is quite natural because the same moulds were often used for bases for lamps, candlesticks and table dishes.

What I say regarding the Sandwich lamps holds equally true in candlesticks, that as these pieces were rarely if ever marked, it is impossible to determine absolutely, beyond a shadow of a doubt, whether they were made at Sandwich, Cambridge, or some of the other glass factories of New England and other states; although many dealers who are constantly handling old glass claim in all sincerity that they can tell by the looks and "feel" of the glass its certain place of origin.

In this group the tallest stick in the center is a beautiful shade of aquamarine blue and is supposed to have been blown in New York State.

The remaining sticks are all attributed to Sandwich. The one on the extreme left with the stepped base is a fine piece of that tint called vaseline yellow and there are two specimens of that opalescent glass which was quite characteristic of Sandwich, the taller one moulded in the figure of a beautiful woman. Of the four in the front row, the tulip-shaped tops you will note are precisely alike, while they are combined with bases in three entirely different patterns.

Plate 72 shows a small but very interesting group of Sandwich candlesticks, most of them of the famous "dolphin" pattern. These were selected from the large collection of this particular design which Mrs. Geo. W. Mitton of Jamaica Plain has gathered together. These range in color from the opalescent stick on the right to ultramarine blue, vaseline yellow and other colors as well as clear glass. The candlestick at the left is a rare pattern in the opaque glass. In the center is a small dish with the dolphin pattern for a standard and back of it a moulded Sandwich peg lamp, placed in a Sheffield holder.

A very unusual and wonderfully beautiful pair of moulded glass candlesticks are shown in Plate 73 by courtesy of the

PLATE 72.

See pages 100, 142

GROUP OF SANDWICH GLASS CANDLESTICKS, MANY OF THE "DOLPHIN" PATTERN
Collection of Mrs. George W. Mitton, Jamaica Plain, Boston

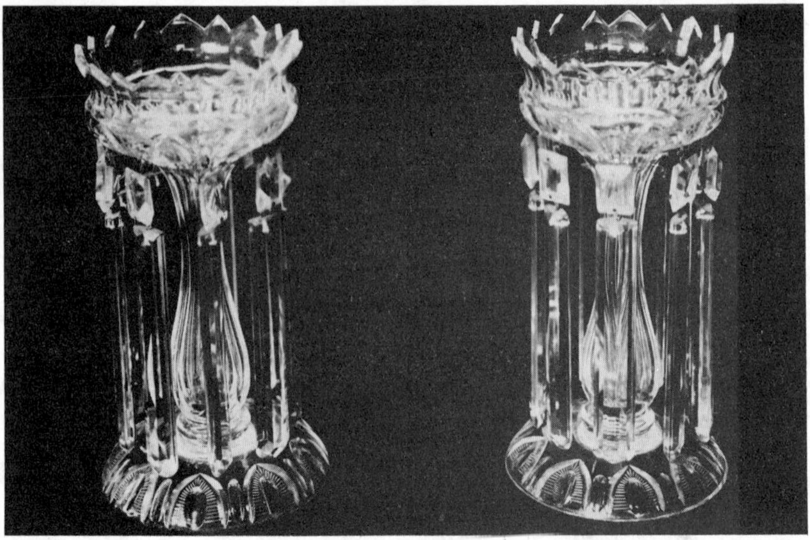

PLATE 73. *See page 100*

Pair Moulded and Cut Sandwich Glass Candlesticks with Lustres

Courtesy of Jordan Marsh Co., Boston

PLATE 74. *See page 82*

Pocket Lighting Outfit — Flint, Steel and Wooden Tinder Box

Photograph by Miss Mary H. Northend

Jordan Marsh Company. Of a rich and graceful design and moulded in that sparkling silvery glass which was a guarded secret at the Sandwich works, they would grace any table or drawing room in which they were placed. The tops have a wide flare where the candles enter and the top edge is cut in points. Their beauty is further enriched by a row of cut lusters which hang on tiny wires from the base of the candle holders, giving an effect of airy grace and beauty which is hard to describe.

There is one more subject which should properly be considered in this chapter and that comprises snuffers and extinguishers.

Snuffers were cutting instruments like scissors for trimming the wicks of candles or lamps. They were made in a variety of shapes and materials, iron, steel or brass for common use and Sheffield plate or coin silver for the more elaborate ones. A small tray was often used with the snuffers on which they were kept, painted tin or iron for the common ones and with the silver usually a tray of the same material to match.

Plate 62 is a photograph of a few items from the collection of Mr. V. M. Hillyer of Baltimore, and I append his own description of the articles in this plate.

" Snuffers are the scissor-like instruments for trimming the wicks of candles or lamps. An extinguisher is a cone-shaped cap for putting out the flame.

" It is a common error to call an extinguisher, snuffers. I have even heard it argued that snuffers was the proper name, although ' extinguisher ' was meant, the expression ' snuff *out* a candle ' being cited as proof. This expression, however, was used to indicate a bungling operation, for it was not uncommon for one unintentionally to put out the candle when snuffing it.

" The burnt wick end was called ' snuff ' and hence the name snuffers. With old-fashioned dip or moulded candles the wick was not entirely consumed and it was necessary to clip off the charred end of the wick more or less frequently, as otherwise it dimmed the flame and made it smoky. Now-a-days, the candle wicks are entirely consumed, making such 'snuffing' unnecessary, but candlesticks, especially the so-called 'Sheffield' are still made with snuffers and extinguishers attached just for ornament, apparently, as they no longer serve any useful purpose.

"The oldest snuffers were simply scissors with one broad blade and a lip to catch the snuff, which was then thrown into the fireplace, on the floor, or — in a more tidy home — into a tray on which the snuffers rested or into a 'wick-end' box. Then came snuffers with a box *on* the blade. This box was elaborate in various ways as shown in the other examples. The last pair of snuffers to the right are for use with an Argand burner in which the wick was tubular.

"Candles were 'extinguished' instead of being blown out to prevent the disagreeable smoke and odor which resulted if an extinguisher was not used and also to put out candles which were out of blowing reach.

"An extinguisher was almost always a simple cone of metal with a projection by which it might be hooked into the socket provided on the candlestick as in the first example. The second extinguisher with the long handle was used to reach a candle enclosed by a 'hurricane' glass or other globe. The third extinguisher had a socket at its side into which a wooden rod was inserted so that candles at a height could be reached. The fourth extinguisher is a more ornamental French one resembling a night cap on which is written the words 'Bon Soir' (good-night).

"Taper sticks, three of which are shown on the back row at the left, are scissor-like tweezers — resembling snuffers elevated on a stand. Indeed so quickly are the customs of a past generation forgotten unless recorded in print, that I have even found dealers who thought such taper sticks were merely a peculiar form of snuffers. Tapers which were simply a thread-like wick soaked in wax or tallow came wound on a spool. They were placed over the upright rod of the taper stick, the tweezers being unscrewed for the purpose, and the end was then held between the jaws of the tweezers. The first taper stick is of iron, the second is of brass with dolphin feet and the third is also of brass."

There were in use generally in the Southern States where the weather conditions favored many open windows, tall glass cylinders, open at both ends and bulging in the middle, often standing from twenty to thirty inches tall, called abatjours or candle shades, which were placed over the lighted candles to protect the flame against draughts and keep the light steady. These were usually of plain blown glass, but later they cut and ornamented them with the emery wheel.

A pair of these glasses over handsome Sheffield candlesticks would give an atmosphere of elegance to an otherwise plain room.

Unfortunately, as they were so large and difficult to handle except with the greatest care, they were easily broken and to-day are among the very hardest of lighting devices to find. I was fortunate to secure the photograph of this beautiful pair in Plate 67 from the collection of Mr. Henry Ford. While they are probably of later date than many, they are an interesting pair, in perfect condition, and show the "hurricane glass", as they were often called in New England, at its most elegant period.

The group of patent candlesticks in Plate 16, also from Mr. Henry Ford's collection, is of interest to the lamp collector. All of the candle tubes are fitted with coiled springs at the bottom. These springs are forced down when the candle is inserted and held in position by the cap over the top. The gentle pressure of the spring keeps the burning wick always in the same position, an arrangement necessary to get the benefit of the reflectors which are on the two stands at the right.

The candlestick at the left has no reflector but in its place a glass globe, ground above and clear below, which steadies the flame.

The first two have an ingenious arrangement of small brass rods which extend just over the opening for the top of the candle and act as automatic snuffers. The stick at the right is made for two candles and has a metal chimney with a flared opening in the center in front. This, painted white or tinned, acts as a reflector for the double flame as well as a protector against disturbing air currents.

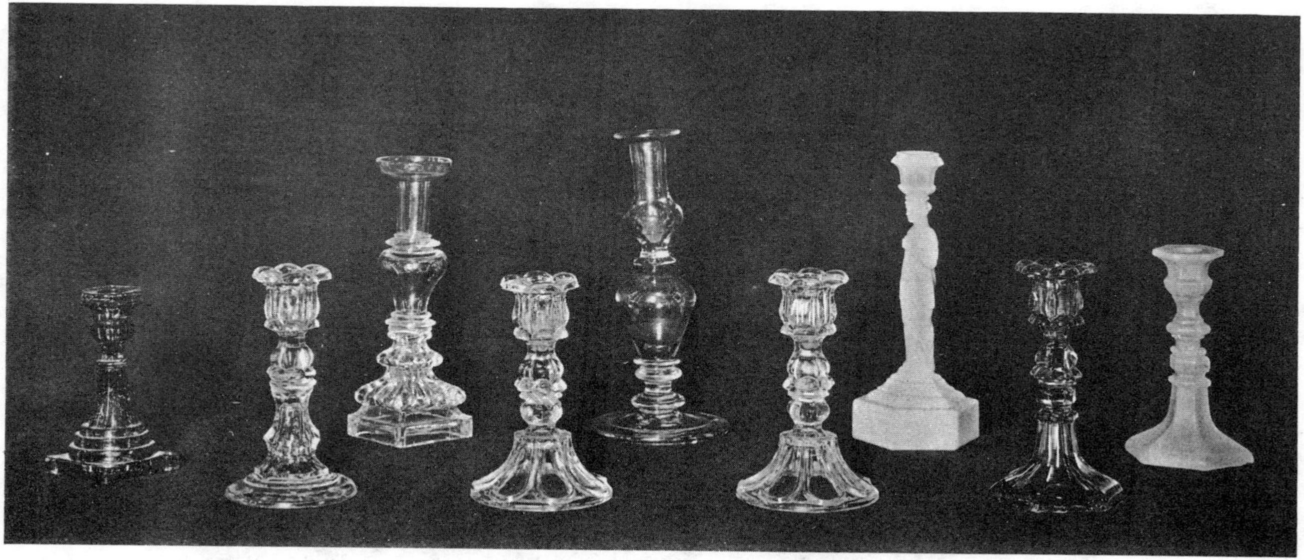

PLATE 75.

GROUP OF SANDWICH CANDLESTICKS IN CLEAR, COLORED AND OPAQUE GLASS
B. N. Gates' Collection, Worcester

See page 99

PLATE 76. *See pages 112, 113*

TABLE AND SPARK LAMPS (MANY OF THEM PROBABLY SANDWICH)
Dr. Norton's Collection

CHAPTER VI

EARLY GLASS LAMPS

NEARLY one hundred years ago, in 1825 to be exact, a few men appeared in one of the little farming and fishing hamlets that are scattered all along the sandy hills of that hook of land running out into the Atlantic from the rocky shores of New England and christened by the Pilgrims Cape Cod. These men purchased a tract of land in the village of Sandwich, built small houses for themselves and other workmen, and erected a furnace for the manufacture of flint glass.

This Sandwich enterprise was not the first venture in the blowing of glass in New England. Several glass works were established quite early. One at Salem, Massachusetts, said to have been started in 1639, did quite a thriving business for a number of years, manufacturing glass bottles and table ware. There seems, however, to be some doubt of the existence of this factory thus early, since its products have entirely disappeared. About 1750 some German workmen started glass works in what is now a part of Quincy, Massachusetts, where they made a large variety of glassware, among which were several styles of lamps. A distinguishing feature of the products of this factory was a peculiar spiral twist which was given to the uprights of the lamps and sometimes also to the handles; but the glass itself was of poor quality.

In 1780, in the town of Temple, New Hampshire, Robert Hewes established glass works and manufactured glass lamps which were said to be of artistic merit. One can distinguish the products of this factory because all were made to use patented burners, with the wick tubes coming through perforated cork, instead of the usual pewter or brass caps.

In 1787 a factory was built in Boston for the manufacture of window and other glass. This factory, which had a struggle for existence for several years, finally established itself, and, we are told, was given the exclusive right by charter to the manufacture of window glass. With increasing business in 1811 they sent to England for more skilled workmen, but when the war with England came on, they were unable to get the men and were obliged to use flint-glass blowers, previously brought over.

About this time another glass blowing company was formed in Cambridge for the manufacture of articles in both porcelain and glass, but this company seems to have been short-lived and was soon on the financial rocks. A new company, known as the New England Glass Works, was formed in 1817 to take over the equipment, was successful from the start, and continued in business in Cambridge until late in the nineteenth century when it moved its factory West.

The founders of the Sandwich factory were undoubtedly workmen from either the Boston or the Cambridge plants. They must have had an accurate and detailed knowledge of the business, for the enterprise seems to have been a success from the start. Commencing — as Mrs. Lenore Wheeler Williams tells us in her interesting little book "Sandwich Glass" devoted to the products of this factory — with some sixty workmen and an equipment of an eight-pot furnace, each pot holding eight hundred pounds, so successful were they in producing at a moderate cost glassware of pleasing appearance, that a steady expansion took place, so that by 1853 the company was employing some five hundred men and running four furnaces of ten pots each, with a weekly melt of approximately one hundred thousand pounds. At this time and for some years following this industry was by far the most important on the Cape.

With this array of workmen, large for those times, one can

readily understand that enormous quantities of glassware of many kinds were produced and liberally distributed through the towns and villages of most of New England and adjoining States. It is even maintained that the company owned and kept one or more sailing vessels with which to distribute their products to the coast towns and cities.

At the commencement of this enterprise, the only means of producing articles in glass was the blowpipe — an arduous, unhealthy vocation, requiring brawny muscles and a high degree of skill. In 1827, a workman at the Cambridge glass factory invented the mould machine which was at once adopted by the Sandwich Company and perfected by them. At first, however, this device still required the use of the blowpipe; for the glass was forced by blowing into the uneven surface of the mould, where the melted glass easily adapted itself to the most delicate and intricate carvings of the soft iron. Later the stamping machines came into general use, substituting for the blowpipes iron ladles with which to pour the molten glass. The use of the pipe in early moulding explains the mystery of the "pontil" mark, or rough place where the end of the blowpipe has been broken off or separated from the article made, which appears often on the bottom of lamps, drinking glasses and other pieces of "pressed" glass. Those articles were made before the machine was used to stamp or press the glass into the mould, while pieces were blown into the mould by the use of the pipe, which left its irregular mark on the bottom. Of course, on the later articles of poured moulded glass no such mark appears.

At the time when this Sandwich enterprise started, the lamps in general use — pewter, tin and brass — had generally adopted the Franklin invention of a double enclosed round wick, and were burning whale oil. The Sandwich Company early realized that a glass lamp of graceful design which could be made to sell for a small sum would probably find a ready and rapidly expanding market all through the countryside. They, therefore, early commenced the making of glass lamps and, to a more limited extent, of glass candlesticks. On this branch of their industry we will focus our attention because this and similar glass companies, to a very large extent, directed the trend of the expansion and improvements in artificial illumination for some few years.

The early lamps were usually quite simple in design, a graceful, flaring, round or square base held an oval font terminating in a brass or pewter cap, the cover of which screwed on and contained two wick tubes that allowed the ends of the wicks to drop down into the oil fonts. Some of these lamps show very plainly the pontil mark at the base. All the early Sandwich glass is noted for the peculiar silvery brilliance, a characteristic which the modern pressed glass rarely or never has. It is said that the early pressed glass was reheated several times, enough to melt a very thin layer at the surface, thus removing any slight roughness which might remain from the mould and making the surface smooth and bright. "Fire-polishing" the process was called.

The silvery luster was also due to the materials used, the formula for the glass differing somewhat from that of the Cambridge plant. In fact, each glass factory used its own formula and guarded with jealous care its secrets that they might not be used by rival plants.

Later, other plants were started in Connecticut, New Jersey, Ohio, Pennsylvania, etc., but comparatively few pieces of domestic glass are found in this part of New England aside from the products of these two plants in Sandwich and Cambridge.

At first the amateur collector is amazed at the quantities and varieties of glass lamps which he finds practically in every antique dealer's shop which he enters; but when he stops to consider the very large output of these two factories — par-

PLATE 77. GROUP OF GLASS LAMPS (MANY SANDWICH)
Author's Collection

See pages 118, 119

PLATE 78.

See page 119

GROUP OF RARE SANDWICH GLASS LAMPS
Collection of Burton N. Gates, Worcester

ticularly the Sandwich one, as indicated by the number of men employed, the size of the weekly melt, and the number of years when it was in active operation — the number of lamps which may be picked up to-day is not so surprising and need not lead to apprehension of counterfeits. Another reason why they are found so scattered all over New England in every little out of the way village and hamlet is the long famous but now almost extinct peddler's cart.

These brightly painted travelling stores with their stock of kitchen utensils, dry goods, notions, and innumerable other articles attractive to the housewives of the country farming districts were once a familiar sight along any country road. With their fat, sleek pairs of horses and shrewd-eyed Yankee drivers, they were the means by which thousands of lamps were taken from the towns along the shores of Maine, Massachusetts, Connecticut and Rhode Island where they had been left by the coasting vessels and distributed all through the less thickly settled sections. Some of the fortunes of to-day received their first start from the contents of the old-time New England peddler's cart.

One curious fact that the antique collector notes is that there seem to be fashions in collecting as in matters of clothing. Some years ago, every one seemed to be collecting the old blue china, particularly historic pieces. I have been in auction rooms in Boston and seen most extravagant prices paid for rare plates, cups, and other pieces by eager collectors who seemed to have no limit to what they would gladly pay for a much desired piece. To-day, though good old blue china always finds a market, no such high prices are asked or obtained.

At another time, the luster wares, copper and silver, were in just as keen a demand, which far outran the supply and consequently kept the prices up. To-day the beautiful old luster wares are almost neglected. If one has the patience to wait and in the meantime quietly enjoy his own collection, the demand for all these will in time come back, probably with renewed vigor. With the constant withdrawal of pieces from the markets into private collections and the constantly diminishing sources of supply — old attics and closets are by now well scoured — the real scarcity of these desirable antiques is likely at any time to start another furor for them.

Just now " hooked-in " rugs and Sandwich glass seem to be most in the public eye — particularly the latter. Some very high prices are being paid for pieces in the rarer designs of Sandwich glass, particularly cup plates. The lamps in this glass are also enjoying quite a bit of popularity along with the other pieces turned out by the factory on the Cape, and signs are not wanting of an awakened interest in early lighting appliances in general.

Since glass lamps are among the easiest to find of all lighting devices and since there is at present such a widespread interest in the old glass in general, I have secured photographs of a large number of the varied designs in which these lamps were made.

I have often heard the question asked, and in fact have asked it myself of dealers who are handling glass all the time, " How can you distinguish Sandwich glass from the products of the Cambridge and other factories? " Most of them will tell you that there is a texture or quality to the glass of one factory different from that of the others which long experience in handling enables them to detect, thus differentiating the one from the others. This is undoubtedly true to a somewhat limited extent; but the keen rivalry between the different glass establishments, the desire to imitate and outdo the successes of their rivals, the going of skilled workmen from one plant to another, carrying of course some of the secrets of formulae and manufacture with them to competing plants, the copying of each other's designs, and the fact that glass made in different places is often absolutely identical to the amateur; — all this makes me think that many times the positive source of a piece is claimed when the evidence is far from conclusive.

I was interested while writing this to see in the *Boston Transcript* a notice of an exhibition by the Society for the Preservation of New England Antiquities — the society, which has done much to save many historic old landmarks, owns outright some six or eight fine old houses, and helps to save and preserve many more. This exhibition was a loan collection of cup plates and other early pressed glass dishes. It was held in the fine old Boston mansion of Harrison Gray Otis, which the society has restored and uses as its headquarters. The account goes on to say, "This collection would probably be classed as Sandwich glass by most collectors. There seems to be no reason to doubt that the greater number are of Sandwich derivation, for they have the iridescent quality which seems to be a feature of much of the glass of that character.

"A number of pieces, however, are somewhat dull in appearance and it may be questioned whether these are Sandwich or from the New England Glass Company's works in Cambridge.

"At one time each of these companies was employing about five hundred hands, so that the output must have been about equal. In spite of this fact, it is the Sandwich Glass Works which has caught the ear of the public and to this factory is ascribed about everything of merit that seems to have a New England origin. Neither public nor private collections have any pieces attributed to the factory in East Cambridge." (I wonder if this is strictly true.) "On November 8th, 1851, in *Gleason's Pictorial* there was published a short article devoted to the East Cambridge plant of the New England Glass Company, illustrated with a picture of the plant as seen from the water."

This article says, "Every description of glassware, from a simple pressed wine-glass to the most elaborately cut and rich plated, gilded, silvered, and engraved glassware is produced here in a style of beauty and excellence unrivalled in the world, and far surpassing in beauty the finest manufactures of Bohemia."

It does seem strange, therefore, that the products of this factory, equipped apparently to do all kinds of most excellent work, should be so very scarce, while that of their rival on the Cape should be found in such abundance. Since it is extremely rare in glass to find a piece bearing the imprint of its place of manufacture, does it not seem reasonable at least to surmise that some of the pieces now masquerading as "Oh, yes indeed, Madam! genuine Sandwich glass without a doubt!" may really have been made here just across the Charles? In Plate 85 is shown a rare old handbill of the New England Glass Co. giving a view of its works along the banks of the Charles River with a brief list of some of its products.

If you have a good piece, I don't know that it makes a great deal of difference which factory turned it out. You may call it Sandwich or New England as you decide; the burden of proof lies with the doubter to show that you are wrong. I should like, however, to see some one competent enough to decide upon a general classification of the output of these two rival plants and to decide upon some standard or formula for a division, if such a thing were possible. Perhaps as interest in the early glass grows, this may be accomplished.

Doctor Norton's collection, most of which is probably Sandwich glass, shows the variety of design which a collector may expect to find. In Plate 76 the tallest lamp in the top row — an interesting piece in itself with its square, many-stepped base and long bulb-shaped oil font — was used by the poet, Henry Wadsworth Longfellow. The tall burners with their brass thimble caps were meant for camphene. The tall lamp immediately under it, numbered 133, has a cut font and a rather unusual-shaped base above the steps. These combina-

PLATE 79.

See pages 45, 119, 120

UNUSUAL GLASS SPARK LAMPS
Collections of Mr. B. N. Gates and Mrs. A. C. Marble, Worcester

PLATE 80. SANDWICH GLASS LAMPS OF RARE PATTERNS
Collection of Mrs. George W. Mitton, Jamaica Plain, Boston

See page 121

tions of partly cut and partly moulded work are not uncommon. This lamp was secured by Doctor Norton from a relative of General Joseph Hooker, who used it in his old home at Hadley, Massachusetts. Numbers 98 and 249 are glass "spark" lamps, the first of a particularly graceful shape. Number 138 is a good example of a glass "peg" lamp. Its cut oil font and camphene burners indicate that it is not one of the very early ones.

"Peg" lamps received their name from the peg-like base, the size and shape of a section of candle, and were intended to be used in the top of a candlestick. Usually they will not stand upright, and, I presume, for that reason were the more easily broken. Good specimens are much harder to find than other lamps. This is the only one which Doctor Norton has.

The first two lamps in this Plate Number 76, not particularly uncommon in their design, both came from the South. Number 99 was used in the State Capitol of Alabama as late as 1855, and Number 227 was found in the Confederate Hospital at Vicksburg, Mississippi, after the siege and surrender of that city. Number 230, a small chamber lamp burning camphene, is one of the many patented lamps spoken of in the next chapter. This lamp is stamped "J. Dreyfus, Pat. May 21, 1867", though just what was patented it is hard to say. The moulded base of the last lamp in the top row is good. The beautiful pair of opaque glass lamps numbered 272 at the end of the second row in this Plate 76 were known as bridal lamps. This opaque glass seems to have been much in demand, for one finds a number of designs in dishes, lamps and candlesticks of this glass coming from the Sandwich factory.

In the second plate (81) from Doctor Norton's collection, the distinguished looking lamp in the center of the top row, Number 307, does not belie its appearance, for it was a gift to Doctor Norton from the poet John Greenleaf Whittier, who had used it in his home in Amesbury, Massachusetts. The very long font is ground and decorated, and the base is the familiar Sandwich step.

Patterns of Sandwich glass were used in various combinations. You will often find two lamps with the same base but entirely different oil fonts, or similar tops with the bases different. Compotes and small fruit and cake dishes also used for the bases a lamp pattern.

It is stated that early in its history the Sandwich Glass Works used oil fonts which were imported from England, welding them (if that is the proper term) on to moulded bases of domestic manufacture. Certainly, lamps occasionally found to-day with bases of an entirely different quality of glass from the tops tend to substantiate this story. I suspect that, if this was the case, as seems probable, the Cape Cod works either could not obtain the metal tops for the wicks or else had no means of fitting them to the lamps which they were making. So they found it easier to buy in England the glass tops ready fitted with metal wick holders and to join them to their own bases, a process, by the way, which few workmen to-day could successfully perform.

The first lamp, Number 145, in the top row of Plate 81 came from the glass works established, much earlier than the Sandwich factory, at Germantown, now a part of Quincy. By looking very closely one can distinguish in the stem at the bottom of the oil font the slight spiral twist which is said to be one of the distinguishing marks of the product of this factory.

The pair of lamps numbered 154, with cut glass fonts, pretty octagonal standards, and square bases formed part of the furnishings of the Governor's private room in the first Capitol building of the State of Maine.

This plate seems to be a page of historic lamps, for almost every one shown here has a history. Number 242, the last on the top row, has a pewter base and a glass camphene burning top. I suspect it may be a peg lamp placed in this pewter candlestick. At any rate, it was a part of the furnishings of the old McLean House at Appomattox Court House, Virginia, and was on the mantelpiece of the parlor when the terms of surrender were arranged there between Lee and Grant on that memorable 9th of April, 1865.

A lamp of equal interest, also closely connected with our great Civil War, is Number 201 in the center of the bottom row. This lamp is in itself unusual in that it has a plain glass, octagonal oil font supported by a fancy brass pedestal on a marble base. The identical lamp used by Mrs. Harriet Beecher Stowe while writing her immortal book "Uncle Tom's Cabin", it was presented to Doctor Norton by her husband, Doctor C. E. Stowe, who certified to the above fact.

The hand lamp numbered 114 gains a prominent place from the fact that it was once the property of Betty Mayberry, one of the local heroines of the War of 1812.

The pair of tall cut-glass Colonial lamps numbered 83 in this Plate 81 have ground decorations on the oil fonts and square step bases. The pair was used in the home of Andrew Clapp, the first mayor of Portland, Maine, in 1832.

The last lamp of this unusual collection, Number 253, is also a Civil War relic. Of the color called vaseline-yellow which is so sought for by Sandwich glass collectors, it formed part of the furnishings of the brick house in Montgomery, Alabama, which was used by President Jefferson Davis and was known as the "White House" of the Confederacy.

The three plates numbered 82, 84 and 88 represent a part of the very extensive collection of Sandwich glass gathered together by the Jordan Marsh Company of Boston, whose antique department contains many interesting and unusual pieces of furniture and china as well as glass. They very courteously allowed Mr. Colby to photograph some of their lamps as good examples of the better known patterns from Sandwich.

The reader by studying this collection may have an opportunity to see for himself what I spoke of earlier — the combining of the same base moulds with different oil font patterns and vice versa. The base of the pair of lamps in the center of Plate 88 is repeated in the bases of lamps in Plate 84 which have entirely different oil fonts. The Sandwich designers seem to have paid more attention to the oil fonts than to the bases, for there are many more different designs for the upper than for the lower parts. The bases of the two outside lamps in Plate 84 are identical but the tops differ. This base appears again in the second lamp in Plate 82 which has still a third top.

Though, no doubt, many of the old lamps were sold, and intended to be used, as pairs, it is somewhat difficult to-day to get two in perfect condition which exactly match. Plate 88 shows three perfectly matched pairs in proof condition. The first two on the left show the " Hob Nail " pattern on a graceful, six-sided base. The central pair, though quite similar in shape and general appearance, have the " hob nails " smaller and the pattern more pronounced. This is called the " Hob Nail Diamond " pattern.

The last two on the right are known as the " Gothic Window " design (one of them being retouched to show the pattern more clearly), a name which fits quite nicely. The remaining smaller odd lamps on this Plate 88 are both severely plain without any attempt at decoration and are known respectively as the " Urn " and the " Balloon " designs.

In Plate 84 the only pair here shown have been modernized by kerosene wicks, glass chimneys, and shades which to my mind detract from the grace and beauty of the old designs. The lamps themselves were so good that I wanted them shown even with the modern improvements (?). They are lovely examples of the much used " Heart " designs for which the Sandwich factory was famous. These " hearts " in a great many different patterns and groupings were used on many of

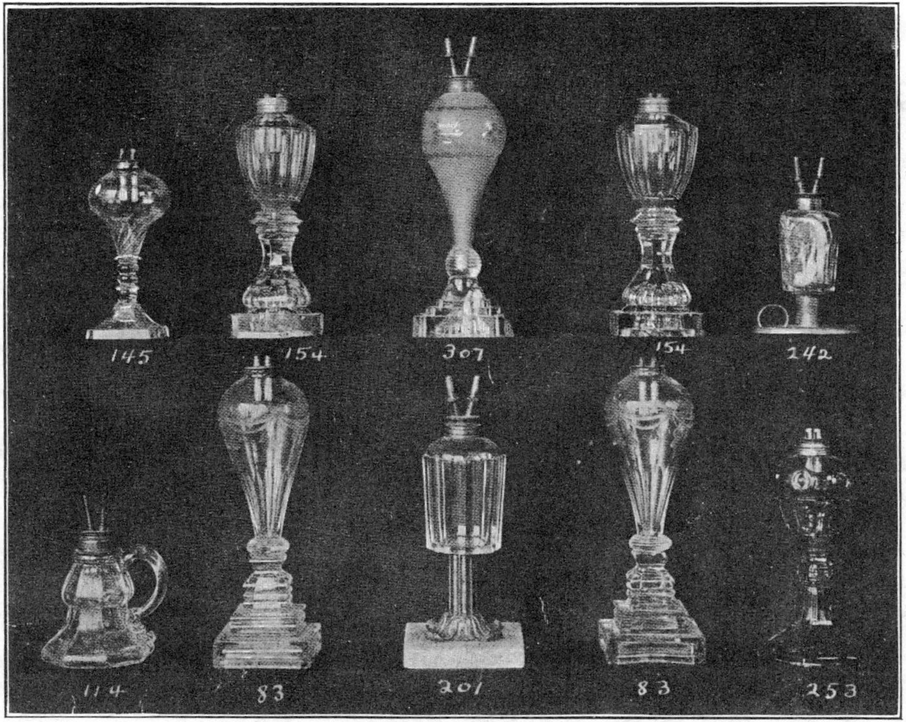

PLATE 81. *See pages 113, 114, 115*

HISTORICAL AND UNUSUAL GLASS LAMPS
Dr. C. A. Q. Norton's Collection

PLATE 82.

Group of Early Sandwich Glass Lamps
Courtesy of Jordan Marsh Co., Boston

See pages 115, 116, 117, 118

the little glass cup-plates which are being so enthusiastically collected at the present time, as well as on larger plates and other dishes.

The first at the left is a fine piece of the " Ripple " design, perhaps suggested by the marks left by the receding tides on the clean white sand of the many beaches along the shores of Cape Cod. The base is of the " Mushroom " type.

This design is repeated again in the last lamp on this page and also in the second lamp of Plate 82. The second lamp on Plate 84 shows the " Star and Full Moon ", not very commonly seen. Number 4, next to the first heart lamp, is an interesting example of the early combining of imported tops and Sandwich domestic bases. The oil chamber is blown and beautifully cut English glass, of an entirely different texture from the base, which is silvery early Sandwich.

Number 5 on Plate 84 is another variety of the " Heart " combined with the " Hob Nail." Number 6 has a " Balloon " font ornamented with the " Long Loop " pattern. Number 8 is a combination " Loop " and " Ring." The last, a very plain, clear, panelled oil receptacle on the pretty mushroom base, makes, to my mind, a very graceful lamp.

The last group from the Jordan Marsh Company collection, shown in Plate 82, comprises single lamps. The first on the left with the plain " Mushroom " base shows a simple " Loop " design on the bowl. The next lamp has a combination " Loop " and " Ring " pattern on the " Mushroom " base already familiar in the other plates. The third is a small camphene hand-lamp with a pretty handle and rather odd-shaped panelled font, an unusually graceful and quaint little chamber lamp. Number 4 has a deeply indented oil font, quite at variance with any of the others shown. This pattern is the " Tulip " design. The base is round instead of six-sided.

The one in the center is a piece of the " Thumb-Print " pattern, indented circles as if one had pressed his thumb over its flat surface at regular intervals. This pattern is more often seen in fruit dishes than in lamps. The author has a large, round fruit dish on a lamp base, the entire surface of which is covered with these indented thumb prints graduated in size, the larger at the top.

Number 6 is the "Heart and Honey-Comb", another variant of the very popular Sandwich "Heart." The second hand lamp shows a modified form of "Hob-Nail" alternating with three "Thumb Prints." The lamp itself is not so pleasing and graceful as the other. The next tall lamp is particularly interesting because it shows well the rare "Cable" design. When the first Atlantic cable was laid, it was a matter of great wonder and immense importance from a commercial point of view. To celebrate the event, the Sandwich people developed this design, using the twisted strands of the cable as a motif. It can be seen distinctly running up and down the sides of the oil font. The last lamp has a striped oil chamber of unusual shape on the "Mushroom" base.

I have spent some time in descriptions and given my readers prints of many lamps that they may familiarize themselves with various designs as much as possible. If they are not already collectors and intend taking up this branch of antique collecting, glass lamps will probably be the easiest to start with. If they have collections of their own, these few pages may help a bit to identify designs and to distinguish older from later pieces.

I am including one Plate 77 of glass lamps from my own collection, not because there is anything especially striking about them, but simply to encourage the beginner and to show what an interesting variety may be picked up to-day at a very small expense. As I recall it, I do not think I paid over three dollars for any lamp here and for some of them much less. Most of them are probably of Sandwich origin, for I picked up nearly all in the Cape Cod country. The lamp on the extreme right may be of English origin. At least the oil font, which is cut, looks like English glass. The tall lamp near the center with the long, straight oil font is unusual in having a small intermediary blown-glass section between the oil-holding top and the solid base. In "Sandwich Glass" Mrs. Williams tells us that "a blown receptacle for the oil fused to a molded base often had a beautiful blown center section." The third tall lamp from the left with two long camphene wicks is an early glass "peg" lamp put into a pewter candlestick base. There are two or three very good specimens of the small glass "sparking" lamps in this group. The slender moulded base and top-shaped oil font on the lamp a little to the right of the center shows an interesting variation from the other more solid and heavy lamps. Although, as I have said, there is represented here nothing of any especial merit, the variety makes a collection from which I derive a great deal of pleasure as I look at it from day to day in my cabinets.

Of much more worth and merit is the group of lamps in Plate 78, beautifully photographed by Mr. Luce from Mr. Gates' collection. If you have familiarized yourself with the patterns on the Jordan Marsh Company's lamps, you will recognize and be able to name some of these. Again you will see some more of the Sandwich base designs and one or two others of especial interest, for example, the bases of the first two lamps and the last two. The central lamp has quite an unusual design — a wine-glass base and round, squat, camphene-burning top. It looks like an aristocrat among commoners.

In Plate 79 the first two lamps, from Mr. Gates' collection, and the last three, from Mrs. Albert C. Marble's, both of Worcester, Massachusetts, are unusual small hand or "spark" lamps.

The first, with an ornamental base, is fitted with a single camphene burner, and, like many of the lamps which were made to burn this explosive fluid, has a tight-fitting brass cap attached by a tiny chain. Camphene lamps were usually extinguished by caps because blowing, the usual method of putting out whale-oil lamps, was dangerous with camphene. Many of the glass camphene lamps have these extinguishers.

The second is a beautiful example of the "Wine Glass", rare in this small size. The central lamp — a night lamp, of later date than the others — has an opaque shade over the tiny flame which gives its small steady glimmer all night long.

The fourth is probably the oldest lamp of the group, a "Wine Glass" with a rounded oil font for a single whale-oil burner. The stem is very interesting as is also the decorative moulding of the glass at the base.

The last lamp is an odd-shaped little "spark" lamp with a glass handle.

Through the courtesy of its owner, Mrs. George W. Mitton, I have been permitted to photograph some lamps from a very extensive collection of the early Sandwich glass now in a beautiful old mansion in a pleasant part of Boston overlooking Jamaica Pond. This collection is particularly rich in the early colored glass which was turned out by this factory, many of the colors of striking beauty.

Plate 83 shows a group of lamps in varied colors. The tall lamp in the center has an opaque glass font, which, being cut away, shows apple green beneath. Just at the left of it in the back row is a tall lamp with a clear glass font on a bronze and marble base, the supporting shaft an ultramarine blue. The lamp with the bronze and marble base at the right of the center has a font of rich ruby glass cut to display the clear glass beneath. The other lamps in this collection range from brown and vaseline yellow to amethyst, light blue, and the very rich deep blue so much sought for. Some of the designs of these lamps, apart from their color, are out of the ordinary, particularly the two at the extreme right.

PLATE 83.

See page 120

Rare Sandwich Glass Lamps in Various Colors
Mrs. George W. Mitton's Collection, Jamaica Plain, Boston

PLATE 84. Some Unusual Patterns in Sandwich Glass
Courtesy of Jordan Marsh Co., Boston

See pages 115, 116, 117

A charming group is shown in Plate 80. Although many of Mrs. Mitton's lamps are in pairs, for lack of space only one is shown in the photographs. There are two pairs in this photograph. The second lamp from the end on either side is a combination lamp with a long-waisted, cut oil font combined with a moulded base. The next pair is an unusual one. The lines of the rich, deep blue glass combined with the clear panels carrying the familiar "Thumb Print" make an odd combination. All the other single lamps in this plate are unusual in design, fine pieces rarely found to-day. The bases are particularly worth careful study.

The last print (Plate 87) of this group from Mrs. Mitton's collection contains an equal variety. Most of the lamps, if not all, are from pairs. The ground glass, balloon-shaped top of one in the right-hand half, on an ornate, clear glass base is pleasing. The small, clear glass one in the center with the wine-glass base is one of the rarest of them all. The shape of the second with its dome top is also interesting and very graceful. The old candlesticks are spoken of elsewhere.

I know of no more interesting study than to compare different groups of these Sandwich glass lamps, noting the combinations of tops and bases and the grace with which the designs are worked out. It is so rare to see one in the least clumsy looking as to speak volumes for the ability of the designers. The quality of the glass and general workmanship of the early products of this factory make the collecting of Sandwich glass one of the most fascinating of hobbies.

CHAPTER VII

ASTRAL AND LUSTER LAMPS AND ORNAMENTAL CANDLE HOLDERS

THE first half of the nineteenth century seems to have been marked by great activity on the part of inventors interested in lamps. It took a tremendously long time for any one to awake to the fact that the old type of open wick lamp was absurdly inadequate to light the progress which the world in general was making; but when in 1783 M. Argand, a Swiss chemist, introduced his great improvement in burners, it started the busy brains of many others to working along similar lines with the result that, in the two or three decades following, hundreds of patents were granted in America for various improvements in lighting devices. In fact, I have seen it stated that between the years 1800 and 1845 more than five hundred patents on whale-oil lamps were granted in America.

The invention of M. Argand was, however, an epoch-making one. Although the single and double burner whale-oil lamps continued to be made and used for more than fifty years — in fact up to the time of the introduction and general use of kerosene — the new principle, simple as it was, introduced by Argand gradually came to be recognized as a long step forward. To-day practically every round wick kerosene lamp is constructed on his idea, which was simply this: the wick, instead of being a flat or solid closely woven or braided one, was made in the form of a hollow tube. This tube was fitted closely into a metal tube of the same shape, which extended downward through the bottom of the oil reservoir, allowing a current of air to come up through the center of the burning wick as well as upon the outside. Argand reasoned that by this means the abundant supply of oxygen being constantly renewed as the heat from the lamp created a draft, the carbon would be entirely consumed, giving a strong bright light without smoke.

His first experiments were with a semi-circular tube for the wick but he soon abandoned it for a circular wick, found to be much more satisfactory. His next advance was some kind of a guide or chimney to direct the draft against the flame. His first chimneys were made of iron with a hood over the flame. The use of glass for this purpose is said to have been the result of an accident. A workman, heating a bottle over a flame, placed it too near, with the result that the bottom cracked and came off. As the bottle had become too hot to hold with comfort, he momentarily set it down over the flame and, to his great surprise, the flame became at once more steady and the light greatly increased. Glass then was at once adopted as the ideal material for lamp chimneys. Glass had the added advantage of utilizing all the rays of light which were formerly shut off by the iron chimney.

This idea of Argand's is the principle upon which all oil-burning lamps to-day are constructed. The flat single or double wicks have perforations under the bottom of the chimney to allow a current of air to be constantly sucked in against the flame. The round wick lamps are made as in Argand's time with the opening through the bottom of the oil font as well as around the outside of the chimney.

In the same year that M. Argand gave his invention to the world, a Frenchman — M. Legus of Paris — had introduced a flat woven wick like a ribbon to take the place of the old braided or solid woven round ones. This new wick permitted a much larger surface to come in contact with the flame so that the free carbon was more generally consumed, giving a brighter flame with much less smoke. At the same time he attached a small spur-wheel which, pressing against the wick, permitted its easy adjustment.

M. Argand's invention in principle was new and it took a long time for its general adoption, people as usual being loath to change old habits and ways. Besides, many who were equipped with the old style lard, whale-oil, or camphene lamps continued to use them down to, and even after, the general introduction of coal oil or kerosene. Gradually, as its merits were recognized, the Argand burner and the glass chimney came into general use.

The artistic skill of the craftsmen of those days produced many lamps whose beauty of line and form are appreciated and admired to-day.

It would be an exceedingly interesting thing to gather together as many different kinds of lamps patented before 1850 as possible. They were a wonderful lot, those patents. A few produced good results; many more, poor results; and the great mass of patents, no results at all. Although in collecting, you rarely find one of these patented lamps, still a glance at a few of the more striking and successful ones may be pertinent and certainly is a matter of no little interest to the student of lamp history.

In 1784 a patent was granted to a Mr. Miles " for his new method of making lamps of different forms, so as to emit an undiminished light however it may be agitated and which may be fixed in halls and shops."

In 1800 Messrs. White and Smithurst patented their " improved lamp burner ", an improvement on the common Argand lamp the object of which " is to afford a more free and plentiful supply of oil." They further explain: " This lamp enables burning common whale or seal oil, which is sold at about half the price of the best spermacite oil; the only inflammable fluid hitherto used in Argand lamps."

When " The Domestic Encyclopaedia " (spoken of in Chap-

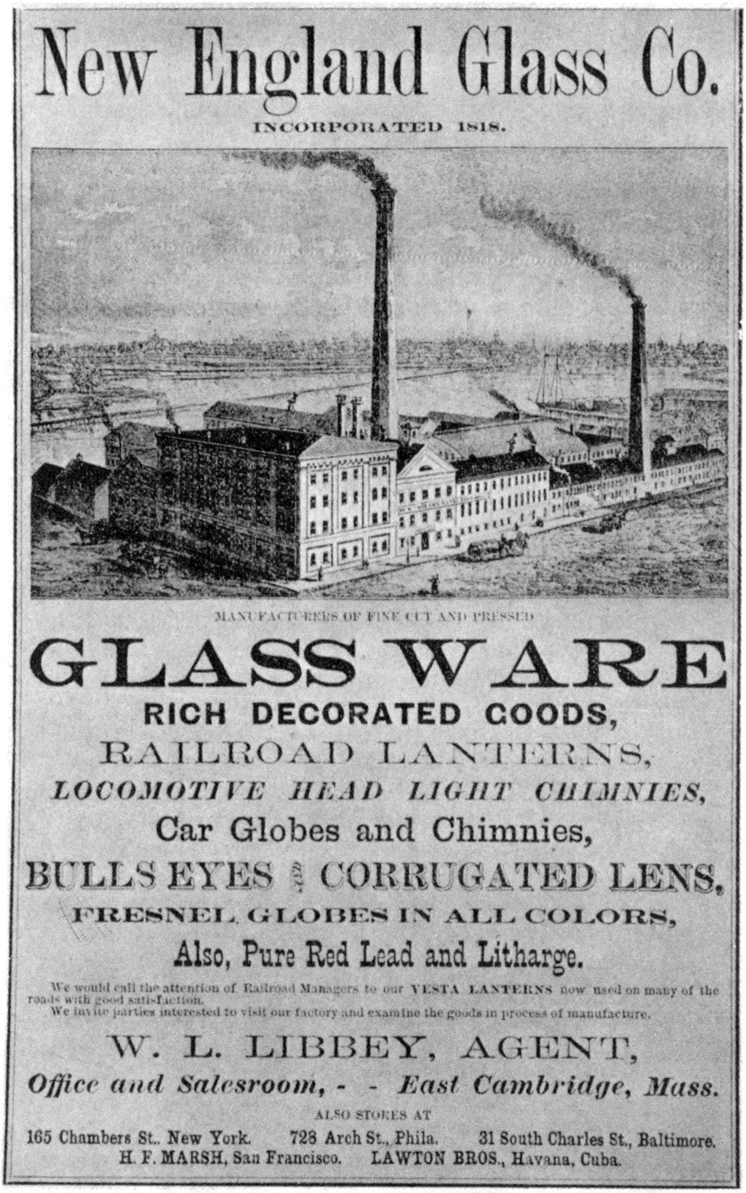

New England Glass Co.
INCORPORATED 1818.
MANUFACTURERS OF FINE CUT AND PRESSED
GLASS WARE
RICH DECORATED GOODS,
RAILROAD LANTERNS,
LOCOMOTIVE HEAD LIGHT CHIMNIES,
Car Globes and Chimnies,
BULLS EYES AND CORRUGATED LENS,
FRESNEL GLOBES IN ALL COLORS,
Also, Pure Red Lead and Litharge.
We would call the attention of Railroad Managers to our VESTA LANTERNS now used on many of the roads with good satisfaction.
We invite parties interested to visit our factory and examine the goods in process of manufacture.
W. L. LIBBEY, AGENT,
Office and Salesroom, - - East Cambridge, Mass.
ALSO STORES AT
165 Chambers St., New York. 728 Arch St., Phila. 31 South Charles St., Baltimore.
H. F. MARSH, San Francisco. LAWTON BROS., Havana, Cuba.

PLATE 85. *See page 112*

Rare Handbill Showing the Cambridge Works of the New England Glass Co. Courtesy of Mr. Burton N. Gates, Worcester

PLATE 86.

GROUP OF PATENTED GLASS LAMPS
Collections of Worcester Historical Society and Mr. Gates

See pages 131, 132

ter V) was published, whale-oil lamps were the common illuminant. Argand burners were coming into use, but were still considered more or less of an innovation and a luxury. The following quotation will be read with great interest — by the light of our 100-watt Mazda electric bulbs: "We have already pointed out the superior utility of lamps, but as the light emitted by them is frequently too vivid for weak or irritable eyes, we would recommend the use of a small screen, which should be proportionate to the disk of the flame and be placed at one side of the light, in order to shade it from the reader's eye, without excluding its effect from others or darkening the room."

Another invention in the same year, 1800, by one Carcel provided a small pump run by clockwork which raised the oil from the base of the lamp to the wick holder, keeping the wick uniformly submerged in oil. This contrivance was, as it sounds, expensive and was only used in large lamps for halls and similar places.

One of the few inventions which seem to have met with considerable success was that whereby a third tube of copper was introduced between the two brass wick tubes. This tube, empty and running down to the bottom of the oil font, was supposed to convey the hot air from the flame down (copper being a good conductor of heat) and was particularly useful on lard-oil lamps, which troubled owners greatly in winter by the congealing of the oil.

It is an interesting fact that lard oil was the common illuminant used in the great lighthouses of the world for many years. It was not until as late as 1880 that a satisfactory burner using kerosene was constructed and adopted.

Another invention early in the century was a perforated disk through which the wick tubes passed. Cemented on the under side of this disk was a cork, which could be fitted to the neck of a glass lamp just as a cork fits into the neck of a bottle. It was used in the very earliest glass lamps brought over to America (1800 to 1810).

One of the most successful and popular improvements was the invention of J. Neal. His lamp was provided with a telescopic sliding cylinder with the wick tubes screwed into a collar which formed the upper part of the tube. When the lamp was filled with oil, a float at the bottom of the tube extended the cylinder to its full length. The wicks were long and reached to the bottom of the cylinder. As the oil was consumed, it had the effect of lowering the float and the cylinder, keeping the wicks uniformly submerged in the oil as long as any remained unburned. This device seems to have been quite generally adopted and was used on lamps of tin, brass and pewter with good results.

Perhaps one of the most ingenious (and, I should think, unworkable) patents was granted in 1839 to J. Price of Nashville, Tennessee, for a lamp which should burn pine knots. In this lamp a large tube having a diameter of about an inch and a half was used, in appearance not unlike a large candlestick. The pine knots were to be cut into small pieces (rather difficult work requiring considerable practice to do well). These pieces of pine were then crowded into the cylinder, at the base of which was arranged a spring to keep them pressed up against the top. When the cylinder was full, a cap or top with a large opening was placed on it, the spring forcing the pine splinters up through the opening in the cap and the ashes falling into a circular pan secured on the upright pedestal. The description further says: "A sheet iron chimney with a broad hood partly surrounding the flame was provided to convey the ascending smoke away from the face of the person using the lamp." Certainly a most curious device!

At about the same time another patent was granted for a device in which balls of cotton or flax saturated with oil or grease were burned. They were held in a claw-like arrangement fastened to an upright coming from the flat base into which the ashes fell.

In 1843 a Philadelphia concern patented what they called a "Solar Lamp", which was a great improvement over any table lamp so far brought out. It was constructed to burn lard oil and was built on the general principle of Argand's. The round wick tube, over which the wick closely fitted, extended through the bottom of the oil font and was provided with openings for the admission of air as in the regular Argand burner, but this burner was so constructed as to diffuse the flame more generally than in the other lamps. The special feature was a glass chimney, bulb shaped, which created a kind of hot air chamber in which the free carbon was consumed. This gave a profuse white, clear, steady light, which was far superior to anything then in use. This firm, Cornelius & Company, made these lamps on quite an extensive scale. They seem to have been used in the homes of the wealthier people.

In 1840 Benkler introduced a lamp, the principle of which was a tube admitting air to the flame. It was placed at an angle so that when the lamp was lighted, the heat produced a current of air which acted as a forced draft and made the light steady and the flame bright because all the smoke was consumed. By this means, the cheaper, heavier oils could be burned without smoke or offensive odors.

These are but a few of the hundreds of devices upon which the active brains of the day were working, but they give a fairly good idea of the progress which was being made.

One of the earliest inventors of prominence was Benjamin Thompson, an American, born in Woburn, Massachusetts, a chemist and physicist of note. He is better known by the title of Count Rumford, which he received from the Elector of Bavaria, in whose service he was for some years. He conducted many experiments, and constructed over one hundred different lamps. He was also the author of an exhaustive treatise on "The Management of Light in Illumination" published in 1789. He invented a machine to measure the relative intensity of light from different illuminants and a burner, which, however, was not a great success. It consisted of a flat wick tube with two flat tubes placed at acute angles on either side of it through which he designed that oxygen should be supplied. He soon abandoned this idea and confined his attentions to the regular Argand burner, which he improved by constructing his "Astral Lamp." In it the oil reservoir was a flat circular tube with radiating arms attached to the base of the lamp proper. His idea was the elimination as far as possible of the annoying shadow cast by the heavy base of the regular Argand lamps. He invented several other improved lamps, particularly ones for large rooms and halls, and was a recognized authority on all matters pertaining to the science of lighting. He was created Count as a reward for his scientific discoveries and valuable services.

Count Rumford's Astral lamps were used extensively in the better class homes together with elaborate candelabra and chandeliers, many of which are greatly prized to-day for workmanship and design of the highest artistic quality.

I have been at some pains to gather together some illustrations showing the tremendous strides which lamp making had made in these few decades since the inventive faculties had been seriously set to work.

Plate 94 shows a beautiful pair of Astral lamps in bronze. Although not so elaborate as some mantel lamps, this pair, with the old ground and cut glass shades, are well proportioned, dignified, and handsome. The main oil fonts are in the tops of the central pedestals from which the oil is conducted through the horizontal arms to the lamps proper. Near the bottom of these cylinders on the arms can be easily seen the openings which admit the air to the center of the wicks. The

PLATE 87. *See pages 121, 142*

FIVE GLASS LAMPS AND TWO CANDLESTICKS, ALL OF RARE SANDWICH PATTERNS
Mrs. George W. Mitton's Collection, Jamaica Plain, Boston

PLATE 88.

THREE PAIRS AND TWO SINGLE SANDWICH GLASS LAMPS OF STRIKING DESIGNS
Courtesy of Jordan Marsh Co., Boston

See pages 115, 116

very small and close wick bases eliminate almost all the shadow and allow the light to extend its full power over the room.

The very ornate and elaborate lamps seen in Plate 100, though very similar, are not mates. A full mantel set usually consisted of a two-branched burner (like the one on the right) for the center of the mantel, with a single-arm lamp to match on either side. These lamps are as elaborate as any that I have seen. Cast in bronze, they show a wealth of elaborate detail without, however, losing their sense of proportion. The double-branched one in particular can bear the closest inspection, for it shows great care in even the tiniest detail, especially the fluted arms, the elaboration of the lamp proper, and even the shade holders. The braces to hold the heavy arms are carefully thought out, the curved motif being repeated on the bell-shaped canopy over the curved shaft.

The crystals on this lamp, together with the odd shaped, beautifully proportioned shades, make a combination which for sheer elegance of design would be extremely difficult to approximate to-day in any of the modern shops. The use of cut crystal lusters for lamps and candlesticks was very general during this period and gave an air of lightness and delicacy to what might otherwise have been a trifle too heavy and solid. The strings of cut button crystals on the single lamp at the left are not nearly so effective, nor is the lamp itself of quite as good a design. They, however, are both fine examples of this type of bronze Astral lamps, and any collector who is fortunate enough to find pieces as good and with a purse long enough to secure them is indeed to be congratulated.

A somewhat similar bronze table lamp of the student type, probably of a later date, is seen in Plate 103. Another fine example of the combination in a pair of Astral mantel lamps of bronze and cut crystals is shown in Plate 93, well designed, finely proportioned lamps, which would add grace and dignity to any home to-day.

Now and then one runs across one of these patented lamps usually tucked away in some dusty corner of a top shelf in an antique shop. They are generally far from ornamental and have no interest for the casual collector, but to any one specializing in lamps they might be an interesting side-line.

In Plate 30 the author shows what was called a "Tumbler Lamp." It is marked at the top of the curious tin, box-like structure on top of the glass (which is an ordinary pressed glass tumbler) "Star Tumbler, Patented Jany. 13, 1874." It was intended to be a physician's or invalid's lamp for heating a little water if needed at night. Just how the necessary air got down into the tumbler to enable the lamp to burn, I can not state. I had never seen one like it until I received some photographs from the collection of the Worcester Historical Society, which show that they possess its duplicate.

The lamp at the left of Plate 40 has a very broad wick, intended evidently for lard oil, coming out of the curious flattened font supported on an open-work, cast-iron base. The wick is unusually broad with three openings where it may be picked up. On one side of the wick at the top is a capped opening through which the lamp is filled and on the opposite side a small open tube, which, I imagine, is for the purpose of conveying heated air down into the font to keep its contents in a liquid state in cold weather. This lamp marked "S. N. & H. G. Ufford, 117 Court St., Boston, Pat. Feb. 4, 1851." is in the possession of the Worcester Historical Society. The writer has in his collection an exact duplicate, except that it has the original small round tin shade painted bronze like the lamp and held over it by two small wire uprights which rest in sockets at either end of the oil font. These sockets may be seen on the lamp in this plate.

The pewter lamp at the extreme right of Plate 40 with the

long double camphene burner is engraved across the front "Saml. Clark, New York" and is unusual in that it has a separate filling hole with a screw cap just below the top of the lamp. This lamp belongs to the Worcester Historical Society.

In Plate 86 — also from the Worcester Historical Society's collection, which seems to be particularly rich in these nineteenth century devices — are several odd patented lamps. The first pair of hand-lamps on the left (the bases of which have a very familiar Sandwich pattern) have curious perforated metal tops which are hinged to the handle and drop down closely over the flame from the single whale-oil burner. These lamps are marked "TOM THUMB DIRIGO Pat. Feby. 1st and Dec. 3rd, 1861. Chas. W. Cahoon."

The clear glass "Peg" lamp lying on its side in the center of this plate is owned by Mr. Gates and is very unusual in that it has a patented device. It is intended for burning camphene, as is shown by the two long wick tubes with their attached brass caps on the cylinder beside it. Inside the lamp and running nearly to the bottom of the extra large, globular oil font is a very fine meshed brass cylinder. Into it is fitted the slightly smaller brass cylinder, also finely meshed, which lies on the table beside it. Just what is accomplished by having the two cylinders it is hard to say, but they evidently acted in some manner to prevent the danger of explosions from the camphene. This lamp is marked "Newells' Patent 1852."

Although camphene as a burning fluid was used for a time quite extensively (as the number of lamps fitted with the long round wick tubes would indicate), many serious burning accidents resulted from the careless handling of these lamps. It was an extremely explosive mixture and if a spark got down into the oil chamber a violent explosion was sure to result. This danger led to the study of various safety devices for minimizing this danger, one of which is evident on the peg lamp above.

The first tall glass lamp on Plate 86 has a pewter burner using three flat wicks which are brought together at the point of flame. This lamp was designed to be used with a chimney and is marked " Schulz & Trull's Patent."

The other two tall lamps are very similar and were evidently turned out by the same factory at about the same time. The bases seem to be identical. Although the fonts are slightly different, all three have the intermediate blown glass bulb between the top and the base which we noted in some lamps in the previous chapter. It is quite likely that these lamps were built by the same firm; for they have a similar pewter burner, using, however, a single round wick instead of the three flat ones. They are designed for glass chimneys. The patent burner has been removed from the lamp at the right and is lying beside it. This burner has a cap on it which, by turning, automatically raises or lowers the wick as desired. This is evidently a patented device, but, unfortunately, the burners are not marked. All of these patented lamps are from the Worcester Historical Society.

While this great change in lamps was going on, much attention was given also to the illuminating fluids used. I have already indicated that the first oil was obtained from the plentiful fish along the shores, that whale fishing from small boats started later, and that finally, after the whales had become scarce along the shore, large sailing vessels were fitted out for long voyages and the industry was worked on a big scale.

The oil from the " right " whale was the common illuminant for nearly one hundred and fifty years. The origin of the name " right " whale seems to be in doubt, but many think it so called because it was the right kind to capture.

PLATE 89. *See page 74*

HALLWAY AT "INDIAN HILL," WEST NEWBURY, MASSACHUSETTS, SHOWING A FINE OLD HALL LANTERN
Photograph by Miss Mary H. Northend

PLATE 90. *See page 140*

PAIR CRYSTAL CANDELABRA FOR THE TABLE WITH WEDGWOOD BASES
Photograph by Miss M. H. Northend

PLATE 91. *See page 140*

ANOTHER PAIR CRYSTAL TABLE CANDELABRA, THE CUT CRYSTALS ARE IN BOTH CLEAR AND COLORED GLASS
Photograph by Miss M. H. Northend

It not only yielded quantities of oil but also a valuable amount of whalebone, obtained from the head.

The oil from the sperm whale which gradually took the place of right oil was lighter oil but usually cost more. When subjected to the refining process it was suitable for the elegant "Astral" lamps of the first half of the nineteenth century and gave a clear, steady, bright flame with little or no odor or smoke.

If one wants to know anything and everything about whaling, New Bedford or Nantucket is the place to go. Just ask for some of the old sea captains, who still may be found of a sunny day in some pleasant room in one of the old warehouses on South Water Street, New Bedford, spinning yarns of bygone days.

A century or two ago whaling was not only an almost exclusively New England industry, but one the extent and importance of which can hardly be realized to-day. New Bedford and Nantucket were the headquarters of rival whaling fleets.

On the water front of New Bedford in the little shop of a maker of whaling guns and lances may be seen a collection of articles relating to this industry really worthy of the name of museum. Here is a long itemized list of goods furnished the New Bedford fleet of sixty-five vessels outfitting in the year 1858. The value of the supplies amounts to nearly two millions of dollars. It was no uncommon thing for nearly one hundred vessels to outfit together in the same season; so one can readily see that the business was of no mean proportions.

Since the whaling voyage meant anywhere from two to five years away from home, an outfit meant, not only the large quantities of provisions necessary for the captain and crew for this period, but trading goods to barter with the natives for fresh meats and other supplies; extra sails, spars and other nautical equipment which might be required to replace that worn out or damaged by storms; huge pots and a large number of barrels to store the oil tried out from captured whales; a full medical chest for the captain who was also the doctor as well as the judge and jury when any disputes arose, and the parson when any one died. Many things may happen in a five-year voyage extending from the frozen ice fields of the Arctic waters to the burning sun, the deadly calms, and the wild tempests of the tropics.

Many people think of whales as fish because they live in the sea and swim, but a whale of course is a warm-blooded animal, bringing forth its young alive, and suckling it like a cow. Its flesh very closely resembles beef, both in appearance and taste and except for now and then a slightly fishy flavor, a good cut of whale meat properly broiled, to many people, could not be distinguished from a fine sirloin steak.

The whales are usually found in schools or " pods ", as they are called, but the whalers sometimes hunt weeks before sighting one.

It is recorded that a lady, talking with an old New Bedford man, spoke rather slightingly of the whale and its uses. He turned to her with the remark, " Madam, you should not speak that way. A woman is more beholden to the whale than to anything under heaven." In answer to her look of amazement he continued: " Three very important things you are dependent upon to the whale — your corsets which give you your style; your cosmetics and your perfumery which give you your beauty and attractiveness." It is not recorded that the lady was pleased, but it is true that, although many things have been tried, nothing has been found equal to real whalebone for ladies' stays.

Ambergris, a mysterious oily, porous substance of a dirty greenish gray color, which is sometimes found cast up on beaches and which comes from the sperm whale, some think as the result of some disease, is used as the basis of many perfumes. Though it has no odor in itself, it has the strange property of absorbing odors to a remarkable degree; hence, its value is more than its weight in gold. In the bony structure of the head of the sperm whale, moreover, is a cavity which yields a very fine grade of oil known as spermaceti; this oil is used as a basis for many cosmetics and ointments as well as for fine candles. It was currently believed that a spermaceti candle would give about double the light of one made from tallow.

The most famous catches of ambergris were made by the schooner *Watchman*, which, in 1858, brought in eight hundred pounds and the bark *Splendid*, which, in 1883, came into port with nine hundred and eighty-three pounds. You may imagine the feelings of the captain and crew when the market price was found to be over five hundred dollars a pound.

Some of the logs of the whalers' captains are interesting even to landlubbers. I recall seeing one by a captain who was something of an artist and had adorned almost every page with a sketch of some kind. .A whale blowing or otherwise deporting itself usually embellishing the pages when whales were plentiful. Any unusual incident to break the monotony such as speaking another vessel or a call at a port for water or fresh supplies, was usually shown. Many of the sketches, though small, were very cleverly done. Sometimes a wounded whale would smash a boat with his powerful flukes, throwing the men into the water, and this would be shown in quite a graphic manner.

When the schools or pods of whales were encountered, the men often worked night and day; for after a whale had been "struck"— as the term is when one is harpooned and finally killed — it was towed up alongside the ship and the work of cutting up the blubber or thick coating of fat just underneath the skin began. This fat, which kept the blood of the whale warm in the frigid waters of the polar seas, was cut off in huge strips by instruments closely resembling sharp spades and, when "tried out" over the fires in the huge kettles, yielded the sought-for oil. But there were often weeks at a time when the lookout aloft swept the seas with his glass in vain for any sign of whales and when time hung heavily on the hands of the crew.

At such times it was often the custom of the men to busy themselves in carving the bones of the whale into strange and unique gifts for the folks back home. One of the favorite devices was the jagging wheel, a fancifully edged wheel on the end of a short handle, somewhat resembling a flattened spur, all carved in more or less intricate designs and sometimes inlaid with mother-of-pearl, according to the skill of the maker. These wheels were used in cutting out and embellishing with fanciful designs the pies and other pastry which were so important a part of every thrifty New England housewife's cuisine.

There were many other articles for domestic use such as bobbins, spools, knitting needles, card cases, work boxes, snuff boxes, and many other things, which the inventive ingenuity of the sailor might suggest, made from the whale ivory.

I have seen the most delicate and beautiful models of ships, the entire hull and spars, deck houses, boats, etc., all cut out of whale ivory, the models being perfect in their proportions and all the complicated ropes and tackle of the rigging exactly reproduced in perfect detail. Several museums — notably that at New Bedford — have extensive collections of these ivory jagging wheels and scrimshaw work, as it was called. A whale's tooth elaborately carved or scratched, the lines filled in with lampblack — often depicting thrilling scenes in the capture of whales — held the place of honor on the mantelpiece or the top shelf of the "what-not" in the parlor of many a seaside New England home.

But the main business of whaling was an arduous one, requiring men of cool heads, stout hearts, iron constitutions,

PLATE 92. *See page 142*

Dining Room at "Indian Hill," Showing a Beautiful Hanging Glass Chandelier
Photograph by Miss Northend

PLATE 93. *See page 129*

Pair Mantel Astral Lamps in Bronze with Cut Crystals
Photograph by Miss Mary H. Northend

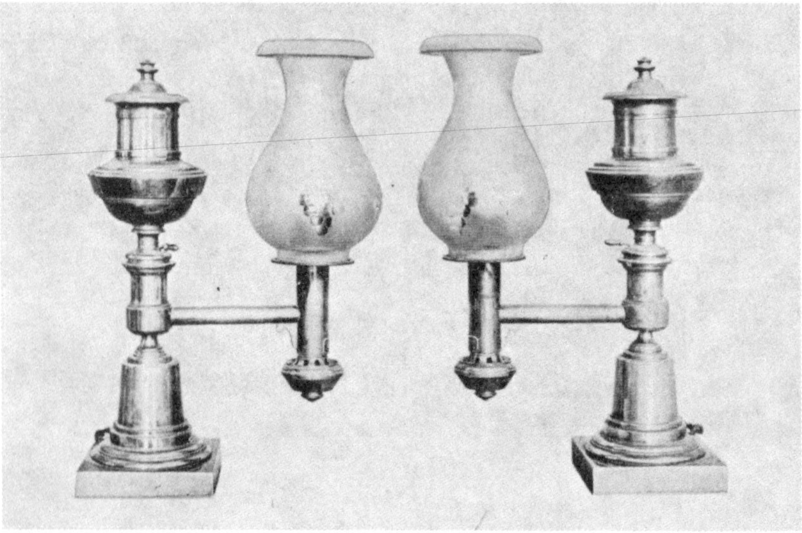

PLATE 94. *See page 128*

Pair Single-Burner Mantel Astral Lamps
Photograph by Miss Mary H. Northend

strong muscles, and steady nerves. The lives of a boatload often depended on the skill and steadiness of the harpooner as he stood in the bow waiting for the exact moment and place to strike.

The vicinity of a whaling vessel while in active operation, with clouds of dense black smoke from the kettles of boiling fat and the penetrating odors of blubber and decaying carcasses of dead whales, was anything but agreeable. Think of years of it, often without letters from home and only the occasional speaking of some other vessel at sea or the occasional call at some port where belated news may be had! It was work only for men of the strongest mental fiber, and such indeed were the men who manned the whaling fleets — splendid specimens of New England's best manhood. Hardly less credit should be given the faithful wives, mothers, and sisters waiting with fortitude and courage through long months of silence for news of their loved ones.

Many interesting books written on the romance and realities of whaling may be found in almost every library. They are well worth reading and tell far better than I the details of this arduous but fascinating New England industry. Such are the works of Herman Melville, which have suddenly revived their popularity of years ago.

But to return from whales to the lamps they lit. Many of the tall table lamps usually classified under the name of "Astral" lamps (though in reality the name properly applies only to the lamps in which a slender arm holding the lamp proper goes off at right angles from the main central oil font) are to be found in the dealers' stores, and may be purchased if one cares to pay the price; for the really good ones command high figures. Care should be taken in buying because many of these lamps with brass or bronze bases, usually attached to a square of marble and sometimes with a row of cut crystal lusters around the shade holder, are not of good proportions and have an awkward appearance. Do not buy a lamp of this kind just because it is old, but wait until you can find one the design and proportions of which will be a pleasure to the eye. I do not quite understand how so many inartistic ones were made since it seems almost as easy to make a lamp of symmetrical proportions as one which offends the laws of grace, but it is a fact that many of the so-called "Astral" lamps which one finds to-day in the various dealers' shops are ungraceful and some are positively ugly.

I give several examples here of what I consider desirable lamps of this type. The designs are good, proportions graceful, and the shades in harmony of design, and in the right relations to the lamp proper. In Plate 102 the tall central lamp is a beautifully designed piece. Its long, perfectly proportioned bronze column resting on a square marble base supports a shade in perfect harmony, and forms a whole which will always be a delight to the eye.

Since many of these lamps are now being bought and fitted for electricity, perhaps this word of caution is not out of place, for a lamp is something which one has constantly before him and a jarring note in design or a false proportion is a matter of constant irritation, to me at least, and I imagine to many others.

In this same Plate 102, beside the tall lamp are two very quaint glass hand lamps in one of the most original designs that I have seen. Shaped something like decanters, the lamp proper is the round glass corresponding to the stopper. The shape is graceful and the handles particularly so, but I think they must have been designed more for ornament than use. They are hardly practical.

The two table lamps given in Plate 108 are from the author's collection and he considers them excellent examples. The one at the left has a French gilt standard on a double marble base and the original old shade is of good shape in proportion to the lamp. The row of lusters, though at first sight rather too short, are of a very elaborate design which is in perfect harmony with the design of the central standard so that the effect of the whole lamp is particularly rich and pleasing. The lamp at the right has a severely plain central column rising from a heavy square marble base and lusters long and severely plain to match. The shade, which is thc original one, is well proportioned and the general effect of the lamp harmonious. A third lamp in the writer's collection in Plate 105 is still more striking. This is the lamp which the writer found in the loft of an old barn, as described in the next chapter. The very unusual shape of the finely cut shade gives it a most distinguished appearance. I give these three as good examples of what to look for in getting lamps of this sort.

The use of cut glass pendants, prisms and drops was probably first introduced by the glass makers of England and Ireland and was copied here by our own workmen, but many of the wealthier people preferred the imported articles. Some wonderfully fine and artistic chandeliers and candelabra adorned the homes of the merchant princes during the first half of the nineteenth century. Plate 99 gives a photograph of a candelabra set consisting of a three-branched candlestick for the center of the mantel and a single candle one to match on either side. This pattern was called the "Paul and Virginia" and was one very much in vogue on account of the great popularity of the novel by that name. The graceful body is cast in French gilt and secured to a square marble base. The broad, elaborately designed collars at the base of the candle holders are encircled by bands of cut and molded lusters. There were numerous designs for the bases of these candelabra, — knights, ladies, castles and cathedrals, shepherds and warriors, baskets of flowers, etc. They may be found to-day, though for a complete set of three in good condition a fairly high price will probably be asked. Since this

French gilt finish did not tarnish readily and they were considered very ornamental, they seem to have suffered less through careless handling than most antiques and are to-day usually part of the stock in trade of most antique stores.

A very fine three-branched one is given in Plate 101. This has the figure of a knight in armor and the long glass lusters are cut in a special design. This candelabrum is shown standing on a handsome carved and gilded eagle bracket, a very spirited piece of work dating probably from about 1800. The candlestick is of a later date.

The three candelabra in Plates 90, 91 and 98 were undoubtedly imported and are probably of Irish or English glass. They are wonderful examples of the graceful designs of those early artists as well as the great technical skill required to produce the designs in glass.

Number 91 is almost entirely in glass. The design for the base of four glass pillars rising from the bronze base is quite unique and is well carried out. Note the grace of the curved glass arms and the cutting of the fancy candle holders as well as the tops of the main shaft. The glass pendants are also unusual, round cut crystals of colored glass, each with its pendent pear-shaped drop of clear cut glass hung about each candle holder and also the glass ornament at the top. The effect of the whole is singularly rich and graceful.

Number 90 is also mainly of glass but of a very different design. The base is bronze or brass enclosing a pottery cylinder of a typical Wedgwood design. The curved glass arms rise from a cut glass bowl and terminate in ornamental glass candle holders. The tall central shaft is connected with the candle brackets by festoons of cut crystals.

The third set shown in Plate 98 has a base of marble with Wedgwood and bronze medallions and the main shaft and candle arms are also of bronze. The lusters which hang from the bases of the candle holders and the top of the central shaft

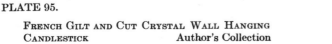

PLATE 95.

French Gilt and Cut Crystal Wall Hanging Candlestick — Author's Collection

PLATE 96.

Gilt and Cut Crystal Candelabrum with Watteau Figure — Author's Collection

PLATE 97. *See page 141*

WALL BRACKET FOR TWO CANDLES IN BRONZE AND FESTOONS OF CUT CRYSTALS

Photograph by Miss Northend

consist of three round cut "buttons" with a long pointed cut drop beneath.

These three, though totally different, are, each in its own way, superb examples of well-balanced and symmetrical design carried out by workmen of great technical skill. I very much doubt if they could be surpassed, or even equalled, in our highest grade shops to-day.

But the work upon the hanging glass chandeliers was even of a more elaborate character. Many of them are marvels of grace and beauty and of the most perfect and exquisite workmanship.

I commend for your study the hanging chandelier for six candles in Plate 104 and the wall bracket for two candles in Plate 97.

Note first the perfect balance and grace of the design and the exquisite cuttings of the balls, pendants, rosettes, and other shapes in crystal which are so effectively worked into the design.

In the breakfast room of Mrs. Mitton's fine old mansion overlooking Jamaica Pond in Boston hangs the chandelier for six candles illustrated in Plate 107. It was made by Wedgwood, the "Prince of Potters" as he was called, and rightly. No one man did more for this fine art than did he. We are told "he modelled many objects himself, his taste and artistic sense being so strong that even the silversmiths followed his models as well as the members of his own craft." This chandelier is an exquisite piece of modelling. The body is that dull, greenish grey which one often finds on Wedgwood vases. The candle holders, ornamented upper edges and bottom, are finished in bright silver luster, a combination as striking as it is beautiful. Its owner has had electricity substituted for the original candles.

Mrs. Mitton is particularly interested in Sandwich glass of which her collection is most extensive. I had photographed only a few of the many choice lamps and candlesticks, all in perfect condition and many of them of extremely rare patterns. Of the famous and graceful "Dolphin" design of the Sandwich works, Mrs. Mitton has many pieces both in clear and opaque glass and in numerous colors.

Plate 72 shows a group, most of which are "Dolphin" candlesticks, some on single and some double bases. The stick at the extreme right is a very rare pattern. The candle holder of opal glass gradually blends into the bell-shaped clear glass base. The stick at the left, of severely classic shape, is all of opaque glass. In the center is a Sheffield candlestick holding a glass peg lamp for two wicks in an interesting design. Just in front the familiar dolphin in colored glass on the round base holds a small shell-shaped disk of opal glass. In the group of lamps from this same collection in Plate 87 are shown two very early blown glass candlesticks on moulded bases. The tops are identical and have the interesting small hollow bulb in the center, but the moulded bases are of entirely different patterns. These plain sticks are seldom found; so this pair in perfect condition is greatly prized by its owner.

They have a very pretty custom on Beacon Hill in Boston of lighting the houses on Christmas Eve with candles at all the windows and other lights in the rooms.

One can wander there on that evening, listening to the bands of carollers singing their old "Noël" hymns, and catch glimpses of beautiful old rooms filled with stately furniture of years gone by. Here and there one catches a glimpse of these rich old glass chandeliers, for there are still some left in those fine old mansions, radiant with the soft glow from many candles, the most beautiful artificial light in the world.

I have secured, through the courtesy of Miss Northend, interior views showing three types of these glass chandeliers.

The simplest one, with its tiers of gracefully curved glass arms, is in Plate 92. This one, with its central rod of brass upon which are strung hollow glass balls alternating with series of glass arms terminating in the candle holders, is undoubtedly of English or Irish glass as are probably the other two. This one hangs in the dining room at "Indian Hill", the fine old residence of the late Ben Perley Poore, at West Newbury. The house, which dates from 1680, has been modernized to some extent, but it still keeps its old-time flavor, helped by the old furnishings throughout, the prized possessions of its late owner, who was a noted and enthusiastic collector.

The remaining two are in modern residences, but so perfectly has the architect and owner environed these pieces as to produce a most harmonious effect. Plate 110 shows the residence of Edward D. Brandegee, Esq., of Brookline, Massachusetts —"Faulkner Farm." This old chandelier, hanging from the center of the ceiling, was originally built for many candles and is a striking example of airy grace in crystal.

Plate 114, the drawing room of "Wechfeld House" at Prides Crossing, Massachusetts, shows a perfect setting for this wonderfully graceful bronze and crystal chandelier. The architects and decorators have evidently used the central chandelier as a keynote upon which the rest of the room is based. Note also the hanging side-lights as well as the perfect harmony in furniture, rug, wall, and decorations.

The church which I attended as a boy in Salem was designed by the famous Salem architect, McIntyre, whose work ranks with that of Bulfinch and Wren. The spire was particularly graceful and was often photographed and studied by architects. The church was built about 1800.

One day while making some repairs in the loft, workmen found, half hidden by rubbish, some large cases. Upon opening them they discovered a wonderful hanging glass chandelier. Some of the older people then remembered that years before a sea captain had brought home from England and presented to the church this elaborate chandelier, which had been hung in the center of the church. For some reason unknown, it had later been taken down, packed carefully away, and in time entirely forgotten. Years and years after (I was quite a lad when I first saw it, and my father did not remember it at all) it was cleaned, polished, put together, and again hung in the center of the church. It was a most elaborate affair as I remember it, hanging, I should judge, at least ten feet in length. There were three rows of curved glass arms — the smallest at the top — alternating with large cut glass globes. The bottom row must have had a spread of six or eight feet and the whole terminated in several fancy glass bowls or globes, diminishing in size. It must have held sixty to one hundred candles and was a wonderful sight to my youthful eyes. Alas! it is no more. On a cold night in winter just as the church was preparing to celebrate the hundredth anniversary of its erection, it burned to the ground and a few half melted scraps of glass were all that was left of my beautiful glass chandelier.

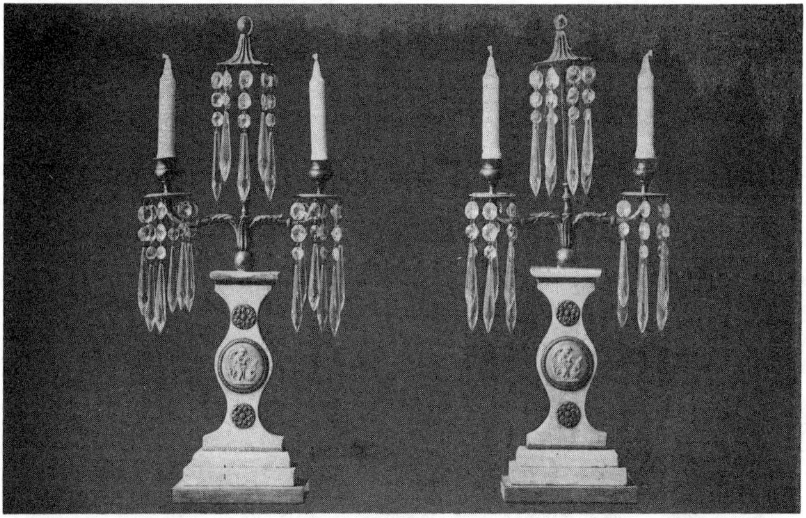

PLATE 98. *See page 140*

PAIR BRONZE AND MARBLE MANTEL OR TABLE CANDELABRA WITH CUT CRYSTAL DROPS Photograph by Miss Mary H. Northend

PLATE 99. *See page 139*

BEAUTIFUL SET OF "PAUL AND VIRGINIA" CANDELABRA WITH ELABORATE CRYSTAL LUSTRES Photograph by Miss Mary H. Northend

PLATE 100. See page 129

Central Two-Burner Bronze Astral Lamp Flanked by One of a Pair of Side Lamps

Photograph by Miss Northend

CHAPTER VIII

RANDOM NOTES ON COLLECTING

I SUPPOSE there is hardly a collector of antiques of almost any kind who has not, at one time or another, had the question asked him by some well meaning friend "What's the good of all that junk anyway?" Perhaps not in just those words, but to that general effect. Well, what is the use of collecting? Let me tell you why I think it a good thing for a man to take up the fad of collecting — not necessarily lamps nor even antiques — but something which will take his mind from the daily grind and care and offer him rest and relaxation.

Nowadays almost every physician advocates for the professional man or any one whose work is of a sedentary nature some form or other of physical exercise: golf, tennis, riding, walking, rowing, swimming, or something else which shall supply the needed physical equilibrium. Why, then, is it not as logical to apply the same theory to the mind and to relieve the pressure of arduous mental work day after day by mental work of an entirely different kind, thus establishing a healthy mental equilibrium?

A fad like collecting will do this, and, if rightly pursued, will bring as much healthy pleasure as a good game of tennis or round of golf.

The best of it is, you can find something exactly to suit your purse as well as your taste. If your means are limited, try something simple like stamp collecting, which affords a great many people pleasure with very little strain on the pocketbook unless they go into it extensively. "Too childish," you say, "just a school-boy's game." But is it? I know a hardheaded business man, who not many years ago ran for Lieutenant Governor of Massachusetts, a shrewd, busy, successful, and by no means sentimental person, who has been for years an enthusiastic collector of stamps. He specializes in those of the Confederate States and his collection must run into many dollars. Another, a successful clothing merchant, has such a large collection that he had a special safe made in which to keep his stamp books. He exhibited his collection of French stamps in Paris to the amazement of the Continental philatelists, who marvelled at such a complete and wonderful showing. Oh, collecting stamps is not child's play!

Some men choose odd things to collect. I have heard of one man who collects old clothes pins — the ones whittled out of hard wood before the days of the five and ten cent stores. I remember when I was a small boy seeing my grandmother using pins which my grandfather had made for her, and very nice pins they were, nearly square on top as I recall them.

A direct descendant of Commodore Thomas MacDonough specializes in "MacDonough's Victory" ware. During the war with England in 1814, his distinguished ancestor defeated a stronger squadron of English vessels in that battle on Lake Champlain which Theodore Roosevelt in his "Naval History of the War of 1812" ranks above every other exploit. After the war was ended, far from feeling any lasting resentment toward America, English potters who were then making quantities of their wares for the American market and decorating them with American views, made a design of ships in battle and called it "MacDonough's Victory." It was carried out in a very rich, dark blue and is one of the historical designs much sought by collectors of such ware. This gentleman has confined himself to the one design and by persistent search has now a collection of more than fifty pieces. When you realize how scarce this design is to-day, you will understand that his collection means a considerable outlay of time as well as money to get such a result. Undoubtedly he has enjoyed it and probably would tell you that the fun was worth all it cost in effort.

There are hundreds of things to collect — mirrors, chairs, Sheffield plate, tables, hooked-in rugs, early American pottery, engravings, worked samplers, old clocks, pewter — just to think of a few out of many which one might collect with satisfaction.

Just now there is a large demand for early American glass, particularly the products of the Sandwich glass works. Genuine pieces of the early pressed or moulded glass, which, when they were first made and sold, could have been bought for a few cents, now often command as many dollars.

Many people are collecting the smaller pieces — salt cellars, small dishes for the table, and particularly cup plates, which were made in many designs and have been a very salable article. These designs were often made to celebrate some political or historical event of interest. Such special plates are eagerly sought and often command very high prices. A short time ago in a New York auction room, a Sandwich pressed glass cup plate which originally might have cost ten or fifteen cents brought twenty-six dollars. I think if one were starting collecting it would be well to select something which was not quite so much in the public eye.

Why not try lamps? They are readily found, the more common ones do not command fancy prices, and one can make a general collection or specialize in one of a dozen kinds as he chooses. There is a wide diversity, as this book indicates and, best of all, a chance for a lot of study and research; for that is really the zest of collecting. As one picks up, bit by bit, knowledge of the particular subject he is interested in, he finds that there is yet a great deal more to learn. When he thinks that he has a fairly good working knowledge of his subject, he runs across some one else who knows so very much more that he decides he doesn't know so much after all and that he had better get very busy and learn more. At least, that is my experience. When I started this book I felt that I had a decently respectable knowledge of the subject. I have learned a great deal more while writing it and realize now that I have yet a long way to go before reaching the ultimate goal of my ambition as to knowledge of lighting devices.

This is an honest confession, but doesn't almost every collector who is honest with himself feel the same way and really isn't that the greatest source of satisfaction in the game? It is not so much getting the actual specimens themselves as acquiring that feeling of confidence in one's own judgment. The feeling that you know what you want and why you want it comes only with study and experience.

What is the first step, then, after you have decided upon your particular field? I should advise visiting antique shops, as many as you can conveniently, and telling the proprietor quite frankly that you are a beginner, know little or nothing of the subject but want to learn. Ask to see his specimens and request any information he can give you. With rare exceptions, I think, the proprietor, be he man or woman, will be very glad to advise you and will give you the special points of such pieces as he has in stock and general idea of current values.

Attendance at auction sales is excellent, even if you are not buying; for it often gives you a very good line on present values, which in the general run are apt to be quite accurate. A great deal of other information may be gained there too. But if you are buying, you should make it a strict rule never to bid on an article without having carefully and leisurely examined it before the sale.

It seems to be the fashion lately among many writers of books on antiques to cast reflections upon antique dealers in general as persons devoid of any desire to tell the truth about

PLATE 101. *See page 140*

GILT AND CRYSTAL CANDELABRUM STANDING ON A CARVED AND GILDED BRACKET — SPREAD EAGLE DESIGN DATING ABOUT 1800
Photograph by Miss M. H. Northend

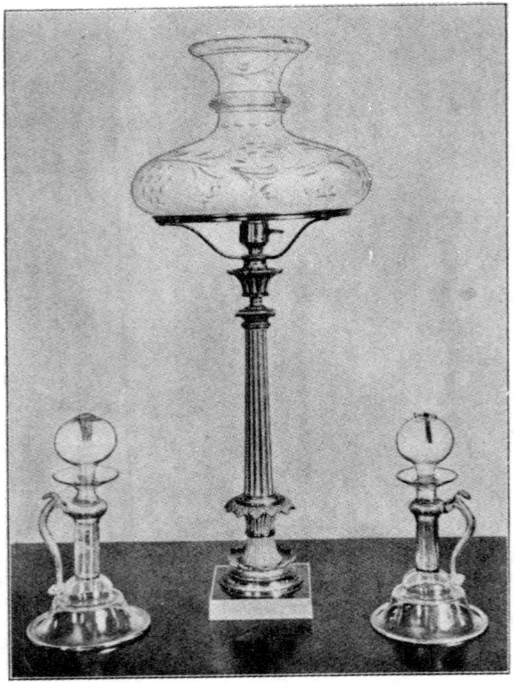

PLATE 102. *See page 138*

TALL GRACEFUL BRONZE TABLE LAMP AND PAIR CURIOUS GLASS HAND LAMPS

Photograph by Miss Mary H. Northend

PLATE 103. *See page 129*

TWO-BURNER TALL BRONZE ASTRAL LAMP (THE ANCESTOR OF OUR MODERN STUDENT LAMP)

Photograph by Miss Mary H. Northend

their wares and to depict them like the proverbial spider, sitting in their nets waiting for the unwary and innocent fly in the guise of a collector that they may devour him. I do not agree with these writers. I have always maintained that if you approach an antique dealer truthfully and honestly, in a perfectly friendly and fair-minded way, you will be met in the same fashion, at least nine times out of ten — perhaps ninety-nine times out of one hundred. In reading an article very recently in an antique magazine, I was glad to note that the writer took the same view, maintaining that the standard of honesty and fair dealing was as high among antique dealers as among any other class of merchants. I have been a general collector of antiques now for a number of years. So far as I know, I have never yet been deliberately sold an imitation or reproduction for the genuine thing. Why should any dealer attempt it (providing, of course, he is not in business intentionally to sell spurious for genuine)? Aside from the purely ethical considerations it is not good business.

If I should purchase an article as genuine which afterward upon further examination I found not to be as represented to me at the time of purchase, that antique dealer would thereby lose a customer. For, confidence in a dealer's honesty once destroyed, hardly any collector would risk further dealings with his shop. Since a customer who buys once almost invariably comes again and again, dishonesty simply means one customer lost. Dishonesty, purely from a dollar and cents view, would not pay. The extra profit from the sale of the "faked" piece usually would be offset many times over by the legitimate profits from the future business of that same customer. The confidence of his customers is the most valuable single asset which an antique dealer carries and most of them realize this. Of course I don't mean to say that there are no spurious articles being offered for genuine — in antiques as in hundreds of other lines of merchandise — but the merchant who does business in this fashion soon becomes known and, I believe, in the long run loses out.

There is this much to be said: perhaps no other line of business lends itself more easily and readily to fraud than does that of antiques in general. And it is not only the customer who gets taken in.

If you have gained the confidence of some dealer whom you have come to know quite well, ask him some time when he is a bit confidential, if he has ever been imposed upon in buying antiques, and if he feels like telling you (most of them do hate to admit that they are ever imposed upon) he will admit that he himself has been deceived more than once. I think I am safe in saying that there are more people in the fraudulent antique game trying to impose on the dealers, people whose business it is to manufacture and place imitations and reproductions, than there are dealers who are deliberately seeking to deceive customers.

I heard recently a story which illustrates this point. I will not vouch for the truth of it. A fine old type of sofa had been handed down in a family as an heirloom. In the course of years it had become badly dilapidated and was finally relegated to the attic or barn. Here the further jostlings of time gradually reduced it to a bare and meagre skeleton of framework on which were three finely carved legs (the fourth had disappeared).

One day a man appeared looking for antique furniture, rummaged about the barn, and chanced upon the dilapidated frame with its three carved legs. An offer was made, accepted after some dickering and the man drove away with the legs tied in a neat bundle. Knowing the type of sofa which went with that style of leg, he constructed three sofas of that original type, using old woods and reproducing the original lines as nearly as possible. Each sofa had one genuine old leg — the rest was all faked. When any one called to buy, and asked any questions, he would say, carelessly placing his hand on the original leg: " Oh, yes, this is absolutely genuine! "

Of course, he didn't tell people that the whole sofa was old. If any one took what he said to mean that, it was no fault of his if they misunderstood. That was their lookout. Sharp practice? Yes. But it occurs in lots of other businesses as well.

Another thing which sets the dealing in antiques apart from most other lines of business is that there is no standard of prices or in fact anything which may establish any set rules for determining prices or values. The price of a thing is usually about what the dealer thinks the public will pay for it. When he buys a piece, the dealer figures what he can successfully charge for it, deducts what he considers a safe margin of profit for himself, and the balance is what he can afford to give for it. Often he has to pay more than he really figures he can afford, the extra amount usually coming out of his profit. Sometimes he buys for less. When he gets the piece to his shop, he may find that it is not as salable as he supposed or may require more work to put it in salable condition. It may remain on his hands for weeks, perhaps months, or longer, so that much of his capital — usually never enough for his business — is tied up where he cannot get it, though he sorely needs it. Perhaps finally he may have to sell at cost price or less to dispose of the goods and release the money which he has invested in it.

Some dealers — of course with the general selling value in view — mark their pieces to be sold at a certain per cent advance over the cost to them. This practice may result in quite marked differences between prices of objects which are of the same value to the collector's eye in different shops in the same town. In such a case, the dealer who had bought at the lower price would probably make the sale, while the other man would either hold his piece, hoping to get his price, or would reduce it to meet the rival dealers' values. Allowing for all these chances which the dealer has to take, I think it will be found in many cases that his margin of profit, which in individual cases may seem large, is not excessive. Fashions also make quite a difference. The buying public's demands and tastes change and shift in collecting as in clothes and many other things. As I said before, one year the demand may be for blue china, the next braided and hooked rugs, the next Windsor chairs, Sandwich glass, mirrors, any one of a hundred things. How does the dealer know? Last year, as I recall, there was a great call for hooked-in rugs and it may be as strong now, though I think the demand is diminishing. Suppose that some dealer has had his agents scouring the country districts for these old rugs and they have brought him a large supply, which they have secured (because they were in demand by many buyers) at heavily rising prices. The dealer now advertises his large and heavy stock of these rugs only to find that the public taste has changed and that they are not buying rugs but demanding Sandwich glass, of which he may have only a meager supply because very few seemed to be interested in collecting glass up to a short time ago. He stands to lose heavily on his stock of rugs and is unable to supply the demand for glass, on which he could perhaps make a large enough profit to cover his loss in rugs if he had the stock.

I mentioned previously reading that at an auction in New York a Sandwich glass cup-plate recently sold for twenty-six dollars. Two or three years ago if a dealer had been offered a dollar for this plate he would have considered that he had made a good sale and rightly, for in all probability the cost of the plate would have been a fraction of a dollar. Then, you say, if a dollar was right then, twenty-six dollars to-day must be robbery! Not necessarily. The law of supply and demand applies here as in everything else. If no one is collecting Sandwich glass cup-plates, the price of one dollar for this one, though it be a very rare pattern, may be so high as to prevent

PLATE 104. *See page 141*

GRACEFUL CRYSTAL CHANDELIER WITH CUT DROPS
Photograph by Miss Northend

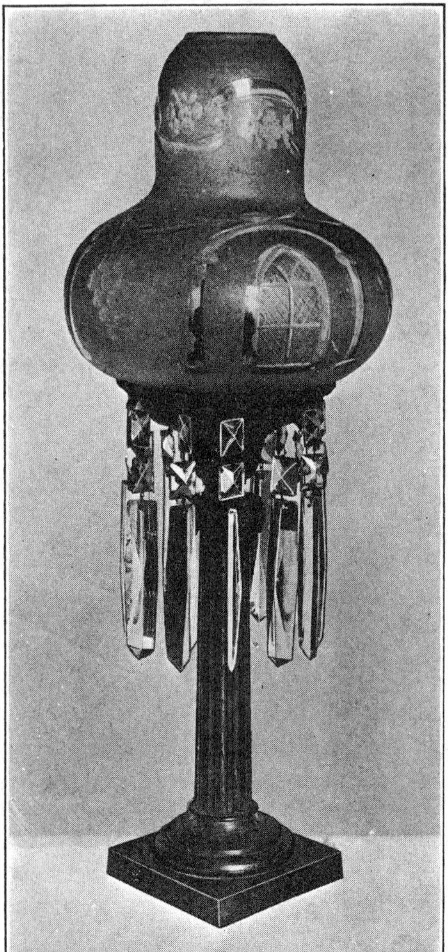

PLATE 105. *See pages 139, 157*

TALL ASTRAL LAMP WITH BRONZE BASE AND UNUSUAL GLASS SHADE
Author's Collection

PLATE 106.

TIN WHALE-OIL LANTERN WITH ORIGINAL GLASS OF STRIKING DESIGN
Collection of Mrs. Ashbel P. Fitch, Quogue, Long Island

sales. On the other hand, when the demand from eager buyers far outruns the supply, twenty-six dollars may be cheap. Fifty collectors, if they had known of this sale, might have gladly paid much more to obtain it.

One of the really lovely phases of collecting is the meeting with some old person who has lived the life of which these lamps and candlesticks are but the symbol. Upon the common ground of reverence and affection for that gone but not forgotten life, such a person will open the gates of memory and allow remembrances of childhood happenings and deeds of later years to sweep over them and you. Better than modern book or magazine are some of the stirring events of their young days, coming in simple, homely fashion from faded lips.

A dear old lady whom I go to see quite often has a rich fund of such tales from her own girlhood days. Although now in her ninetieth year, under a crown of most lovely wavy white hair her bright eyes will light up with merriment and her chuckling laughter will mingle with yours at some episode of her girlhood. One day we had just been looking at an old iron candlestick, one of those early ones with a lip on the top of it by which it could be hung from the slat of a ladder-back chair. This particular stick had been discovered in the back part of a brick oven in an old New England farm house which dated back at least two hundred years. When, or by whom, it had been placed there was entirely a mystery. It was a fine old piece, one of those which country people called "hog-scrapers" because they were convenient in killing time to remove the bristles, after his hog-ship had been immersed in the boiling water.

We were speaking of the old lights and she said she perfectly remembered seeing her mother "dipping" the winter's supply of candles in the kitchen of the old "down-east" farm house which was her girlhood home.

What an arduous task it was, with the great kettles of fat

and the sticks with the wicks looped over them hanging ready for the numerous dippings! When it was over, she said, her mother carefully placed the sticks full of new candles over the backs of two chairs near together, that the candles might dry slowly and evenly and not crack.

Many are the tales which she has told, as, sitting in her high-backed rocking chair, she has lived over again the days of her childhood in a contented home on a big, prosperous farm in Maine. The family was large: father, mother, eight brothers and sisters, and aunts, uncles, and cousins near by, so that the home life was always a busy and merry one. The father, she proudly told us, was reputed one of the best and thriftiest farmers of the country-side. His potatoes and apples were the biggest and best and his corn the fullest eared of any round. When winter came, his bins were full of all kinds of vegetables for the family use, his pork barrels filled, his sheds piled to the eaves with stacks of cut wood all dried for the winter's needs. What good times they had at Thanksgiving gatherings and husking bees after the corn was harvested! How her face lights up as she recalls vividly those days of long ago! One peculiar custom of which she told us I had never heard of elsewhere. In the springtime, when the sap was commencing to flow, the children would get up a "slivering" party as they called it. Going into the pine groves, they selected young vigorous trees, and, after removing the outer bark, pulled off long slender "slivers" of the tender bark which was then full of the newly running sap. She said it was as sweet as sugar when one chewed it. Making birch bark baskets, they filled them with the fresh tender pieces and took them home. Sugar maples were not so common in that part of Maine, so pine slivers probably satisfied the children's longing for sweets in days when candy, as we have it now, was entirely unknown.

Her great-great-grandfather (possibly another great) obtained a grant of land, took his family and yokes of oxen, and started off into the trackless wilderness to fell the trees, build his log house, clear the land, and plant his farm. He established an outpost of that civilization which spread in ever-widening circles from that tiny beginning on the shores of Massachusetts Bay. With Indians and wild creatures her ancestors became very familiar in those first years in the great forest when they wrested a living from a reluctant soil. Many were the tales of those early days which she heard from the lips of her parents and grandparents as the tales had been handed down from generation to succeeding generation.

Early in that forest life, one day while the men were at work in the wood cutting and clearing, as was their custom, they left a boy in charge of their guns, placed conveniently near as they worked. For eternal vigilance was necessary in a land in which the painted face of the savage was no uncommon sight. This day the boy was sleepy or careless and before he could give warning the savages were between him and the guns. The men fled for their lives, but most of them were killed. One young man, her great-grandfather, was captured and carried away. As his body was not found with the others, his fate was unknown to his young wife and children. Not hearing from him, in time they gave him up as one who had shared the fate of the others. More than five years later, he appeared one winter's day alive and well. It seems that the Indians had for some unknown reason treated him kindly and taken him with them on a long march north, far into the Canadian woods. Here he lived with them, learned their language, dressed and seemed like an Indian. In time they put much trust in him, sent him on long journeys to obtain needed supplies, and relaxed the vigilant watch which they had formerly kept over all his movements. In the winter, his chance came. He was sent on skates on a long errand. Supplying himself with as much food as he could obtain without attracting attention, he skated away, on and on down through Canada, across the border, and, after suffering untold hardships, finally made his way home to his family.

At another time a young woman, scarcely more than a girl, was left alone in the house while the rest of the family were obliged to be absent for some reason or other. Just as it was getting dusk, she chanced to hear an unusual sound out of doors. Peering through the chinks between the logs in the wall of the cabin, she saw several of the dreaded Indians in the woods circling the house. After securing the doors and windows, she blew out the candle she was using and banked the fire on the hearth that there might be no bright light to show to the prowling Indians that she was the sole occupant. Then, in a loud voice, she commenced conversations with Tom, Dick, Harry, and other imaginary members of her family. So well did she manage that the Indians were deceived into believing that there was so numerous a company of men that they did not dare attack. When her family returned on the following day, they saw in the snow the prints of moccasins circling the house and their tracks leading away that showed quite a numerous band. The house and probably the life of the young woman had been saved by her quick wit and brave spirit. Of such fiber were the pioneers.

At another time, this same woman was going down to the spring for a jug of water and looking up she saw just before her a mother bear and her two little cubs who had also come to the spring. Needless to say, she allowed them all the time they needed and waited until they had ambled away before venturing to get her own supply.

I have often been interested, in reading books on collecting, by a wonderful tale of finding some very rare piece in the bottom of a barrel in a junk shop, or tucked away under the eaves in an old barn or attic, and buying it for little or nothing. I have wondered then if such luck would ever be mine.

Not long ago it was my task to close up a house for an aged

PLATE 107. *See page 141*

RARE WEDGWOOD HANGING CHANDELIER WITH DECORATIONS IN SILVER LUSTRE
Collection of Mrs. George W. Mitton, Jamaica Plain, Boston

PLATE 108. *See page 138*

Two Graceful Types of Astral Lamps
Author's Collection

PLATE 109. *See pages 50, 93*

(Left) Early Iron Rush-Light Holder on Wooden Base
Collection of Mr. C. L. Cooney, Saugus
(Right) Tin Lard-Oil Lamp with Tin Reflector
Collection of Mrs. A. A. Dana, West Orange, New Jersey

relative who had moved West. The house, which had been his home for many years, had a large garden, although it was in the city. At the back of the garden, a small stable had formerly been the home of a favorite driving horse.

My relative sent me a long list of the contents of the house which he wished shipped to him. The balance, which he said was of not much value, I was to sell, give away or dispose of in any way I saw fit. About a carload the movers boxed and shipped. The rest I disposed of as he said. Some I sold, some I gave away, and delivered up the rest to the ash barrel and bonfire.

The barn had not been used as a stable for many years and the hay loft had the usual accumulation of decrepit furniture and other things, not usable, but " too good to throw away " as the thrifty New England housewives put it. This was cleared out in short order. In taking one last look about to see that everything was gone, for the place was to be sold, we discovered in a dark corner under the eaves and covered with dust the bronze and luster lamp shown in Plate 105. Of course, we were delighted at the discovery. This lamp had evidently been there for years and its owner had probably long since forgotten its existence. We were so glad to get the lamp, of course, but — if only we had the shade! But, no. That was broken long ago. We groped around, nevertheless, in the semi-darkness still farther, and, wonder of wonders found the shade buried in dirt, but without a nick or scratch! And a wonderful shade it is you will agree with me. So I am reading these tales of extraordinary finds with more optimism, now that I have one such story of my own.

I think it is much better for one beginning to collect not to attempt to specialize just at first. If you are, let us say, interested in lamps, I should advise a general collection. Then as you get better acquainted with the different kinds and periods, you will naturally be more attracted to certain kinds or groups. It may be that your opportunities of location will enable you to obtain some kinds much more readily than others and will kindle interest in that branch; but a general knowledge — which can best be obtained by a general collection of lamps, lanterns, and the like — will be almost indispensable even if you have decided to confine your collecting eventually to only one sort of lighting devices.

A friend of mine told me a short time ago of an interesting and amusing experience which befell him in London. He is, by the way, one of the most indefatigable and successful collectors of lighting devices that I know. He has now been interested in them for years, not only in American lamps but in lighting devices of every period from all parts of the world. His collection now numbers, I think, well over seven hundred specimens and he has journeyed to nearly every country on the globe in his favorite pursuit. Some time ago he was in London and met there a titled Englishman, who, he was told, was a fellow collector of illuminating devices. The Englishman, with the customary reticence of that nation upon meeting a stranger (or is it a touch of suspicion of Americans?), had scarcely anything to say and my friend had to do all the talking, which naturally fell upon the subject of their mutual interest. He expatiated at some length on the many points of excellence of his collection, its choice pieces, etc. Gradually he warmed up to his subject, while the Englishman sat smoking in stony silence, broken only by a "humph" now and then, otherwise evincing no particular interest.

My friend, after talking about an hour, without apparently making the slightest dent in the Honorable's armor, literally stopped for breath. His companion looked up then and in a bored tone asked him what he specialized in. "Oh, I haven't specialized in any one line in particular," my friend replied; "I'm interested in the whole field of lighting appliances."

The Englishman shook his head. "That won't get you

anywhere," he said; "I know, for I have tried it. If you want to do anything really worth while in collecting, you must specialize."

This, of course, was not particularly encouraging to the American, who, by the way, really has a most wonderful collection but he pulled himself together and went on talking until the Englishman looked up and interrupted.

"How many chuck-mucks have you?"

My friend looked at him aghast.

"Beg pardon, but I don't think I got your question."

"I said, 'How many chuck-mucks have you?'" again repeated the Englishman.

This was a poser. Not only did my friend not have any "chuck-mucks", but he hadn't the faintest notion what they were. The Englishman evidently noted his consternation at his query, for the slightest suspicion of a twinkle appeared in his eye and his face relaxed just a wee bit. My friend did the only sensible thing to do under the circumstances. He burst into a hearty laugh, confessed openly that he had "no sich animile" and hadn't the faintest idea what it was. Would the specialist in "chuck-mucks" kindly tell him all about them? The Englishman, having discomfited the "blooming American", proceeded to do so at length.

Lest any of my readers remain as ignorant as I was while my friend was telling me this story — for I had never heard the word before and had no idea of its meaning — it seems that "chuck-muck" (I am not sure of its spelling) is the Chinese name for a kind of tinder box which was used in China long ago. The Englishman had made the collecting of "chuck-mucks" his particular hobby and had two hundred and fifty of them in his collection! And my American friend didn't even know there was such a thing!

In the end they became very good friends and just before he sailed for home his English friend proposed they take a walk together, for, he said, "Let's see if we can't find a 'chuck-muck.'" They visited a number of curious little shops in out of the way places and finally their search was rewarded. They found a real specimen, upon which, after careful examination, the Englishman set his stamp of approval and my friend purchased it. "Now," said the Englishman, "if any one asks, you have a chuck-muck in your collection." Since then, I think he told me, he has added a number; so that now he has about a dozen of these curious objects.

I have told this story for two reasons, or perhaps I might say that this tale has two morals. First, never — well, I won't say brag or boast; for of course a really truly collector never does that — I'll say, never monopolize the conversation about the excellence of your own collection until you have had a peek at least at the other man's. It is more than possible that your collection may not look so extraordinary after seeing his. There are people who have good collections and don't always talk about it. Secondly, just when you get to the point where you feel that you are really pretty well posted on that particular subject, the chances are you will run across some one who knows so very, very much more than you do that your knowledge will dwindle to a mere pin point and you will feel like starting to learn all over. This is a very healthy state of mind to be in; for in collecting, as in many other things in life, the knowledge that there is a great field ahead, unknown, and yet to be explored, is the finest possible stimulus and makes the sport of collecting what it is to-day — a sport for "princes as well as ploughmen."

There is another side to collecting which perhaps some overlook. Many people have an idea that collecting, if one follows it at all ardently, is a very expensive fad, entailing a large outlay, and can only be pursued by one with plenty of money to spare. This, I think, is quite a wrong conception. A much fairer way is to consider your collection, of whatever it

PLATE 110. *See page 143*

FINE EXAMPLE OF ENGLISH OR IRISH CUT CRYSTAL CHANDELIER, NOW IN HOME OF EDWARD D. BRANDEGEE, ESQ. AT " FAULKNER FARM," BROOKLINE, MASSACHUSETTS
Photograph by Miss M. H. Northend

PLATE 111.

Two Unusual Tall Lamps, One Pewter and One Glass, with Original Shades. Sheffield Candlestick
Author's Collection

may consist, as a savings bank, your deposits being the items which you add from time to time. If you buy intelligently and wisely — which you will undoubtedly do after the newness has worn off and you acquire a good working familiarity with your particular hobby — you will find that your bank is paying you a fairly respectable rate of interest in the natural and inevitable increase in values as the years go by. One will realize this when a few facts are considered. First, the supply of genuine antiques cannot increase. It is true that there are undoubtedly some pieces now hidden away in closets and attics and out-of-the-way houses, which are at present unknown to dealers and collectors. Their numbers, however, must be comparatively small. Practically all the finer antiques are now known and tabulated, since the country has been combed so many times by keen-eyed searchers that the per cent undiscovered must be small. Secondly, the known supply is gradually diminishing. Fire, decay, and accidents take their toll each year. The number of collectors, on the contrary, is increasing year by year. As the supply gradually diminishes and competition to possess becomes keener and keener, more people are attracted each year, so that the inevitable result is gradually increasing prices for those pieces which do find their way to market. Collectors will find that the better the pieces, the more rapidly values go up. Almost any dealer will tell you to-day that the difficulty is not in selling his stock — but in replenishing it. The demand has overtaken the supply. Ten or twenty years ago it was just the opposite, plenty of antiques but few buyers; to-day, more buyers than goods. Under these conditions what better or safer use is there for your spare change than an intelligent, conservative investment in some form of antiques?

You have the satisfaction of acquiring, the pleasure of daily enjoyment in the sight or use of those things in which you delight. If your circumstances change, or you tire of your particular branch of collecting, or for any other reason wish to dispose of your collection, you will undoubtedly find that you can realize your entire outlay with a handsome margin of profit besides. The enjoyment of ownership for all the intervening years has cost you nothing.

I think that this is much the better and more correct way of considering the entire field of collecting and I am sure an intimate knowledge of many of the sales of later years, both private and public, will bear me out in my statements. But laying all monetary considerations aside, I feel perfectly safe in saying that at least ninety-nine out of every hundred collectors will tell you that the pleasure of seeking and finding outweighs the cost many times over.

A phase of this sentiment for the antique, often overlooked, merits our consideration. It is a sad but noticeable fact that many of the places where people live to-day are not homes in the truest and deepest sense of the word. Too often they are merely convenient stopping places where one sleeps and snatches hasty meals between the claims of the office, store or shop and the more absorbing pleasures of the theater, dance, party, movie, game or what not.

Our dwellings often sadly lack that genial atmosphere of hospitality, comfort, and good cheer which we of the older generation remember in the homes we knew and loved. So little care or thought seems to be given to-day to the contents or arrangement of our modern dwellings that it is not to be wondered at that our young people are found anywhere but in their homes.

Picture a fair-sized living room, its fireplace filled with sweet smelling hardwood sticks sending forth their cheerful blazing warmth and comfort; some comfortable old chairs and a sofa or two invitingly near; a secretary of fine old wood reflecting the light of the fire from its polished surface and old brasses, and behind its panelled doors gleaming bits of old china, silver,

PLATE 112. *See page 73*

Two Fine Hanging Hall Lanterns
B. N. Gates' Collection, Worcester

PLATE 113. *See page 73*

Hanging Hall Lantern with Colored Glass Globe
Photograph by Miss Northend

PLATE 114. *See page 143*

WONDERFUL OLD CHANDELIER (NOW FITTED FOR ELECTRICITY) WITH CUT CRYSTAL PENDANTS. NOTE ALSO BRACKETS ON SIDE WALLS
Photograph by Miss M. H. Northend

and pewter; slender-legged antique tables here and there laden with books, magazines and a quaint old lamp or two. Old rugs in soft colors lie on the floor and a few good engravings mellowed with years hang on the walls. An elusive but plainly perceptible home atmosphere clings to those fine old pieces of furniture. On Sunday nights, the family and any chance visitors gather around the fire while the hostess from the convenient tea tray serves in grandmother's best, gold band wedding china. Can you estimate the refining influence of such an atmosphere on the casual visitor and still more upon the child growing up in such surroundings?

Are not the virtues of care and thoughtfulness for the aged and infirm, of hospitality toward one's friends and neighbors, of respect and love for parents and of desire to make the most of one's self through life more easily cultivated into strong, sturdy growths in such environments than in the atmosphere of some of the homes we know to-day?

That the world to-day is in a most unhappy condition is self-evident. I believe there is at the present time in America a crying need for the real, old-fashioned, Christian home, a home bright with loving thoughtfulness for others rather than self, warm with the glow of genuine welcome for friends and neighbors, rich in the seeking of ways of service to the less fortunate, of kindnesses to the shut-ins, the sick and particularly the aged; a happy, peaceful home where the vexations and bickerings of a great self-seeking world are left outside the door, and where within its portals the aim of each is to help and cheer; a home that we leave with regret and return to with eager anticipations,— that neighbors and friends love to visit — a true home.

Tennyson's biographer said, "He felt with Wordsworth that upon the sacredness of the home life depended the greatness and stability of a people." If only somehow we could get back to a nation of real homes, many of the social and industrial problems which vex us so sorely at the present time would solve themselves and our influence upon the other peoples of this world would be tremendously increased for real and lasting good. I cannot do better in closing than to echo the words of one of our loved New England poets —

> " O make Thou us, through centuries long,
>   In peace secure, in justice strong;
> Around our gift of freedom draw
>   The safeguards of Thy righteous law;
> And cast in some diviner mould,
>   Let the new cycle shame the old! "

Colonial Chandeliers

Supplement by

JAMES R. MARSH

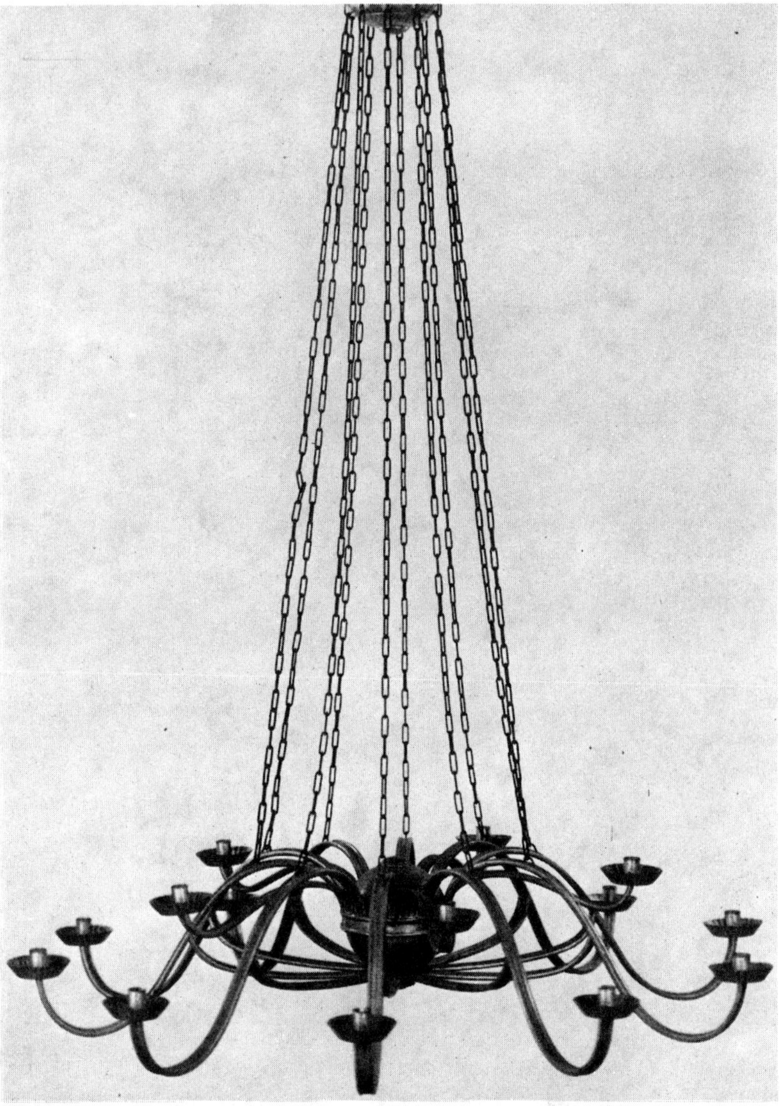

PLATE 1

A rare twenty-light tinned chandelier with central sphere. Note there are five short arms and special supports for ten longer arms, creating an elaborate design suspended by many links of chain. American, nineteenth-century.
Owned by The Henry Ford Museum, Dearborn, Michigan

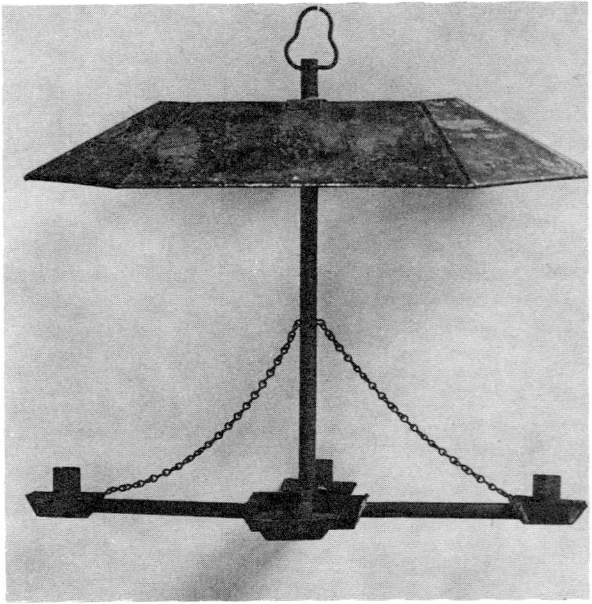

PLATE 2

Tinned four-light ceiling device with glass-lined hood for reflection of light. Pennsylvania, c. 1800.

Courtesy of The Metropolitan Museum of Art, Gift of Mrs. Robert W. de Forest, 1933

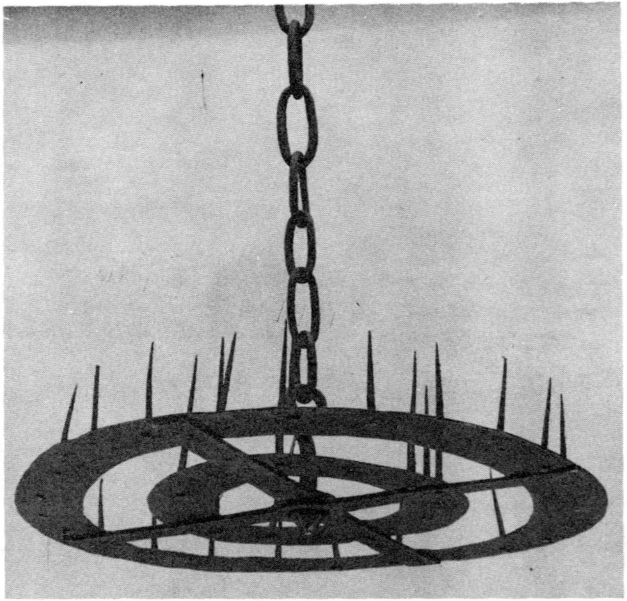

PLATE 3

Primitive in form, this chandelier is entirely the work of a blacksmith who forged spikes, cross bars, hook, bottom button and formed the rings.

Courtesy, Old Sturbridge Village

PLATE 4

A large sheet iron ring with edges crimped at top and bottom. Holds fifteen candles and is suspended from a thin iron rod handle.

Courtesy, Old Sturbridge Village

PLATE 5

An interesting eighteenth-century chandelier of wood-turned center and sheet metal arms with characteristic crinkled cups. Note the staggered placement of the arms. *Courtesy, Old Sturbridge Village*

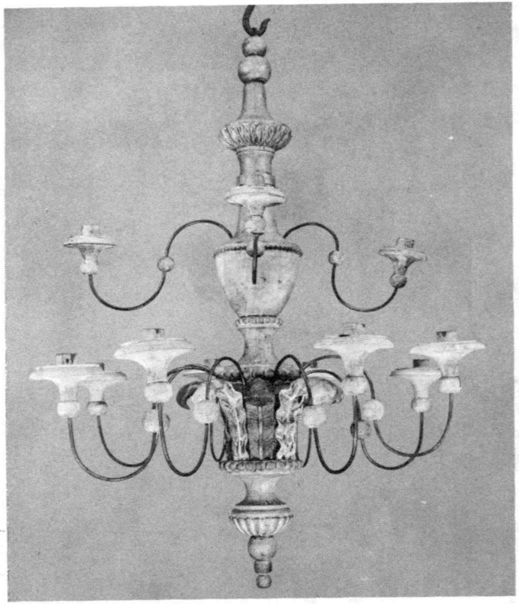

PLATE 6

A fine example of wood turning and carving that has the elegance of the eighteenth-century Flemish and English bronze and silver prototypes.

Courtesy, Old Sturbridge Village

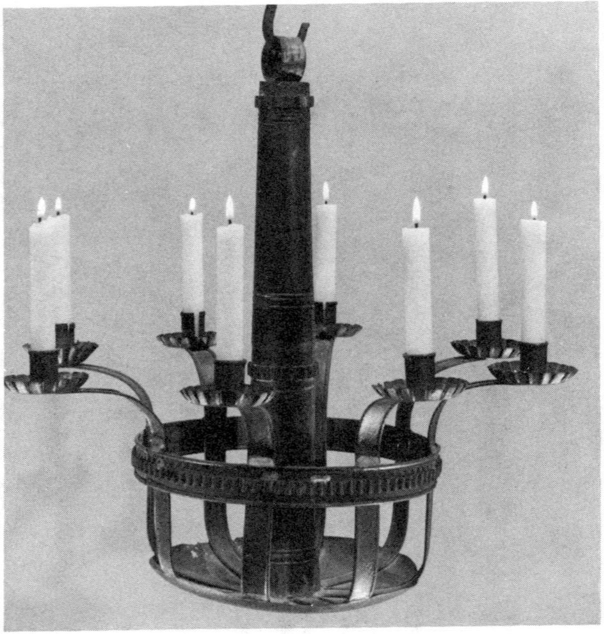

PLATE 7

Severe in design, this shape is interesting and the construction sturdy. It is made entirely of sheet metal.

Courtesy, Old Sturbridge Village

PLATE 8

A simple form of the tinsmith's craft. Note the rolled top edge of the main band in which a stiffening wire is inserted for strength. The design is so simple it could be regarded as modern. *Courtesy, Old Sturbridge Village*

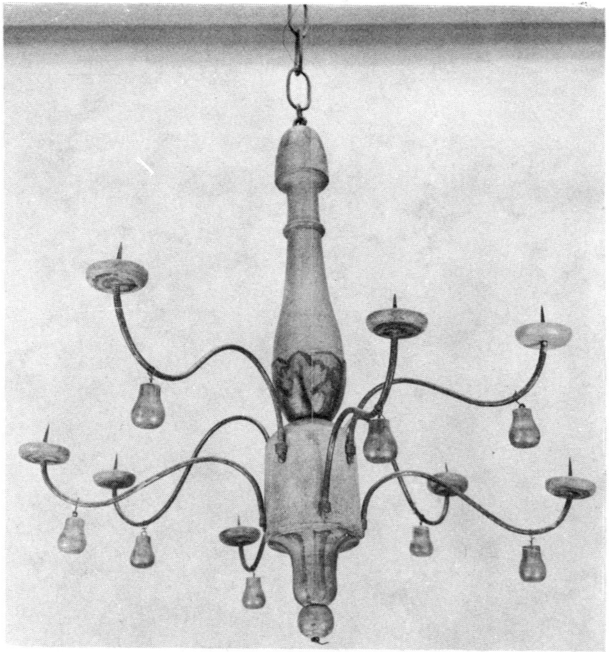

PLATE 9

A predominantly wood-turned chandelier including pear-shaped drops and painted leaves for decoration. Note the forged spikes to hold candles.

Courtesy, Old Sturbridge Village

PLATE 10

The long leaves, fastened to each arm in two sections with metal ribbons, create a highly decorative design when combined with ornamental wood turnings.

Courtesy, Old Sturbridge Village

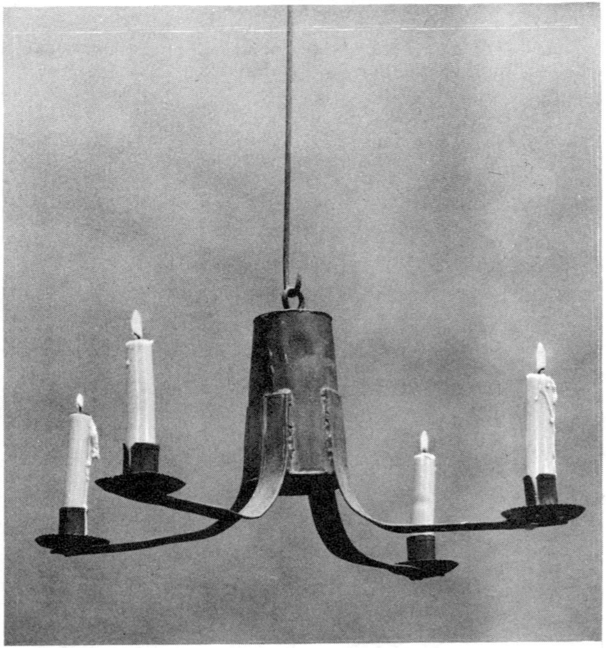

PLATE 11

A primitive design in sheet iron. The solder joints remind one of today's welded sculpture.

Courtesy, Old Sturbridge Village

PLATE 12

A handsome ring chandelier made of sheet metal bands the edges of which are beaded for both strength and decoration. The ring was pierced wih hand punch and die. Chain links are made of sheet metal strips.

Courtesy, Old Sturbridge Village

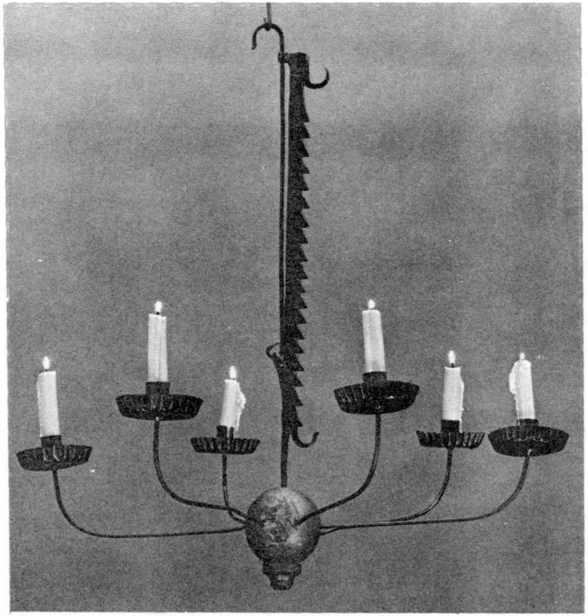

PLATE 13

A combination of wrought iron trammel, wood center and wire arms makes this decorative and utilitarian chandelier a collector's item.

Courtesy, Old Sturbridge Village

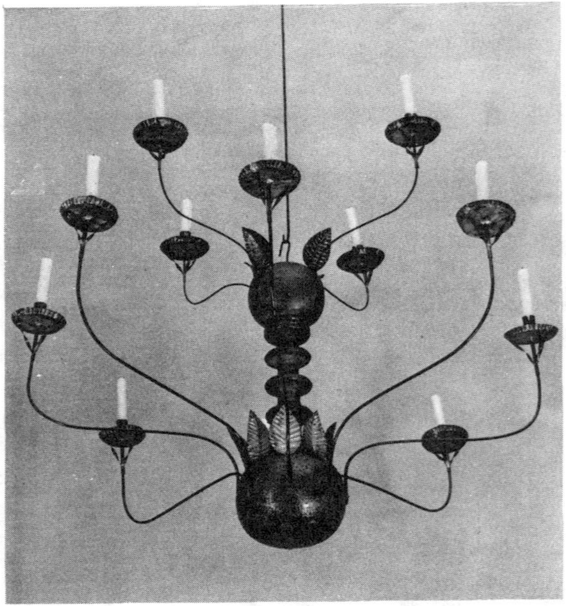

PLATE 14

An exceptionally well organized design with graceful arms flowing from a seventeenth-century style wood turning crowned with leaves. A similar chandelier is in the collection of the Henry Ford Museum.

Courtesy, Old Sturbridge Village

PLATE 15

A stylish design using the characteristic double cone bottom finial and tubular stem with fluted cup as top.

Courtesy, Old Sturbridge Village

PLATE 16

A primitive twelve-light ring chandelier made of tinned sheet iron with wire supports and chain links. Note the attractive veined candle cups.

Courtesy, Old Sturbridge Village

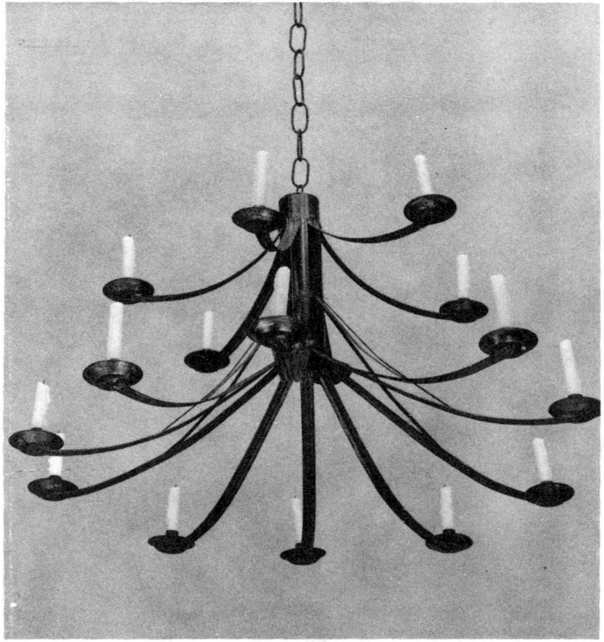

PLATE 17

A large primitive sixteen-light chandelier made entirely of sheet metal. Note the supporting braces for the lower tier.

Courtesy, Old Sturbridge Village

PLATE 18

A fine example of an eighteenth-century meeting house or ballroom chandelier. Both wood turning and carving are generously used, as well as gilding.

Courtesy, Old Sturbridge Village

PLATE 19

A nine-light double tier tinned chandelier with cylindrical centers relieved by curving arms and fluted cups. Eighteenth-century.

Courtesy, Henry Francis du Pont Winterthur Museum

PLATE 20

Interior of the Meeting House, Old Sturbridge Village, showing three beautiful chandliers made of painted wood with turned and carved centers and candle cups and iron arms.

Courtesy, Old Sturbridge Village
Photo by Samuel Chamberlain

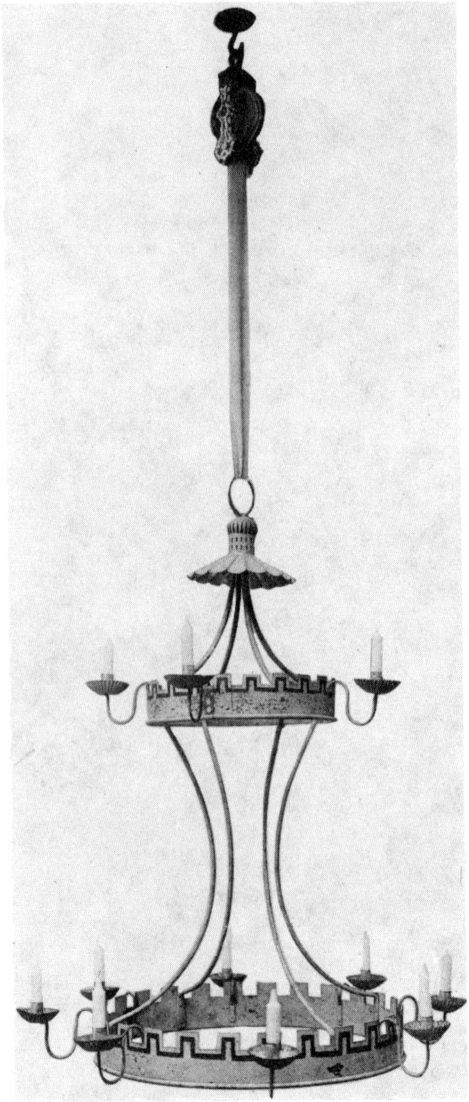

PLATE 21

A painted double ring chandelier in the Greek Revival style. From St. John's Church, Hebron, Connecticut; gift of Mrs. J. Insley Blair.

Courtesy of the Cooper Union Museum

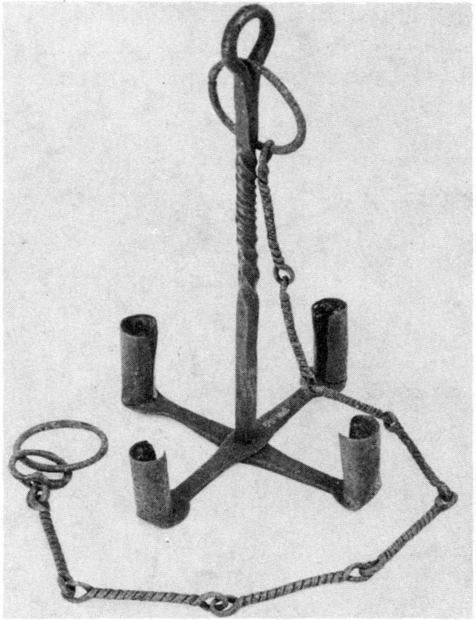

PLATE 22

A completely hand forged design of wrought iron. Almost every inch has been beaten and twisted by the blacksmith.

Courtesy, Colonial Williamsburg

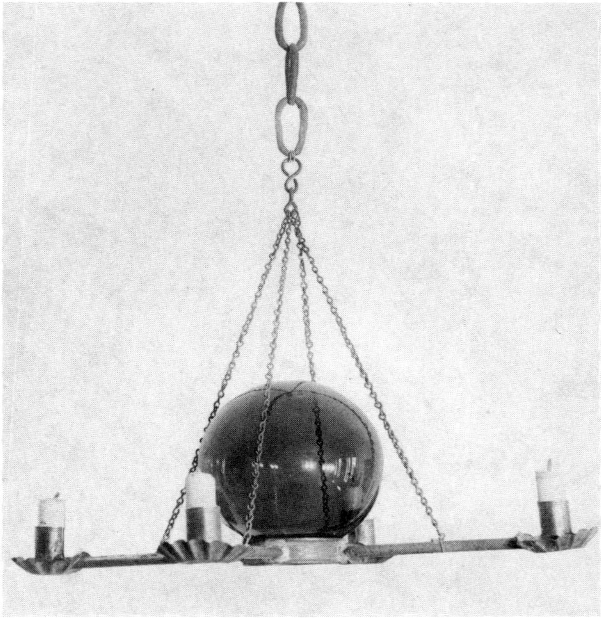

PLATE 23

A rare tinned chandelier with a glass ball to increase illumination by reflection.

Courtesy of the Cooper Union Museum

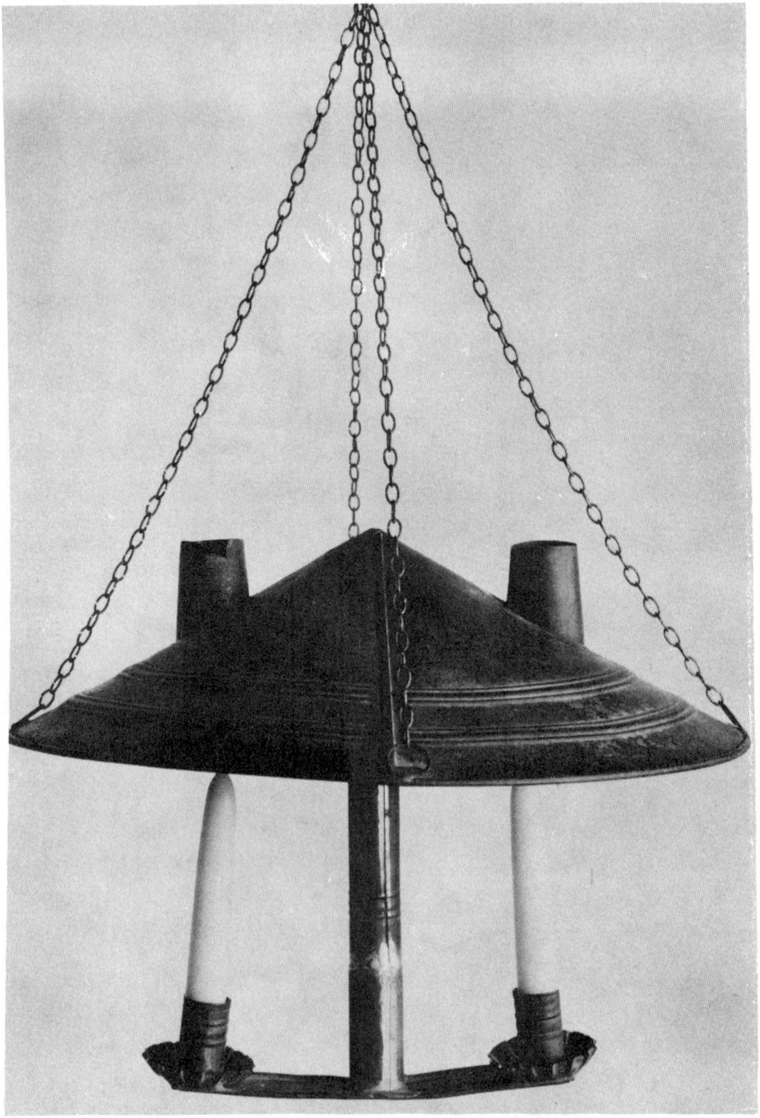

PLATE 24

The vented conical hood serves as a reflector for the two candles. With the exception of the chain, the entire fixture was made of tinned sheet iron.
Courtesy of the Cooper Union Museum

PLATE 25

A handsome chandelier with carved wood shaft in the form of leaves, turned wood candle cups and little balls placed on curved wire arms. Painted and gilded. From New England.

Owned by The Henry Ford Museum, Dearborn, Michigan

PLATE 26

A festive twelve-light tinned chandelier with applied leaves and fluted cups and corrugated strips. A decorative work of imagination and craftsmanship.

Courtesy of the Cooper Union Museum

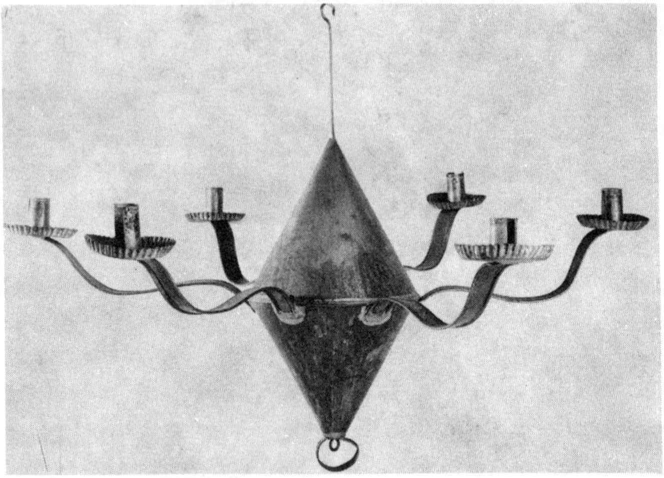

PLATE 27

The geometric form of the double cone contrasts well with the free-curving arms, the edges of which are folded over for strength. Various forms and combinations of the cone were frequently used.

Courtesy of the Cooper Union Museum

PLATE 28

The shape of this central wood turning was used quite often on chandeliers, especially with curved sheet metal arms as shown. The wood was painted yellow and the arms originally were tin coated. American, c. 1800. This now hangs in the old kitchen of Clinton Inn at Greenfield Village.

Owned by The Henry Ford Museum, Dearborn, Michigan

PLATE 29

An interesting central ring supporting curved arms and top finial. The chandelier is composed entirely of beaded sheet iron strips and is tin coated. American, early nineteenth-century. It now hangs in the Tap Room of Clinton Inn at Greenfield Village.

Owned by The Henry Ford Museum, Dearborn, Michigan

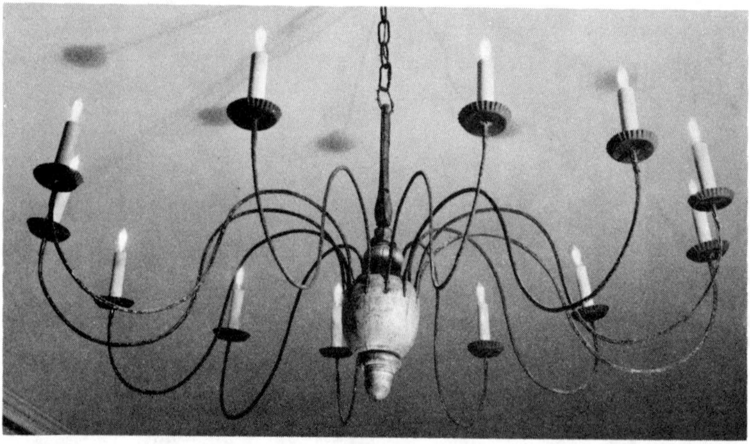

PLATE 30

An early meeting house chandelier based on the Flemish counterpart which was made of silver or bronze. Center shaft turned of wood, arms and cups of iron.

Courtesy, Henry Francis du Pont Winterthur Museum

PLATE 31

An interesting chandelier with eight double arms terminating on the metal shaft of a series of cones, creating a unique design. From a church in New York State, c. 1800.

Marsh Collection

PLATE 32

A double tier wood and metal chandelier with built-up core. Painted red. New England, eighteenth-century. Note the unusual treatment of curved segments of wood backing the contour of the central metal frame. This chandelier hangs in the dining room of Susquehanna House in Greenfield Village. Also illustrated in Wallace Nutting's book, *Furniture Treasury.*

Owned by The Henry Ford Museum, Dearborn, Michigan

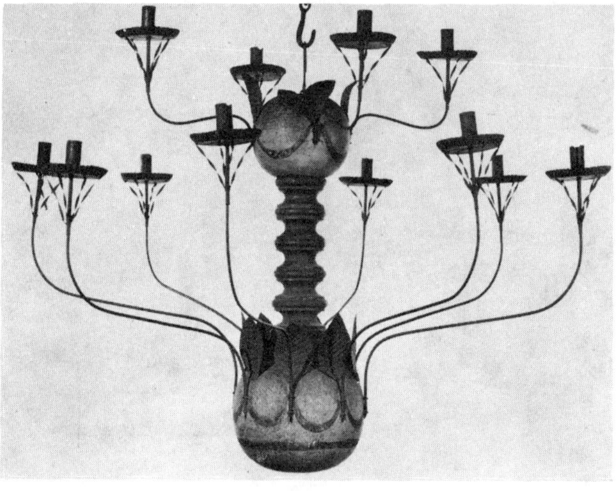

PLATE 33

A truly decorative chandelier with fancy turned wood center, painted festoons, metal leaves, twisted metal ribbons supporting fluted cups, and well shaped wire arms. A similar design is in the Old Sturbridge Village Collection. American, c. 1800.

Owned by The Henry Ford Museum, Dearborn, Michigan

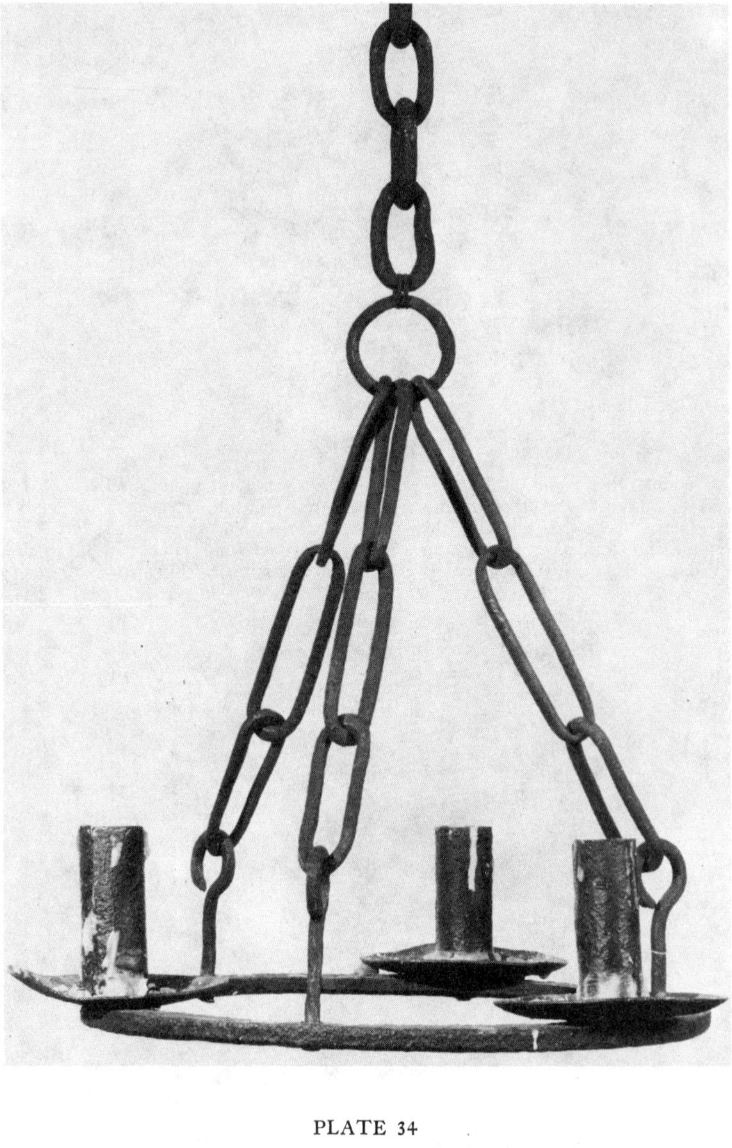

PLATE 34

This wrought iron chandelier was forged in a blacksmith shop. American, eighteenth-century. It now hangs in the kitchen of Susquehanna House at Greenfield Village.

Owned by The Henry Ford Museum, Dearborn, Michigan

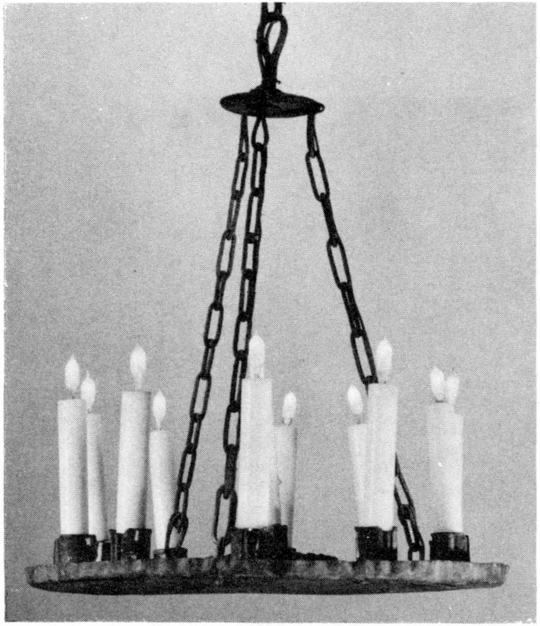

PLATE 35

An eleven-light chandelier made of sheet iron in the form of a round tray with turned up edge. Simple but effective.

Courtesy, Henry Francis du Pont Winterthur Museum

PLATE 36

A rare and decorative wrought iron trammel chandelier. Although eighteenth-century it has characteristics of ancient and contemporary sculpture.

Courtesy, Henry Francis du Pont Winterthur Museum

PLATE 37

Primitive, but stylish and decorative. The candle cups and looped arms converge on a ring ban embellished with painted leaf work.

Courtesy, Henry Francis du Pont Winterthur Museum

PLATE 38

A William and Mary style gilt wood English chandelier, c. 1700, from the H. H. Mulliner Collection. An exceptionally fine example of ornamental wood carving. Location, Palace, Governor's Office, Colonial Williamsburg.

Courtesy, Colonial Williamsburg

PLATE 39

An early eighteenth-century bell metal chandelier from Ashburnham Place, Sussex, England. Unusual scroll-shape arms, fine craftsmanship. Location, Capitol, Committee Rooms, Colonial Williamsburg.
Courtesy, Colonial Williamsburg

PLATE 40

A fine eighteenth-century example of the blacksmith's skill in making a "hot" twist uniform and round in the forge.
Courtesy, Henry Francis du Pont Winterthur Museum

PLATE 41

This is one of the most characteristic designs of the period. The double cone center, turned-edge arms, fluted cups and wire links are entirely the handwork of the tinsmith on tin-coated sheet iron. It now hangs in the Printing Office, Press Room, Colonial Williamsburg.

Courtesy, Colonial Williamsburg

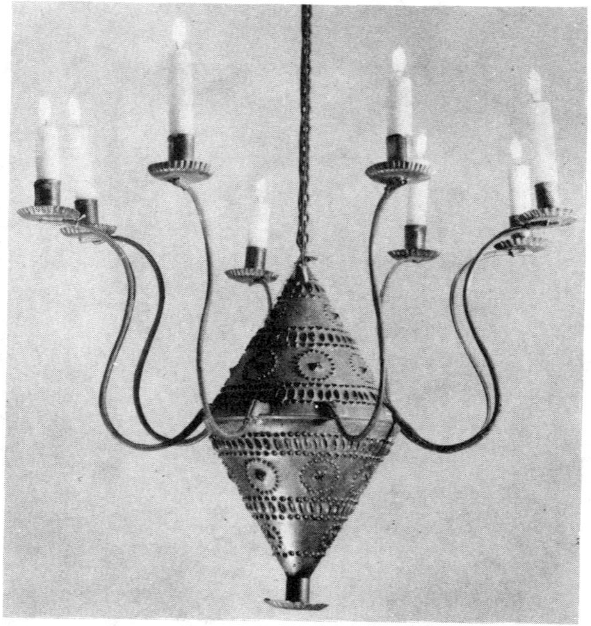

PLATE 42

This uplifting curve of the arms and decorative perforations of the double cone center create a unique and graceful eight-light chandelier. Eighteenth-century.

Courtesy, Henry Francis du Pont Winterthur Museum

PLATE 43

An eighteen-light chandelier of superb design and craftsmanship in tinned metal that was influenced by the Flemish and English bronze chandeliers. It hangs in the American Wing of The Metropolitan Museum of Art in New York.

Courtesy of The Metropolitan Museum of Art, Sylmaris Fund, 1937

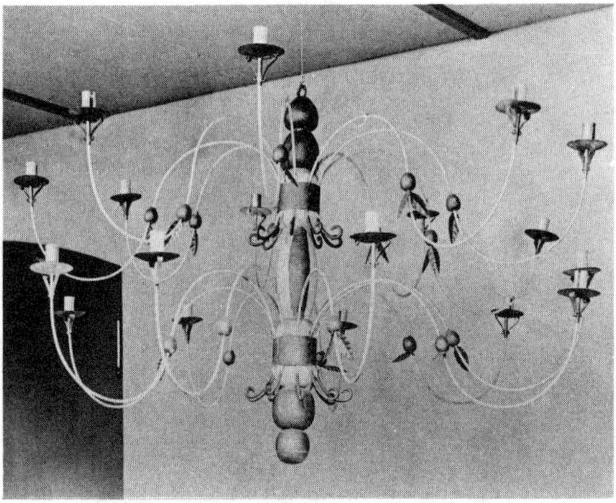

PLATE 44

Eighteen gracefully curved arms, grouped in two tiers, converge onto a slender wood shaft painted in gay colors. This is the design mentioned in the Introduction to the Dover Edition. One came from a church in Virginia, two from a church in Connecticut, while two are in the ballroom of the Frary House in Old Deerfield, Massachusetts and one in the Marsh collection.

Courtesy, Wadsworth Atheneum

PLATE 45

Influenced by the European bronze and silver chandeliers, the urn-shaped wood turning gives this design an elegant touch without the formality of polished metal. Location, Christiana Campbell's Tavern, Colonial Williamsburg.

Courtesy, Colonial Williamsburg

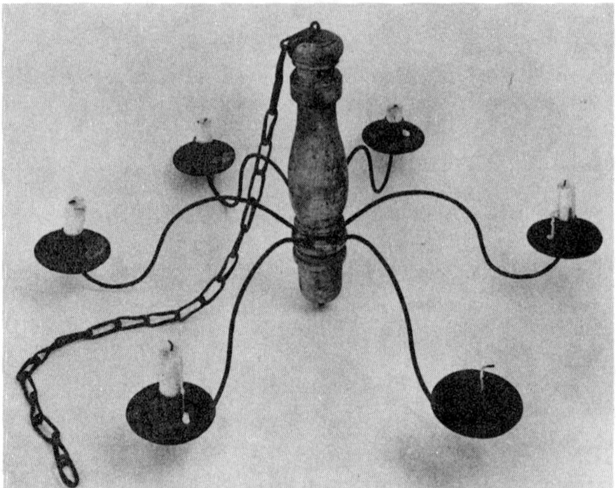

PLATE 46

The delicate arms, generous candle cups and turned wood shaft combine to make a handsome and simple design.

Courtesy, Colonial Williamsburg

PLATE 47

An ornamental design probably of European origin. Its construction includes the crafts of wood turning (top finial), tinsmithing (cups and leaves) and blacksmithing (iron ring and frame holder).

Courtesy, Old Sturbridge Village

INDEX

THE END

A CATALOG OF SELECTED

DOVER BOOKS

IN ALL FIELDS OF INTEREST

A CATALOG OF SELECTED DOVER BOOKS IN ALL FIELDS OF INTEREST

DRAWINGS OF REMBRANDT, edited by Seymour Slive. Updated Lippmann, Hofstede de Groot edition, with definitive scholarly apparatus. All portraits, biblical sketches, landscapes, nudes. Oriental figures, classical studies, together with selection of work by followers. 550 illustrations. Total of 630pp. 9⅛ × 12¼.
21485-0, 21486-9 Pa., Two-vol. set $25.00

GHOST AND HORROR STORIES OF AMBROSE BIERCE, Ambrose Bierce. 24 tales vividly imagined, strangely prophetic, and decades ahead of their time in technical skill: "The Damned Thing," "An Inhabitant of Carcosa," "The Eyes of the Panther," "Moxon's Master," and 20 more. 199pp. 5⅜ × 8½. 20767-6 Pa. $3.95

ETHICAL WRITINGS OF MAIMONIDES, Maimonides. Most significant ethical works of great medieval sage, newly translated for utmost precision, readability. Laws Concerning Character Traits, Eight Chapters, more. 192pp. 5⅜ × 8½.
24522-5 Pa. $4.50

THE EXPLORATION OF THE COLORADO RIVER AND ITS CANYONS, J. W. Powell. Full text of Powell's 1,000-mile expedition down the fabled Colorado in 1869. Superb account of terrain, geology, vegetation, Indians, famine, mutiny, treacherous rapids, mighty canyons, during exploration of last unknown part of continental U.S. 400pp. 5⅜ × 8½. 20094-9 Pa. $6.95

HISTORY OF PHILOSOPHY, Julián Marías. Clearest one-volume history on the market. Every major philosopher and dozens of others, to Existentialism and later. 505pp. 5⅜ × 8½. 21739-6 Pa. $8.50

ALL ABOUT LIGHTNING, Martin A. Uman. Highly readable non-technical survey of nature and causes of lightning, thunderstorms, ball lightning, St. Elmo's Fire, much more. Illustrated. 192pp. 5⅜ × 8½. 25237-X Pa. $5.95

SAILING ALONE AROUND THE WORLD, Captain Joshua Slocum. First man to sail around the world, alone, in small boat. One of great feats of seamanship told in delightful manner. 67 illustrations. 294pp. 5⅜ × 8½. 20326-3 Pa. $4.95

LETTERS AND NOTES ON THE MANNERS, CUSTOMS AND CONDITIONS OF THE NORTH AMERICAN INDIANS, George Catlin. Classic account of life among Plains Indians: ceremonies, hunt, warfare, etc. 312 plates. 572pp. of text. 6⅛ × 9¼. 22118-0, 22119-9 Pa. Two-vol. set $15.90

ALASKA: The Harriman Expedition, 1899, John Burroughs, John Muir, et al. Informative, engrossing accounts of two-month, 9,000-mile expedition. Native peoples, wildlife, forests, geography, salmon industry, glaciers, more. Profusely illustrated. 240 black-and-white line drawings. 124 black-and-white photographs. 3 maps. Index. 576pp. 5⅜ × 8½. 25109-8 Pa. $11.95

CATALOG OF DOVER BOOKS

AMERICAN CLIPPER SHIPS: 1833–1858, Octavius T. Howe & Frederick C. Matthews. Fully-illustrated, encyclopedic review of 352 clipper ships from the period of America's greatest maritime supremacy. Introduction. 109 halftones. 5 black-and-white line illustrations. Index. Total of 928pp. 5⅜ × 8½.
25115-2, 25116-0 Pa., Two-vol. set $17.90

TOWARDS A NEW ARCHITECTURE, Le Corbusier. Pioneering manifesto by great architect, near legendary founder of "International School." Technical and aesthetic theories, views on industry, economics, relation of form to function, "mass-production spirit," much more. Profusely illustrated. Unabridged translation of 13th French edition. Introduction by Frederick Etchells. 320pp. 6⅛ × 9¼. (Available in U.S. only) 25023-7 Pa. $8.95

THE BOOK OF KELLS, edited by Blanche Cirker. Inexpensive collection of 32 full-color, full-page plates from the greatest illuminated manuscript of the Middle Ages, painstakingly reproduced from rare facsimile edition. Publisher's Note. Captions. 32pp. 9⅜ × 12¼. 24345-1 Pa. $4.95

BEST SCIENCE FICTION STORIES OF H. G. WELLS, H. G. Wells. Full novel *The Invisible Man,* plus 17 short stories: "The Crystal Egg," "Aepyornis Island," "The Strange Orchid," etc. 303pp. 5⅜ × 8½. (Available in U.S. only)
21531-8 Pa. $4.95

AMERICAN SAILING SHIPS: Their Plans and History, Charles G. Davis. Photos, construction details of schooners, frigates, clippers, other sailcraft of 18th to early 20th centuries—plus entertaining discourse on design, rigging, nautical lore, much more. 137 black-and-white illustrations. 240pp. 6⅛ × 9¼.
24658-2 Pa. $5.95

ENTERTAINING MATHEMATICAL PUZZLES, Martin Gardner. Selection of author's favorite conundrums involving arithmetic, money, speed, etc., with lively commentary. Complete solutions. 112pp. 5⅜ × 8½. 25211-6 Pa. $2.95

THE WILL TO BELIEVE, HUMAN IMMORTALITY, William James. Two books bound together. Effect of irrational on logical, and arguments for human immortality. 402pp. 5⅜ × 8½. 20291-7 Pa. $7.50

THE HAUNTED MONASTERY and THE CHINESE MAZE MURDERS, Robert Van Gulik. 2 full novels by Van Gulik continue adventures of Judge Dee and his companions. An evil Taoist monastery, seemingly supernatural events; overgrown topiary maze that hides strange crimes. Set in 7th-century China. 27 illustrations. 328pp. 5⅜ × 8½. 23502-5 Pa. $5.95

CELEBRATED CASES OF JUDGE DEE (DEE GOONG AN), translated by Robert Van Gulik. Authentic 18th-century Chinese detective novel; Dee and associates solve three interlocked cases. Led to Van Gulik's own stories with same characters. Extensive introduction. 9 illustrations. 237pp. 5⅜ × 8½.
23337-5 Pa. $4.95

Prices subject to change without notice.

Available at your book dealer or write for free catalog to Dept. GI, Dover Publications, Inc., 31 East 2nd St., Mineola, N.Y. 11501. Dover publishes more than 175 books each year on science, elementary and advanced mathematics, biology, music, art, literary history, social sciences and other areas.